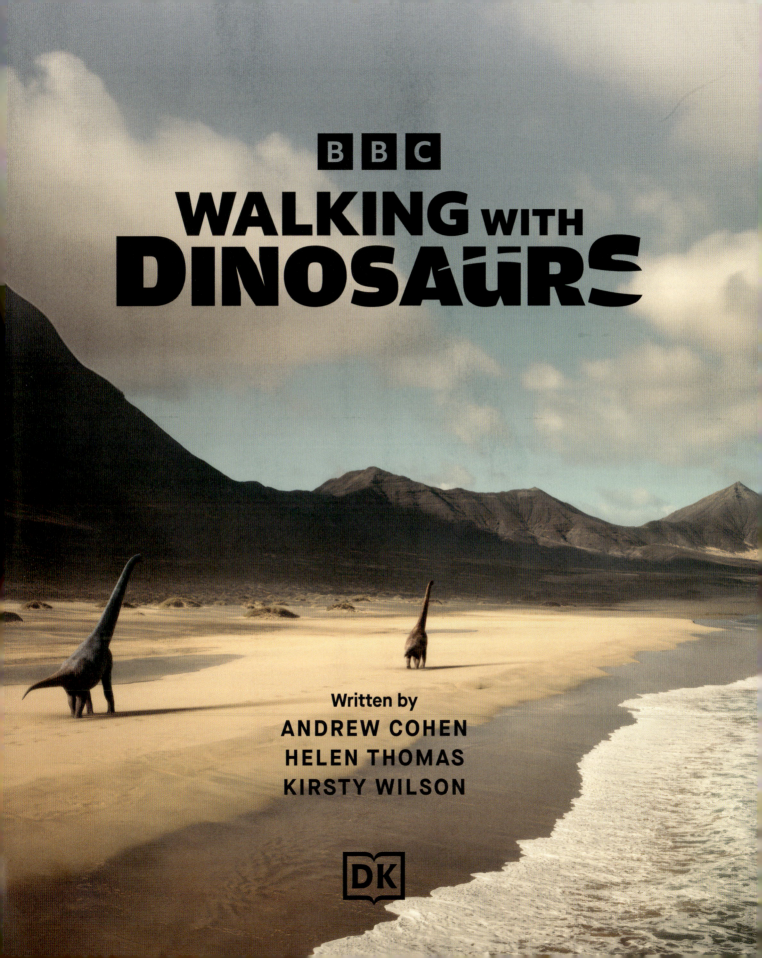

BBC
WALKING WITH DINOSAURS

Written by
ANDREW COHEN
HELEN THOMAS
KIRSTY WILSON

DK

Edited for DK by Rona Skene
Designed for DK by XAB Design
Picture Research for DK by Jo Walton
Consultant Dr. Dean Lomax

Editor Sophie Dryburgh
Production Editor Siu Yin Chan
Senior Production Controller Lloyd Robertson
Managing Editor Tori Kosara
Managing Art Editor Jo Connor
Art Director Charlotte Coulais
Publisher Paula Regan
Managing Director Mark Searle

Jacket designed by Jo Connor

First American Edition, 2025
Published in the United States by DK Publishing,
a division of Penguin Random House LLC
1745 Broadway, 20th Floor, New York, NY 10019

Page design copyright © 2025 Dorling Kindersley Limited
25 26 27 28 10 9 8 7 6 5 4 3 2 1
001–351296–June/2025

BBC, BBC EARTH and WALKING WITH DINOSAURS (word marks and logos) are trade marks of the British Broadcasting Corporation and are used under licence. BBC logo © BBC 1996. BBC EARTH logo © BBC 2008. WALKING WITH DINOSAURS logo © BBC 2010-2025. Licensed by BBC Studios.

All rights reserved.
Without limiting the rights under the copyright reserved above, no part of this publication may be reproduced, stored in or introduced into a retrieval system, or transmitted, in any form, or by any means (electronic, mechanical, photocopying, recording, or otherwise), without the prior written permission of the copyright owner.

No part of this publication may be used or reproduced in any manner for the purpose of training artificial intelligence technologies or systems.

Published in Great Britain by Dorling Kindersley Limited

ISBN: 979-8-2171-2803-7

DK books are available at special discounts when purchased in bulk for sales promotions, premiums, fund-raising, or educational use. For details, contact: DK Publishing Special Markets, 1745 Broadway, 20th Floor, New York, NY 10019
SpecialSales@dk.com

Printed and bound in Canada

www.dk.com
www.bbcearth.com

This book was made with Forest Stewardship Council™ certified paper—one small step in DK's commitment to a sustainable future.
Learn more at www.dk.com/uk/information/sustainability

AUTHORS' DEDICATIONS

Andrew would like to thank Dylan and Charlie for reminding him that monsters really do exist.

Helen would like to thank Dave for his dry wit and unwavering support; her inspirational friends for all the chats and litres of EG tea; and the world's best brother Robert, Sylke and nephews Max, Ben and Zac for the competitive board gaming, laughter and endless chaos!

Kirsty would like to thank her incredible family; doing this job wouldn't be possible without their endless support. And a very special thank you to her very own Coco-saurus, there's no one more roarsome.

CONTENTS

FINDING LOST WORLDS	6	**THE DEADLIEST PACK**	134
		Albertosaurus	138
THE BIGGEST KILLER	26	Coastal Forests	148
Spinosaurus	32		
Wetland World	38	**THE EPIC MIGRATION**	158
		Pachyrhinosaurus	162
TERRESTRIAL TITAN	62	Mountains and Forests	170
Lusotitan	68		
An Island Habitat	74	**THE LAST DINOSAURS**	190
		T.rex	194
THE CREATURES OF GRAND COUNTY	96	A Humid Swamp	202
Utahraptor	100	Triceratops	220
Plains and Forests	108		
Gastonia	118	**MAKING *WALKING WITH DINOSAURS***	230
		Glossary	248
		Index	250
		About the Authors	254
		Acknowledgements	255

FINDING LOST WORLDS

INTRODUCTION

> For a select group of people, time travel is not a daydream, but their everyday reality.

STEPPING BACK IN TIME

For most of us, time travel seems impossible. We are firmly anchored to the here and now, unable to venture back into the past or leap forwards to peer into the future, except in our imaginations. The dream of stepping back into an ancient world has to remain just that, a fantasy. But for a select group of people, time travel is their reality and part of their everyday business.

To be clear, we are not referring to your police-box, sonic-screwdriver, flashing-light, flux-capacitor type of time lords; the time travellers we are talking about are much more modest than that. They are the scientists who dedicate their lives to the endless quest of understanding the deep history of our planet. These people spend their days hunting for places on Earth where a window can be opened into the prehistoric past, allowing us to travel back millions of years in search of real-life monsters — in search of the dinosaurs.

▼ **Feeling the heat**
In Utah, USA, scientists work under makeshift shade at a dig site during filming of *Walking With Dinosaurs*.

8   INTRODUCTION

◀ **Manual worker**
In Alberta, Canada, a palaeontologist expertly uses a pickaxe to chip a specimen out from a rocky cliff.

In this book we want to give you a taste of what it's like to be one of those dinosaur-hunting explorers of past worlds. Palaeontology is not an endeavour for the faint-hearted; to delve this far back in time requires grit and determination, trekking to locations that are some of the most beautiful on Earth but also some of the most inhospitable. Once there, the work is anything but easy. It most often starts with the removal of tonnes of rock, digging day after day in the heat, dirt, and dust. This is time travel through hard labour, digging down into millions of years of dense geological history. And then, when these explorers come within touching distance of their target, all that brute force is replaced by a much more delicate process — the painstaking task of scraping away layer upon layer of ancient earth and soil until the prize hidden beneath can finally be revealed.

▼ **Brushing away the past**
In Utah, a member of the dig team uses a soft paintbrush to clear away loose debris from a newly unearthed fossil.

It's at this moment that the most ancient of bones can once again see the light of day, glimpsed for the first time by human eyes, they open a window directly into a lost world. To the untrained eye, it can be difficult to comprehend what it is that is actually lying in the ground. The fossilized shapes in the dirt often appear at first sight to be nothing more than rocks. But to the eye of a palaeontologist, each bone is not only a clue to the anatomy of a lost creature, it also paints a picture of a long-forgotten world and a life story that is just waiting to be told.

FINDING LOST WORLDS

AGE OF THE DINOSAURS

For most of Earth's history, its only life forms were single-celled organisms. Then around 600 MYA (million years ago), multi-celled animals appeared and an incredible diversity of life evolved — including, for the 165 million years of the Mesozoic Era, the dinosaurs.

BRACHIOSAURUS (150 MYA)
One of the heaviest and tallest sauropods; remains found in North America

COELOPHYSIS (212 MYA)
Carnivorous theropod with slim, pointed jaws; fossils have been found from North America to Africa

SCELIDOSAURUS (190 MYA)
Plant eating dinosaur in the thyreophoran group — the first armoured dinosaurs

HERRERASAURUS (231 MYA)
Bipedal hunter from Argentina; one of the earliest known dinosaurs

GUANLONG (160 MYA)
From China, one of the tyrannosauroid group of theropods. Grew to 3 m (10 ft) long

PLATEOSAURUS (220 MYA)
European "prosauropod" up to 8 m (26 ft) long; unlike later sauropods, walked on two legs

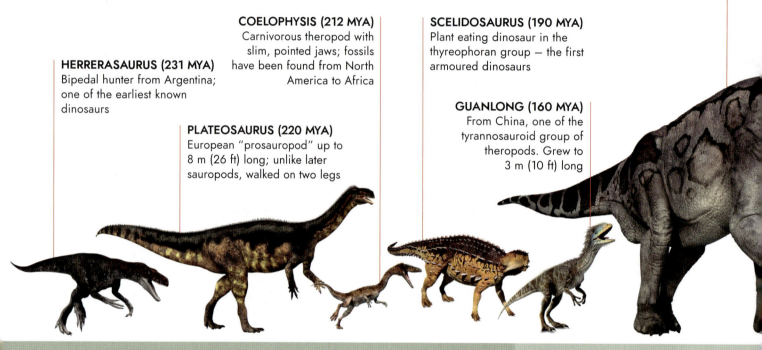

TRIASSIC LIFE 252–201 MYA

At the start of this period, life was recovering from the world's most devastating mass extinction, and conditions were harsh. More than 70 per cent of the life on Earth had been wiped out and it took about 10 million years for ecosystems to recover. During the period, the surviving reptile groups spread widely over the supercontinent of Pangaea and the first true dinosaurs appeared, about 230 million years ago. The Triassic ended with another mass extinction event, probably as a result of volcanic activity. More than 75 per cent of animal life did not survive.

JURASSIC LIFE

By now, the supercontinent Pangaea had begun to break into two large landmasses and the Atlantic Ocean was forming. Moist ocean winds brought rain to deserts and plants began to grow where deserts had been, providing plenty of food for new kinds

MARINE REPTILES

Marine reptiles held sway in the oceans of the Mesozoic Era. There was huge diversity, but the three main groups were ichthyosaurs, plesiosaurs, and mosasaurs. Almost all marine reptiles did not survive the Mesozoic Era — however, sea turtles did make it and their close relatives are still alive today.

ARCHELON
This Late Cretaceous reptile is the largest recorded sea turtle.

PTEROSAURS

The first vertebrates to evolve powered flight were pterosaurs; they flourished throughout the Mesozoic. Although not dinosaurs, the two groups did share some characteristics. Their bodies were feathered, but they flew using their forelimbs, which had a membrane attached and stretc hed between one elongated finger and a foot.

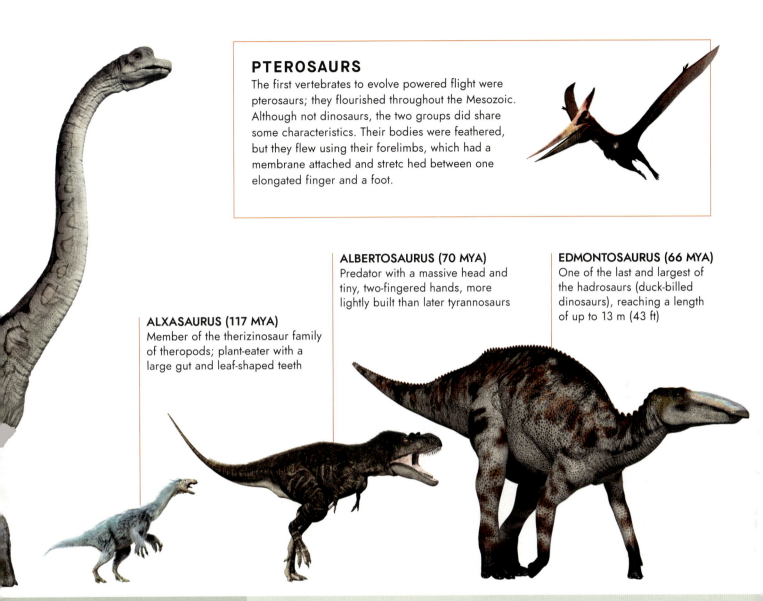

ALBERTOSAURUS (70 MYA)
Predator with a massive head and tiny, two-fingered hands, more lightly built than later tyrannosaurs

EDMONTOSAURUS (66 MYA)
One of the last and largest of the hadrosaurs (duck-billed dinosaurs), reaching a length of up to 13 m (43 ft)

ALXASAURUS (117 MYA)
Member of the therizinosaur family of theropods; plant-eater with a large gut and leaf-shaped teeth

201–145 MYA

of dinosaurs. Sauropods and theropods flourished and ornithopods, stegosaurs, and ankylosaurs all appeared. The Jurassic Period did not end in cataclysm, but with gradual climate change and the emergence of new life forms as the planet cooled.

CRETACEOUS LIFE 145–66 MYA

In this period, the two huge continents split apart and the first flowering plants and grasses appeared. Dinosaurs continued to diversify and some grew to truly gargantuan size. Other life forms also flourished, including birds and the modern insect groups. The end of the Cretaceous Period came with a cataclysmic asteroid strike. In the dark, cold, climate-changing aftermath, more than half of all life on Earth perished, including all non-avian dinosaurs. Those dinosaurs that survived evolved into the birds that populate the planet today.

ELASMOSAURUS
This four-flippered reptile was one of the plesiosaur group.

MOSASAURUS
The mosasaurs were massive, huge-jawed predators.

ICHTHYOSAURUS
Ichthyosaurs were dolphin-like, air-breathing reptiles.

EARTH'S LONG LIFE

Travelling this many millions of years into the past can be a disorienting experience, particularly when we are so used to measuring time in tens or, at most, hundreds of years. Before we get going, we need to put the scale of such deep time into some sort of perspective, allowing us to comprehend

▶ **Ancient wonder**
The Great Pyramid is one of the world's oldest built structures; however, it represents modern history when compared to the age of the dinosaurs.

just how far back we are about to travel. So let's start with something that is often used as a touchstone of ancient history, the Great Pyramid of Giza. Few monuments represent the deep past as powerfully as this extraordinary construction — and yet it was completed just 4,600 years ago. Stretching a little further back, we come to the last Ice Age, when much of Earth's northern hemisphere was covered by vast, slow-moving glaciers. This period ended around 11,500 years ago. The last of our Neanderthal cousins disappeared around 40,000 years ago and it was around 315,000 years ago that our species, *Homo sapiens*, first walked on the planet.

All of this helps to take us further and further back into the past, to a time before humans even

▼ **Early human species**
A Neanderthal skull (left), compared to *Homo sapiens* (right). It's thought that the two species coexisted in northern Europe for several thousand years.

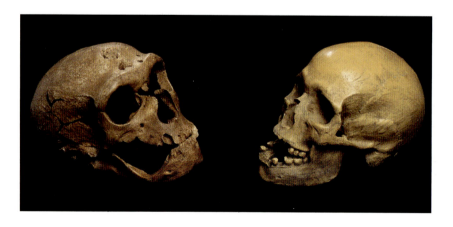

12 INTRODUCTION

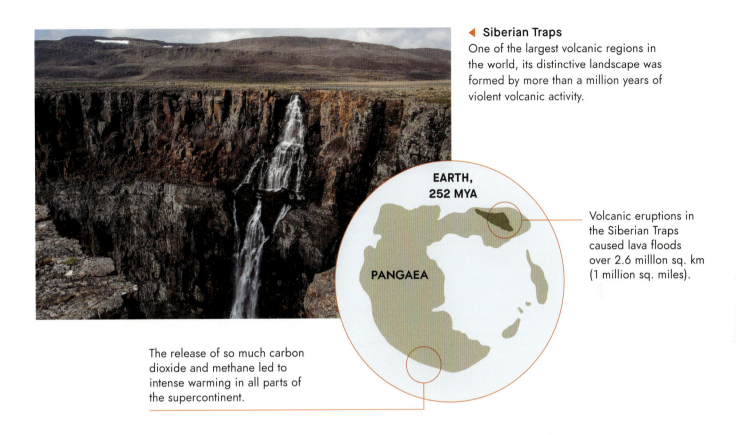

◀ **Siberian Traps**
One of the largest volcanic regions in the world, its distinctive landscape was formed by more than a million years of violent volcanic activity.

Volcanic eruptions in the Siberian Traps caused lava floods over 2.6 million sq. km (1 million sq. miles).

The release of so much carbon dioxide and methane led to intense warming in all parts of the supercontinent.

existed; and yet in the geological timescale, and for anyone in the business of hunting for dinosaurs, these are all events that may as well have happened just yesterday.

The landing zone for our journey back in time begins a staggering 252 million years ago in a geological time period known as the Late Triassic. This was a time when Earth was just beginning to recover from perhaps the most cataclysmic event since life began on our planet. The Permian-Triassic extinction, as it is known, accounted for the disappearance of well over 80 per cent of species. The event was triggered by massive volcanic activity in an area that is known today as the Siberian Traps. The eruptions and their aftermath led to a devastating change in climate, which transformed the oceans and atmosphere from nurturers of life into a toxic hell. And yet out of this catastrophe, a new world began to emerge.

A devastating change in climate transformed the planet from nurturer of life to toxic hell.

FINDING LOST WORLDS

13

CLASSIFYING DINOSAURS

Dinosaurs are usually divided into two main orders; ornithischians and saurischians. This distinction, based on observed hip shape, was first proposed by English biologist Harry Seeley in 1888, and has been used ever since. Around 1,500 species of dinosaur have been identified so far, but this is a fraction of the number of species that have ever existed.

FIRST DINOSAURS
The earliest dinosaurs evolved from archosaurs — dinosaur-like reptiles — such as Nyasasaurus. The earliest dinosaur bones found so far are 233 million years old.

Nyasasaurus

SAURISCHIANS
("Lizard-hipped")
The name given to this group refers to the fact that many of these dinosaurs had pelvic bones like those of lizards. However, we now know that some did not. Saurischians had longer necks than ornithischians.

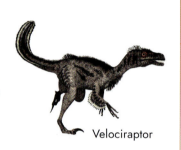
Velociraptor

ORNITHISCHIANS
("Bird-hipped")
Ornithischians were so named because their pelvic bones seemed to early palaeontologists to be like those of birds. They had beaks supported by an extra bone in the jaw, leaf-shaped teeth with large serrations, and fleshy "cheeks".

Stegosaurus

DIFFERENT HIPS
Dinosaurs were divided into two main groups according to the formation of their hip bones. In most saurischians, the pubis bone was lizard-like and pointed forwards, while the ischium pointed backwards. In all ornithischians, the bird-like pubis and ischium both pointed backwards. Confusingly, modern birds are actually saurischians and not closely related to the ornithischians.

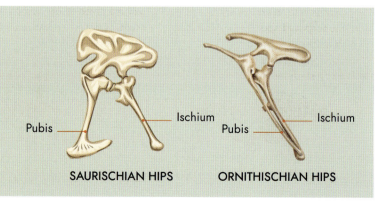
SAURISCHIAN HIPS   ORNITHISCHIAN HIPS

INTRODUCTION

THEROPODS
This group was bipedal, and most were carnivorous, with sharp, serrated teeth. Modern birds are evolved from theropods.

T.rex

SAUROPODOMORPHS
Most members of this plant-eating group walked on four legs. This group included the sauropods, which were mostly giant, long-necked grazers, with pillar-like legs.

Diplodocus

STEGOSAURS
These heavily-built thyreophorans sported rows of distinctive bony plates and spikes that ran down the back. They walked on all fours.

Gigantspinosaurus

THYREOPHORANS

ANKYLOSAURS
The low-slung, pot-bellied, plant-eating ankylosaurs were armoured with bony plates and spikes. Some had heavy tail clubs that they could use as defensive weapons.

Gastonia

MARGINOCEPHALIANS

ORNITHOPODS
These were highly successful herbivores with beaks. Later ornithopods had specialized teeth, which helped them to grind through tough plants. Some had a showy crest on the head.

Iguanodon

PACHYCEPHALOSAURS
Plant-eating pachycephalosaurs had massively thick, dome-shaped skulls, which often had extra frills. They walked on two legs.

Pachycephalosaurus

CERATOPSIANS
These horned, plant-eating dinosaurs had hooked, parrot-like beaks, and walked on all fours. Most had large heads with horns and big, bony frills.

Pachyrhinosaurus

FINDING LOST WORLDS

THE FIRST DINOSAURS
Around 231 million years ago, the first dinosaur remains appear in the fossil record — and one of the best locations on the planet to find evidence of these early dinosaurs is in the Ischigualasto Formation, in northwestern Argentina. It's here that we've discovered the remains of some of the earliest dinosaurs, including Herrerasaurus, a predator 350 kg (770 lb) in weight and 6 m (19.6 ft) long, that prowled the forests of the Late Triassic. Herrerasaurus would have shared its world with other theropod dinosaurs, such as Eodromaeus and the diminutive Eoraptor which, at just 1.6 m (5.2 ft) long, was perhaps one of the most confusing of the first dinosaurs. Its three toes were uncannily similar to those of T.rex, yet it had the teeth of a plant-eater, and so the debate continues as to its classification.

▶ **Lunar landscape**
The distinctive rock formations of the Ischigualasto badlands have earned it the nickname *Valle de la Luna* ("Valley of the Moon").

The Late Triassic Period marked the beginning of the age of the dinosaurs, which would stretch across the next 170 million years; a vast expanse of time during which thousands of species of reptile ruled the land. The story of the dinosaurs would be played out over three acts; the Triassic Period transformed into the Jurassic, which lasted from 201–145 million years ago. In turn, the Jurassic gave way to the Cretaceous Period, which continued until the age of the reptiles came to an abrupt end 66 million years ago. Together, these three geological periods are known as the Mesozoic Era, a name that is derived from the Greek for middle (*Meso*) and life (*zoon*). As we will see in the following chapters, the variety of dinosaur species that lived through the Mesozoic Era is vast. From the fossil evidence we have uncovered we first began to realize the bones belonged to dinosaurs, and we've since been able to uncover and identify around 1,500 different dinosaur species on the landmasses of every modern continent on Earth. These egg-laying creatures could be peaceable herbivores or deadly carnivores. They could be bipedal, quadrupedal, or in some cases able to switch between the two. They could be unimaginable giants, 33 m (131 ft) long and 18 m (59 ft) tall – the largest land animals ever to walk the Earth. But they could also be diminutive creatures no more than 10 cm (4 in) in length. And it wasn't just in size that there was so much diversity across the dinosaur kingdom; horns, crests, feathers, and spines created an array of different physical characteristics. These features played an integral part in the behaviour of these extraordinary animals; from the attack and defence strategies of predator-prey relationships to complex courting rituals using elaborate displays – this was a natural world filled with endless wonder.

Eoraptor stood upright on muscular back legs.

▲ **Eoraptor**
With its name meaning "early plunderer", Eoraptor was one of the earliest dinosaurs to evolve.

EARTH'S ERAS

Eoarchean	4–3.6 billion years ago
Paleoarchean	3.6–3.2 billion years ago
Mesoarchean	3.2–2.8 billion years ago
Neoarchean	2.8–2.5 billion years ago
Paleoproterozoic	2.5–1.6 billion years ago
Mesoproterozoic	1.6–1 billion years ago
Neoproterozoic	1 billion–541 million years ago
Paleozoic	541–c. 252 million years ago
Mesozoic	c.252–66 million years ago
Cenozoic	66 million years ago–present

◄ **Geological time scale**
Earth's 4-billion-year history is divided into 10 separate eras, primarily based on stratigraphy, which is the study and classification of rock layers.

FINDING LOST WORLDS

PLANET OF THE DINOSAURS

Throughout the Mesozoic, the tectonic plates that make up Earth's crust pushed together to make new continents and pulled apart to form oceans and seas. These changes created new climate conditions and habitats — and the dinosaurs were among the animals who were best able to adapt and thrive.

TRIASSIC EARTH

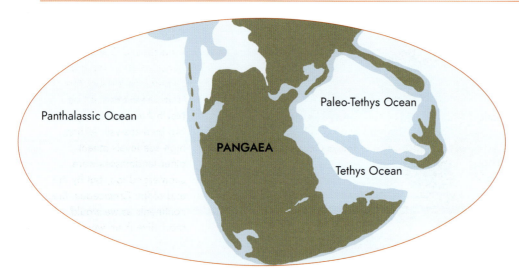

252-201 MYA
In the first of the three periods that make up the Mesozoic Era, all the continents that had existed before joined up to form a single landmass, which stretched from pole to pole. This supercontinent is known as Pangaea. Lush forests fringed the huge ocean, but the vast interior of Pangaea was largely desert.

JURASSIC EARTH

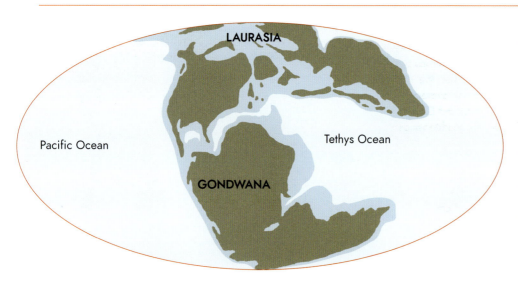

201-145 MYA
During the Jurassic, Pangaea split apart to form two landmasses, Laurasia and Gondwana (which would become Africa and South America). This separation of the supercontinent transformed the climate, allowing moist air to reach more of the land and turning deserts into flourishing forests, teeming with life.

ANCIENT OCEAN

As Pangaea broke apart, the Tethys Ocean formed, separating the continents that would become Africa and Asia. It disappeared about 24–21 million years ago. Today, the Black and Caspian Seas, seen in this satellite image, are the last remnants of this vast ocean.

CRETACEOUS EARTH

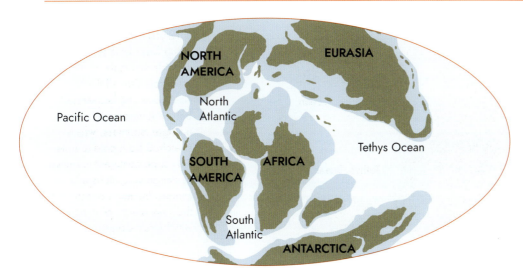

145-66 MYA

Laurasia and Gondwana began to break up and for much of the period, the landmass that would be North America was split in two by a seaway. At first, high sea levels meant other landmasses were submerged too, but by the end of the Cretaceous, the continents as we would recognize them were taking shape.

EARTH TODAY

There are seven separate continents on Earth today, and all are still on the move. As plate tectonics push the Indian subcontinent and Asia together, the Himalayas mountain range grows by an average of 1 cm (0.4 in) a year, and when Africa and Europe collide in 50 million years' time, the Mediterranean Sea will close up altogether.

Australia is moving north by around 7 cm (2.7 in) every year.

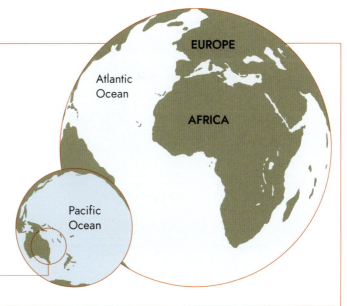

FINDING LOST WORLDS

A DIFFERENT WORLD

Throughout the Mesozoic, it was not only the animals that made this era so distinct from our own. In the hothouse climate that prevailed through this time, plant life looked very different as well. The species that proliferated more than any other were the gymnosperms — woody, flowerless, seed-bearing plants, which we would recognize today in the shape of conifers, cycads, and ferns. The age of the dinosaurs was not just largely devoid of flowers; those now-ubiquitous plants, the grasses, barely featured in the landscapes that they would cover today.

> The age of the dinosaurs was not just largely devoid of flowers, but of grasses, too.

In fact, so much that we take for granted was different through this time; even the continents looked nothing like the familiar landmasses we see today. Instead, across those 170 million years, the ground was slowly but relentlessly shifting beneath the feet of the dinosaurs as the single massive supercontinent, known as Pangaea, broke apart on its way to the formation of the seven continents we see on Earth today.

The rise of the dinosaurs is just one example of life creating a seemingly unstoppable force. The history of our planet is littered with moments like this, when one particular life form seems to ascend and seize for itself the title of ruler of the world. There have been periods of time during which the natural world was dominated by giant insects, giant sponges, and even giant fungi; and yet despite these life forms seeming to be, in their respective times, completely unassailable, every one of these examples of biological dominance ultimately failed and lost their crown. And as we know, despite 170 million years of supremacy, the dinosaurs' time would also pass.

▶ **Triassic trees**
The Petrified Forest in Arizona, USA, is strewn with fossilized remnants of the Late Triassic forests in which early dinosaurs roamed.

◀ **Uncovering the past**
A palaeontologist examines a Triceratops jawbone. Every find has the potential to add to, or even transform, the current knowledge base.

UNFOLDING STORY

Just as the age of the dinosaurs was ushered in with a catastrophic event, so it ended with another one. Around 66 million years ago, with the dinosaur party seemingly in full swing, a city-sized rock came hurtling towards Earth from across the solar system, impacting the surface of the planet in what is now the Yucatán peninsula of Mexico. An event, we now know, that once again sent the Earth into climatic chaos and resulted in the mass extinction of much of its animal and plant life — including almost every species of dinosaur.

And so, as the curtain fell on this grand act in the drama that is Earth's history, the evidence of these extraordinary creatures disappeared into the dirt and dust, with just a precious few of their remains preserved in the ground through the seemingly miraculous process of fossilization. Soft tissue decomposed to leave a skeleton that, in just the right conditions, would be transformed into bones made of solid rock.

Under the ground, the mineralized bones would lie for tens or hundreds of millions of years, waiting for our time-travellers to turn up and uncover them. Armed with their panoply of palaeontological tools — some almost as old as humankind itself and others harnessing cutting-edge technology — palaeontologists seek, on our behalf, to discover the secrets of those long-lost worlds and the incredible animals that inhabited them for so long.

There is, as yet, no end to this story — as long as we remain curious and there is ground left to break, there will be intrepid, time-travelling detectives searching for clues to solve the mysteries of Earth's dinosaurs.

FOSSILIZATION

The process that transforms organic matter into rock — mineralization — is the most common type of fossilization. It can occur in different ways, depending on the conditions and environment in which the animal or plant lived and died. More durable body parts such as bones and teeth are more likely to last long enough to become fossils.

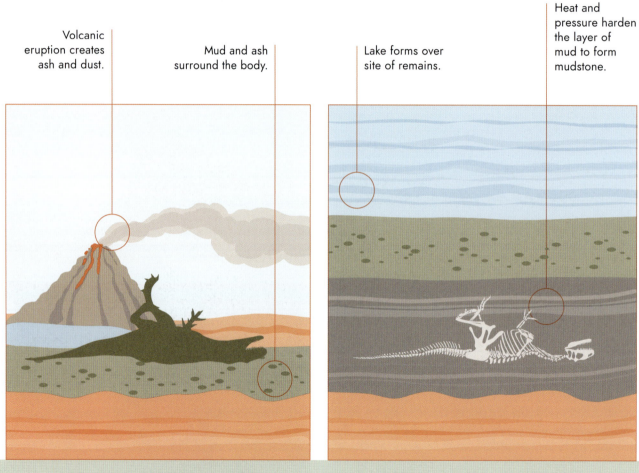

147 MILLION YEARS AGO

100 MILLION YEARS AGO

DEATH

At the end of the Jurassic, an Allosaurus dies. Its body lies in soft mud by a river. Nearby, a volcano erupts, pouring out lava and ash, covering the body.

BURIAL

Protected from scavengers by layers of sediment from the river, the soft tissues decay, leaving bones. More sediment builds up over the skeleton.

Ancient ocean-dwellers

The most commonly found fossils are of ancient marine life, such as ammonites — small, sea-dwelling creatures that first appeared 450 million years ago. The fossil remains of their spiral shells are found in large numbers all over the world.

Fossilized bones or footprints may form in newer layers of rock.

Layers of rock build up and mountains may form on older rock.

Erosion has exposed part of the fossilized dinosaur.

2 MILLION YEARS AGO

5 YEARS AGO

MINERALIZATION

Minerals in the surrounding layers seep into the bones, which turn to rock over time. Wind and rain start to erode the top layers of rock.

EXPOSURE AND DISCOVERY

Erosion and weathering continues to wear away and move the rock. Part of the fossil is exposed and discovered. The rest of the skeleton is then unearthed.

FINDING LOST WORLDS

TYPES OF FOSSIL

There are many ways in which living things leave behind evidence of their existence. Fossils are either the bodily remains of animals, plants, or microbes, or traces of them, such as footprints, nests, or droppings. Most fossils do contain a life form or object itself — they are copies or impressions left on, or in, rock.

1 Mineralized fossils
This Compsognathus skeleton is a well-preserved example of the most common form of fossilization — mineralization. This is when organic material, such as bone, is replaced by minerals that harden into rock in the same size and shape.

2 Impressions
An impression fossil is an imprint of an organism that is no longer there, because the original life form decomposed entirely — as was the case for these fern leaves.

3 Tracks
Preserved footptints occur where a dinosaur stepped in mud or sediment, and the track was quickly covered with more sediment before it could disappear.

4 Eggs
Eggs could fossilize if they were laid on sand or soft ground, then covered by sediment. Shells and embryos of unhatched dinosaurs have been discovered as fossils.

5 Total preservation
When an environment has no oxygen, a dead organism cannot decay. The entire body of this mosquito has been preserved in amber (solidified tree resin).

6 Moulds and casts
This trilobite's exoskeleton dissolved during fossilization, leaving a space the exact shape of the creature. Sediment then filled that space to form a cast.

FINDING LOST WORLDS

CHAPTER ONE

THE BIGGEST KILLER

THE "LOST" SPINOSAURUS

When a story is more than 100 million years in the making, it can be difficult to know where to begin. But in the case of the story of Spinosaurus, perhaps the biggest predator ever to walk on Earth, we're not going to start in the Late Cretaceous Period, nor in the early 20th century, when the first remains of this extraordinary creature were discovered in the Egyptian desert, but on the night of 24 April 1944 — a night when war continued to rage across Europe and much of the world. Some 234 Lancaster Bomber aircraft and 16 Mosquito fighters left the RAF bases of southern England on one of the most significant bombing missions of World War II; their target was the Bavaria region of Germany. Together with the US Air Force, the RAF planes made up a force of more than 800 Allied aircraft, all with Munich and its surrounding area in their sights.

> This Spinosaurus story begins not in the Late Cretaceous, but on an April night in 1944.

On the target list of the RAF's Bomber Command were a mixture of industrial manufacturing sites and airfields scattered around the city. This would turn out to be one of the last air battles of the war when the *Luftwaffe* — Germany's air force — was effective enough to be able to mount a serious defence. But despite the loss of nine Lancasters, the RAF inflicted extensive damage, with 80 per cent of the buildings in their target area destroyed. But as was almost always the case with such indiscriminate "carpet bombing" raids, many other buildings were also hit that night, resulting in thousands of casualties and the loss of hundreds of civilian lives.

▶ **Lancaster Bombers, 1944**
The Lancaster was the RAF's most successful long-range bomber plane. Its 9,979-kg (22,000-lb) "grand slam" bomb was the heaviest carried by any WWII plane.

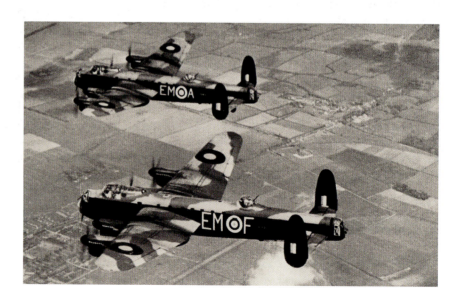

28

CHAPTER ONE

◀ **Munich in ruins**
More than 90 per cent of central Munich was destroyed in the Allied bombings. This photo shows Marienplatz, around 500 metres from the Alte Akademie building, where Markgraf's finds were housed.

Undoubtedly an interesting story, but you may well be wondering what on Earth this has to do with an enormous predatory dinosaur that lived more than 94 million years ago. Well, the answer lies in the opening of one of those Lancasters' bay doors, and the dropping of one bomb amongst the thousands that rained down on the city that night. A single bomb that missed its intended target, and instead struck the building that housed the Palaeontological Museum of Munich.

The museum held some of the most precious fragments in the history of palaeontology. It included a collection of material discovered by a German palaeontologist, Richard Markgraf, whilst on an expedition in the Bahariya Formation of western Egypt in 1912. Markgraf was one of the world's most prolific fossil-hunters of the early 20th century, having fallen into the bone-hunting business whilst working as a pianist in the bar of a fashionable Cairo hotel.

▲ **Shepheard's Hotel, 1906**
The most famous hotel in Cairo was a hub for expats, tourists, and visiting foreign dignitaries.

Career development in the field of palaeontology was a little different then; being in the right place at the right time was almost as likely to make a dino-hunter of you than years of academic research. And so, with no formal training, Markgraf was able to utilize his knowledge of Arabic and the contacts he made at the hotel to manoeuvre himself into the fossil business.

THE BIGGEST KILLER

▶ **Richard Markgraf**
Markgraf's successful partnership with Stromer ended with the outbreak of war in 1914. He died in Cairo just two years later, at the age of 46.

Once Markgraf had mastered the basic techniques, he became almost unstoppable. After working with a number of respected palaeontologists, Markgraf partnered up with the German aristocrat Ernst Freiherr Stromer von Reichenbach, more usually known as Ernst Stromer. The academic Stromer came from a very different background to Markgraf; his father was mayor of Nuremberg and the extended family was strewn with the glittering careers of politicians, scientists, and lawyers, all making the most of the privileged position they held in Bavarian high society. So it was with the confidence of kings that Stromer led a series of expeditions to Egypt at the turn of the 20th century.

Starting in 1901, Stromer and Markgraf travelled across much of the Western Desert in search of undiscovered fossil beds. One of their final trips together was an expedition to the area known as the Bahariya Oasis, where they arrived in January 1911, after what was reported to have been an extremely difficult and taxing journey. This was not helped by the fact that Markgraf was far from a well man. His long history of ill health included bouts of typhoid, malaria, and dysentery — all of which left him a long way short of the levels of physical resilience needed to dig, day after day, in the desert. But the two men had become close friends and Stromer knew that, for all Markgraf's vulnerabilities, the risk of bringing him into the field was far outweighed by the increased chance he created of them striking palaeontological gold. It turned out to be a gamble that rapidly paid off.

DIG DEEPER

Stromer's bones
As well as Spinosaurus, Stromer's notable finds in Egypt included the large herbivore Aegyptosaurus and two predators, Carcharodontosaurus and Bahariasaurus. In the image above, he is holding a Bahariasaurus femur.

Within days they had unearthed the partial remains of what seemed to be a giant theropod dinosaur. The incomplete skeleton included fragments of jawbone, teeth, vertebrae, and perhaps most strikingly of all, giant neural spines, the longest of which measured 1.65 m (5.5 ft).

On 18 February 1911, Stromer left Egypt and headed home to Germany, where he spent the next few years drawing and describing the finds before publishing details of his discoveries in 1915. By this time, Markgraf was a very sick man with only a few months to live, and so it would be Stromer alone who would be left to introduce the world to the extraordinary and strange new predatory species of a dinosaur he called *Spinosaurus aegyptiacus* – "spine lizard of Egypt".

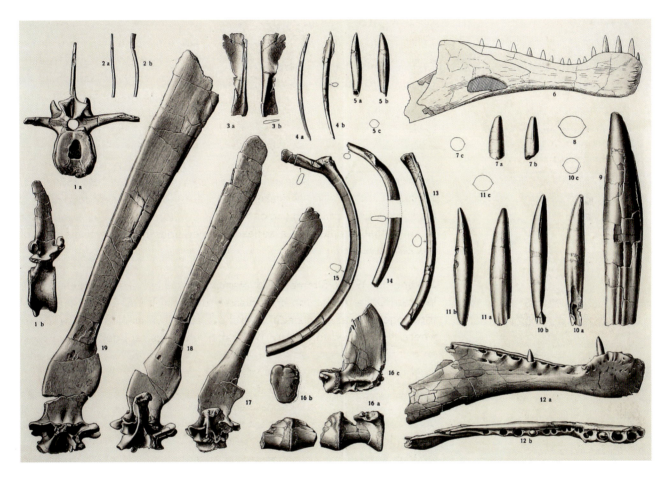

▲ **Spinosaurus fossils, 1915**
In Stromer's 1915 paper in the *Abhandlungen* (Discourses) of the Bavarian Academy of Sciences, he presented detailed drawings of the bones. The key gives Stromer's original descriptions.

KEY
1 Caudal vertebra
2 Small lateral gastral element
3 Left angular (jaw) bone
4 Gastral rib
5 Smallest tooth
6 Left mandibular ramus (lower jaw)
7 First left lower tooth
8 Second largest isolated tooth
9 Largest isolated tooth
10 Middle-sized, posterior tooth
11 Middle sized, posterior tooth
12 Right mandibular ramus (lower jaw)
13 Single-headed right rib
14 Two-headed flat right rib
15 Two-headed large right rib
16 Sacral (lower back) vertebrae
17, 18, 19 Neural arches with neural spine

THE BIGGEST KILLER

SPINOSAURUS

This huge carnivore was longer than T.rex and considerably taller. Enormous, skin-covered dorsal spines formed a gigantic "sail" on the back. The spines were anchored by muscles and composed of dense bone with few blood vessels. This suggests that the sail was meant for display and not to trap heat or store fat.

Sail would have been visible even when the animal entered the water.

Position of nostrils enabled breathing while the animal was partly submerged.

Small pores in the snout may have held pressure sensors for detecting prey.

Long, flexible neck enabled Spinosaurus to strike fast with its snapping jaws.

DATA FILE

SCALE

Name: Spinosaurus
Type: Theropod
Length: 14 m (46 ft)
Weight: 6–7 tonnes (6.6–7.7 tons)
Diet: Carnivore
Found in: North Africa

TRIASSIC	JURASSIC	CRETACEOUS
252 MYA	201 MYA	145 MYA

SPINOSAURUS TIMELINE: 112–97 MYA

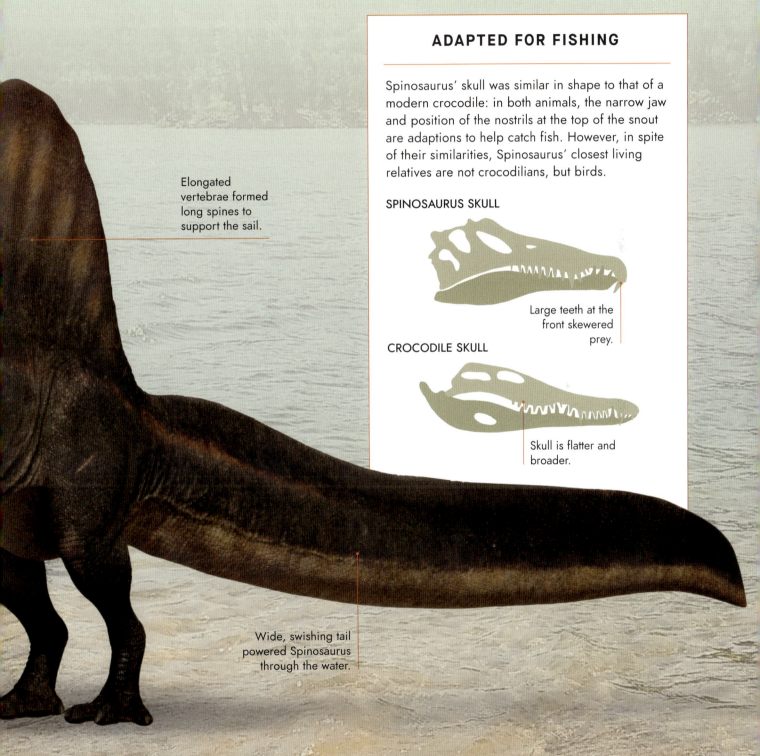

Elongated vertebrae formed long spines to support the sail.

Wide, swishing tail powered Spinosaurus through the water.

ADAPTED FOR FISHING

Spinosaurus' skull was similar in shape to that of a modern crocodile: in both animals, the narrow jaw and position of the nostrils at the top of the snout are adaptions to help catch fish. However, in spite of their similarities, Spinosaurus' closest living relatives are not crocodilians, but birds.

SPINOSAURUS SKULL

Large teeth at the front skewered prey.

CROCODILE SKULL

Skull is flatter and broader.

Spinosaurus is not the easiest of dinosaurs to get your head around. A hodge-podge of a creature, it seems to have borrowed a range of body parts to create a patchwork monster, both puzzling and terrifying in equal measure. Based on his partial collection of bones, Stromer was the first to describe, in his 1915 paper, this extraordinary creature. Around 14 m (46 ft) in length, with a flat, crocodilian-like skull housing the giant jaws of a carnivore, this was an animal that seemed perfectly formed for a piscivorous (fish-eating) lifestyle. Walking on two powerful hind legs and with a giant structure on its back constructed around enormous neural spines, it's easy to see why this new discovery caught the imagination. "One might think of the existence of a large hump of fat to which the [neural spines] gave internal support", wrote Stromer as he tried to make sense of this creature's extraordinary anatomy.

> For the second time in its long history, the skeleton of this ancient creature was buried out of sight, and this time it was gone forever.

With a new genus and species introduced to the world, one that was up with the largest predators so far known to walk the Earth, it seemed that Stromer had made the discovery of a lifetime. But with only an incomplete skeleton to investigate, many questions remained unanswered and a full image of this dinosaur remained tantalizingly out of view. Further fragmentary remains would be discovered in the same region 20 years later, including vertebrae and hind limbs, and these added a little to our understanding of this enormous predator. But with no more finds after that, Spinosaurus was a dinosaur still wrapped in many layers of mystery and myth — a collection of bones that rightly held pride of place within Stromer's extensive fossil collection.

And so it came to be that, 100 million years after the animal's death, the only physical evidence of its existence was stored in that Munich museum on that April night — right in the path of that Lancaster and the single bomb that made its way through the building's roof. This direct hit brought about the destruction of almost all of Stromer's priceless collection, including the remains of his Spinosaurus. That night, for the second time in its long history, the skeleton of this ancient creature was buried out of sight, and this time it was gone forever.

▼ **Stromer's reconstruction**
More than 20 years after he published his findings, Stromer produced this reconstruction of a Spinosaurus; the shaded bones represent those he recovered.

34

CHAPTER ONE

With the destruction of Stromer's collection, almost all traces of Spinosaurus disappeared from the palaeontological record. Left frozen and only partly understood in the annals of science, Spinosaurus became an almost mythical creature, impossible to investigate beyond the few photos, papers, and memories that remained after the bombing.

For Ernst Stromer, the long years of war brought far more pain than the loss of his life's work; it also took two sons from him, with a third presumed dead but who had actually been captured and held as a prisoner of war in the Soviet Union until 1950. When Stromer died in 1952, he took with him the last first-hand memories of the majestic creature that he and his colleagues had witnessed rising from the ground.

THE SECOND COMING

For the next four decades, any further evidence that would help unlock the secrets of Spinosaurus remained firmly hidden from view, buried beneath the ever-shifting desert landscape of North Africa. In that time, no other palaeontologists had the skill, or perhaps luck, of Stromer and Markgraf in finding Spinosaurus bones beneath the sands of Egypt. Gradually, the search moved further west, across the 9 million square kilometres of parched Sahara earth to the western edge of that great desert.

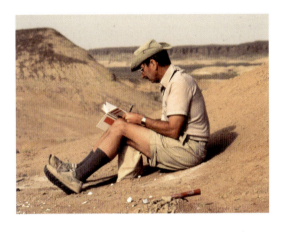

▲ **Russell in China**
This 1989 photograph was taken in the field while Dale Russell was working on the China-Canada Dinosaur Project, a collaboration between scientists from the two countries.

In the mid-1990s a group of fossil-hunters, led by renowned North American palaeontologist Professor Dale Russell, began to take a particular interest in the eastern dunes of Morocco — a region known as the Kem Kem. Even for these modern-day dino-hunters, this remained (and remains today) one of the most inhospitable environments on Earth, but for those who dared, the area proved an intriguing new gateway to a lost world.

The Kem Kem is of particular geological interest to Spinosaurus hunters because the rocks that are exposed in this eastern region of Morocco date back to the Late Cretaceous Period; the fossil beds here are of a similar age to those Egyptian formations in which Stromer and Markgraf had enjoyed so much success.

Around 100 million years ago, when dinosaurs dominated the land, this region of northwestern Africa couldn't have looked more different to the endless sands we see today. At this time, the continents were recognizable as the landmasses we see on a modern world map.

▶ **Late Cretaceous Africa**
By the Late Cretaceous, the continent of Africa had largely taken its modern shape. The area that would become North Africa was a region of shallow, warm seas and extensive wetlands.

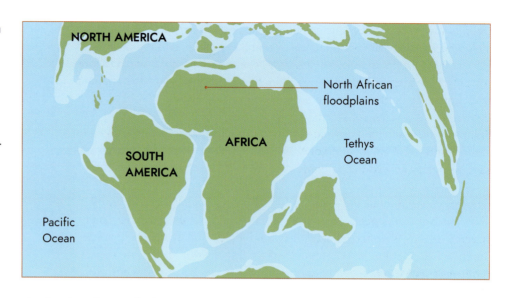

The familiar shape of Africa had emerged from Gondwana, the supercontinent that had dominated the Earth's surface for hundreds of millions of years. And as this new continent emerged, the environment in this particular corner was far from the barren desert it is now; instead, it comprised a massive network of flowing waterways.

▶ **Trionyx**
This soft-shelled turtle thrived all over the Cretaceous world; it survived the Great Extinction and can be found today in Africa and the Middle East.

These waters supported large areas of scrub and forest; it was a tough environment, but one that nonetheless could support an abundance of life. A plethora of freshwater turtles, frogs, and crabs made their home in these wetlands, hiding amongst the tangled root systems of the mangrove-like trees that populated the riverbanks. In this hot, humid environment, there were just enough trees and ferns to provide some essential shade from the intense Cretaceous sun for those Kem Kem inhabitants that lived on the land.

Many millions of years later, it was the search for the inhabitants of these lost, watery worlds that drew palaeontologists to dig in the dirt and dust of the Kem Kem. In 1996, Russell and his team were the first to find evidence to suggest that one of the area's ancient inhabitants was a giant, long nosed, fish-eating predator with a massive sail on its back; they had uncovered the first new evidence of Spinosaurus since Ernst Stromer's fossils had disappeared in the rubble of war-torn Munich 50 years earlier.

Deep in the Moroccan Sahara, the team discovered fragments of a skeleton including three vertebrae, some teeth, and the remains of a neural arch. It was enough for Russell to surmise that these were, in fact, the precious remains of a Spinosaurus — albeit with subtle differences to the creature that Stromer had pulled from the ground 80 years earlier. A detailed analysis of the neck bones led Russell to suggest that this was a different species of Spinosaurus, one with a significantly longer neck. And so, when it came to announcing the find to the world, the animal was given its own unique species name, *Spinosaurus maroccanus*.

Two years later, Russell and his colleague Philippe Taquet published another find, this time in Algeria, of a snout that seemed to belong to the same species. The desert sands were finally beginning to give up their precious Spinosaurus secrets, with a series of enticing finds slowly emerging, particularly from across the Kem Kem fossil beds. These discoveries included dental fragments in 2002, a small fragment from the top of the skull described in 2005, and 1-m- (3.3-ft-) long piece of a snout, also shared with the world in 2005. Each fragment hinted at the extraordinary physiology of the Spinosaurus, but none of them offered the same deep level of insight into an individual animal that Stromer's skeleton had fleetingly provided.

These new finds didn't come out of the ground without controversy. Palaeontology is a science that often sees different interpretations of the same evidence, which is understandable when you consider that the evidence is made up of fragments that are tens of millions of years old. Some experts suggested that the creature found and named by Russell as S*pinosaurus maroccanus* was not, in fact, a different species, but another specimen of Stromer's *Spinosaurus aegyptiacus*. Others agreed with Russell and felt that the existence of two separate species of Spinosaurus was a valid interpretation of the sparse evidence available. Without being able to refer back to the destroyed Stromer specimen it was difficult, if not impossible, to resolve this debate.

The confusion wasn't helped by the fact that Stromer's initial description of Spinosaurus, published in 1915, was also challenged by modern palaeontological analysis. In 2000 the discovery was made of some photos, detailed drawings, and descriptions of the Egyptian specimen, which had somehow survived the upheavals of World War II. Two photographs, one of the lower jaw and one of the mounted entire specimen, were of particular interest to scientists.

DIG DEEPER

Philippe Taquet
In his distinguished career, French palaeontologist Taquet has described a number of new dinosaur species of Cretaceous North Africa, as well as describing the largest-ever crocodilian, *Sarcosuchus imperator*.

WETLAND WORLD

Around 100 million years ago, the area of Morocco now known as the Kem Kem was part of a massive river system in the northern regions of the landmass that would become Africa. The environment was dominated by coastal plains, swamps, lakes, humid forests, and scrubland — all nestled alongside a shallow ocean.

COELACANTH
Common in Kem Kem waterways, coelacanths were thought to have become extinct at the end of the Cretaceous, until a close relative of the ancient species was discovered alive in 1938.

SHARING A HABITAT

The region was home to a variety of dinosaurs adapted to wetland conditions, such as Carcharodontosaurus, as well as flying pterosaurs and aquatic reptiles. Giant fish, including lungfish and coelacanths would have been common prey items for Spinosaurus. Onchopristis, the 4-m- (13-ft-) long sawskate shown in the main image, was a less frequent target — Spinosaurus would need to remove the saw first before eating the rest of the fish.

THEN AND NOW

Spinosaurus' home territory could not have been more different to the desert it is today — the climate was hot and sultry, its tidal flats, river systems, and mangrove forests teeming with life. Today, the area is part of the Sahara desert, forming part of the border between Morocco and Algeria.

CHAPTER ONE

This mangrove swamp in the Great Sandy Region, Northern Australia, is a similar ecosystem to the Kem Kem in the time of Spinosaurus.

The Kem Kem is located in an area of the Sahara where average high temperatures regularly exceed 40° C (104° F) during the summer months.

THE BIGGEST KILLER

After studying the rediscovered images, a US-German team of researchers came to the conclusion that Stromer's 1915 paper was not an entirely accurate description of the bones. Further analysis then suggested that the partial skeleton put forward as the holotype specimen (the one to which all others are compared) was, in fact, made up of bones from three different dinosaurs, including vertebrae and neural spines from a carcharodontosaurid similar to Acrocanthosaurus, and tooth fragments from Baryonyx or Suchomimus. Although this analysis was rejected by a number of palaeontologists, it continued to cast a shadow over Stromer's findings and his claims about them.

> Finding monsters in the dust has a history that goes back hundreds, if not thousands, of years.

With only the Russell team's fragments and the rediscovered Stromer documents to work with, it seemed impossible that researchers would be able to truly step back in time to bring Spinosaurus to life and let it walk again. But that changed in 2014 with the discovery of the remains of a gigantic predator that had lain in the dusty rock of the Kem Kem for almost 100 million years. This Spinosaurus would once again open the world's eyes to this extraordinary animal and reveal more about how it lived and died than we could have ever imagined.

IN THE BEGINNING

Finding monsters in the dust has a history that goes back hundreds, if not thousands, of years. Giant bones have been discovered and documented since at least the third century CE in Europe, China, and beyond. But for

▶ **Stromer's bones**
The only surviving photographic proof of Stromer's discovery of Spinosaurus was uncovered by an American researcher in the archives of Munich's Museum of Palaeontology.

almost all that time, the true nature and scale of these discoveries have been impossible to grasp by those holding the wondrous bones in their hands. And so, as is often the case, myth and legend filled any voids in knowledge, leading those looking for explanations towards creatures of folklore or religion, be they dragons, monsters, giants, or creatures from holy scriptures. Even when the scientific revolution opened our eyes in the middle of the last millennium, transforming our understanding of the world, scientists were still a long way from making the connections necessary to work out the true origins of the bones that lay in front of them.

◀ **Robert Plot**
The success of Plot's natural history book led to his appointment as the first Keeper of Oxford's Ashmolean Museum. He later became the first ever Professor of Chemistry at Oxford.

The naturalists of the 17th century used early scientific principles to make tentative progress with their investigations of these strange specimens before stumbling back into the darkness. For instance, the English naturalist Robert Plot was correct when he identified an enormous bone discovered in a limestone quarry in Oxfordshire as part the femur of an animal so large it couldn't belong to any known living species. Plot wondered if it might have come from an elephant "brought hither during the government of the Romans in Britain", but subsequent comparisons with contemporary elephant bones that Plot had managed to source quickly dispelled this hypothesis. When he finally announced his find, along with the first known illustration of a dinosaur bone, in his 1677 publication *The Natural History of Oxford-shire*, Plot described the specimen as a bone from a giant human, perhaps even a Titan from Greek mythology. Back then, even Oxford professors couldn't get their heads around the idea that it wasn't giant humans, but giant lizards, that had once ruled the Earth.

Two decades later in 1699, the embryonic science of palaeontology took another step forward when Edward Lhwyd, an assistant to Robert Plot at the Ashmolean, published the first ever catalogue of fossils, the *Lithophylacii Britannici Ichnographia* ("British Figured Stones"). Lhwyd had found

▼ **Plate from *The Natural History of Oxford-shire*, 1677**
This plate includes an image of the huge thigh-bone (Fig. 4), thought to be the first published image of a dinosaur fossil.

THE BIGGEST KILLER

▶ **Edward Lhwyd**
Lhwyd succeeded Plot as Keeper of the Ashmolean Museum, and was also a distinguished scholar of linguistics, botany, and geography.

▼ **Plate from Lhwyd's *Lithophylacii*, 1699**
This page showcases an array of fossillized teeth — the *Rutellum* tooth is on the second row, third from left.

almost all these fossils in his local Oxfordshire area and managed to convince his friend, a certain Isaac Newton, to fund the publication of the catalogue. Lhwyd's collection is still held at the Ashmolean; the most noteworthy specimen is a single tooth, which was collected in the village of Caswell, near Witney in Oxfordshire.

This tooth has a place in palaeontological history because Lhwyd described and named the creature it came from as *Rutellum impicatum*; this was the first time in history that a name was given to a creature that we now recognize as a dinosaur. We would later learn that the tooth was from a sauropod, possibly a cetiosaurid, that lived in the Middle Jurassic around 170 million years ago. But that fact, as well as the names that would define this group of dinosaurs, would not become a part of the scientific knowledge base until almost 150 years later.

It was not until the beginning of the 19th century that scientists began to piece together the evidence in these ancient bones in ways that allowed a picture of the true nature of their origins and age to begin to emerge. Setting out on this path required an almost superhuman leap of imagination.

Imagine for a second that you are an inquisitive naturalist in the late 18th century, unknowingly holding the bone of a dinosaur. The anatomical structure of the creature to whom this bone belongs is difficult enough for to you to visualize, but the eons of time that stretch between this animal's lifetime and yours would be nigh on impossible to grasp with the knowledge available to you.

This was still an age when the theological idea of Genesis — the Bible's story of the creation of Earth and all the life on it — held firm amongst the vast majority of people, including the educated and scientifically literate. Equally widely established was the "scientific" belief that Earth's creation had occurred some 6,000 years earlier, largely based on the theories of James Ussher, a bishop in the Church of Ireland. This would not be not an easy position for you, the would-be naturalist, to break out from and theorize that the bones you are holding might be more like 100 million years old. But that was all about to change.

Towards the end of the 18th century, some maverick scientists began challenging the accepted set of beliefs, and in doing so transformed the understanding of Earth's age and origins. Just as Copernicus had (heretically) demolished the universally held theory that Earth was the supreme, central body amongst the stars, so revolutionary geologists such as William Smith, often called the Father of English geology, began to find evidence to suggest that the life story of Earth had more chapters than suggested in the Bible. In the 1790s, Smith had begun exploring layers of rock and fossils in the Mearns Pitt coalfield at High Littleton in Somerset, England. As he began to recognize patterns in these rock layers that seemed to repeat across multiple locations, he formulated a hypothesis. If the same types of fossils were found in layers of rock in different locations, then it seemed reasonable to Smith that the fossils, and therefore the layers (or strata, as Smith named them), were of the same age.

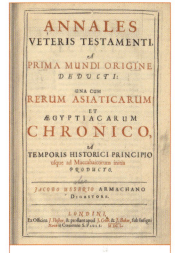

DIG DEEPER

Save the date
Irish cleric James Ussher worked out an exact date for the birth of Earth as 23 October 4004 BCE. His calculations, based on the ages of biblical figures, were set out in 1650 work, *Annals of the Old Testament* (above).

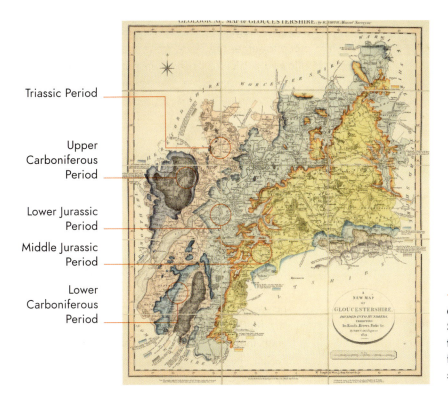

- Triassic Period
- Upper Carboniferous Period
- Lower Jurassic Period
- Middle Jurassic Period
- Lower Carboniferous Period

◀ **Smith's geological map of Gloucestershire**
Self-taught geologist William Smith is thought to have produced the world's first colour-coded geological maps, showing different strata of rock.

THE BIGGEST KILLER 43

DIG DEEPER

John Phillips
A talent for groundbreaking geology ran in William Smith's family. His nephew John Phillips published the first global geological timescale — a description of Earth's history, based on analysis of rock strata. He identified three distinct geological eras, based on the most prevalent forms of life at those times and named them the Palaeozoic, Mesozoic, and Cenozoic eras; terms scientists still use today.

▶ **Cross-section of the Thames Valley, 1871**
This plate from John Phillips' *The Geology of Oxford and the Valley of the Thames* demonstrates how he built on Smith's colour coding to show the rock composition of the Thames Valley.

Exploring this hypothesis further, Smith discovered that the strata were arranged in predictable patterns and found in the same positions in different locations. It led him to his principle of faunal succession, which holds that the strata of rocks denote age and the layers get older the deeper you go — and it follows that the fossilized life forms within those strata must get increasingly older, too. It seems obvious to us now, but from a starting point of the biblical creation story, this would have been a truly radical view. Smith's strata provided a timeline with which you could calculate the relative ages of the life forms entombed within them. And something else emerged from Smith's work; the further back in time you went, the more the fossilized creatures seemed to differ from the animals alive today. Look at Smith's strata and life on Earth could be seen to be evolving before your eyes.

This pioneering work was crucial in underpinning an emerging explanation of the development of life on Earth — one that would ultimately come to be defined by Charles Darwin with his theory of evolution by natural selection. In the early 1800s, Darwin's theory and all the understanding that it would engender was still decades away, but that didn't stop William Smith's work having enormous influence on people's view of life on Earth, and specifically of the timeline of the dinosaurs.

Assigning a colour to each different rock formation made it easier to compare the makeup of different parts of the valley.

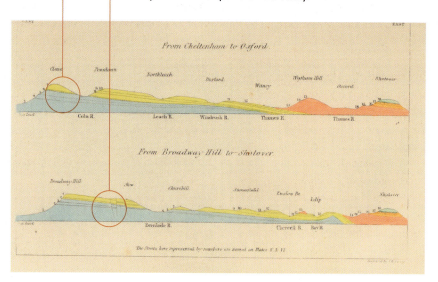

One of the people inspired by Smith's principle of faunal succession was a man not only of rock but also of the cloth. William Buckland, Dean of Westminster and amateur geologist and palaeontologist, would travel down the two roads of religion and science his whole life. In much of his research, he attempted to reconcile the deep discrepancies between these two systems of understanding — perhaps most intriguingly in his search for valid scientific evidence to support the biblical account of the Great Flood and Noah's Ark.

In the early 19th century Buckland, amongst others, developed theories that sought to reconcile the worlds of religion and scientific enquiry. Key to the success of this would be taking a less literal view of the Bible, which would allow the biblical and scientific timelines to sit a little more comfortably together. This was achieved by redefining the word "beginning", as used in the creation story in the Book of Genesis, as a long, undefined period between the origin of the Earth and the creation of all contemporary life.

> Buckland created a space for the emerging narratives of science to sit more comfortably within a biblical context.

This created a space for the emerging narratives of science to exist without directly contradicting the Bible — a space during which Buckland believed there had been a long series of extinctions and creations, with new kinds of plants and animals appearing and disappearing through time. This radical new interpretation of Earth's timeline helped to explain the strange fossils that were coming out of the ground at the time, including the widely reported discovery of ancient bones in a Yorkshire cave. Buckland's analysis of these remains as ancient hyenas and their prey catapulted him to the very summit of scientific fame.

▼ **Megalosaurus model, 1854**
This speculative reconstruction was based on the scant information gleaned from Buckland's fossil find. Although a creditable attempt, we now know it to be largely inaccurate.

But it was Buckland's work on one extraordinary set of bones, which had been discovered in a quarry in the village of Stonesfield, Oxfordshire, that would cement his place in palaeontological history. Around 1815, Buckland acquired these remains, leaning on his lofty position as the first Professor of Geology at Oxford University.

Kem Kem Formation
These sandstone cliffs in Morocco contain a treasure trove of Late Cretaceous fossils, including the first Spinosaurus to be discovered in almost a century.

THE BIGGEST KILLER

In 1824, Buckland published a paper in which he described the finds. The paper accurately described the fossilized bones of a giant reptile he named Megalosaurus, from the Greek for "great lizard". This was the first-ever full scientific description of what we now call a dinosaur and with that, the scientific age of the great lizards had truly begun.

Fiction and folklore were rapidly being superseded by fact to explain the origin of the growing number of great lizard fossils being found across Europe and North America. These discoveries fuelled a flood of interest in the burgeoning new science of palaeontology. One of the scientists to have his head turned by the buzz around bones was the English biologist and palaeontologist Sir Richard Owen. Years before he became the driving force behind the establishment of the Natural History Museum in London, Owen coined the word that would go on to make the museum famous around the world. Speaking at a meeting of the British Association of the Advancement of Science in 1841, Owen described the characteristics of three giant reptiles; a plant-eating Iguanodon, an armoured Hylaeosaurus, and Buckland's carnivorous Megalosaurus. Bringing this evidence together for his audience, he concluded by declaring:

"The combination of such characters ... will, it is presumed, be deemed sufficient ground for establishing a distinct tribe or sub-order of Saurian Reptiles, for which I would propose the name of..."

We can only imagine that Owen might have taken a breath before finishing that sentence — and when he did, he gave the world a name to describe the group of ancient reptiles that had emerged from mythology into the scientific realm; a name that would capture the collective imagination of generations to come. As Owen uttered the final word, "... Dinosauria", the "terrible lizards" had truly arrived on the scientific scene. Things would never be the same.

BOX OF BONES

Almost 200 years after Owen gave a name to this clade of extraordinary reptiles, digging for dinosaurs is now a global endeavour, taking place in pretty much every corner of the planet. Today, modern palaeontologists employ an increasing array of cutting-edge technologies to increase

▼ **Sir Richard Owen, 1856**
One of the most celebrated and gifted naturalists of his era, Owen was also an outspoken critic of Charles Darwin's theory of evolution by natural selection.

48　　　　　　　　　　　　　　　　　　　　　　　　　　　CHAPTER ONE

their chances of striking dinosaur gold. But in a world of hi-tech, high-stakes research, the most important component of any discovery can still be a very large piece of luck.

Luck was exactly what came Nizar Ibrahim's way when a man offered the young palaeontologist a seemingly unremarkable cardboard box full of dinosaur fossils in a Morocco marketplace in 2008. After examining his purchase more closely, Ibrahim began to think his purchase might be more noteworthy than the seller had realized; the bones all looked to be the same age and, even more interesting, it seemed possible that they all belonged to the same animal. But for this 26-year-old, still at the beginning of his career in palaeontology, there was little else to go on — no location for the find, no more bones, only his sense of a hunch, a gut feeling that this assortment of fossils could turn out to be more than just "quite interesting".

Ibrahim's next stroke of luck came a year later, when visiting the Natural History Museum in Milan. He was invited to look at some unusual bones in the basement, which had been donated to the museum — an invitation like

◀ **Fossil-hunter**
Nizar Ibrahim holds a Spinosaurus tooth. Among his other finds in the Kem Kem are fossil footprints and a giant pterosaur, *Alanqa saharica*.

◀ **Milan's museum**
After losing almost its entire collection in wartime bombing raids, Milan's Natural History Museum has amassed an impressive fossil collection and become a hub for cutting-edge palaeontology research.

this is nothing less than catnip to a curious palaeontologist. Making his way beneath the beautiful galleries of the museum, through a warren of dusty rooms and corridors, Ibrahim inspected the collection of bones along with two Italian academics working at the museum, Cristiano Dal Sasso and Simone Maganuco.

After examining the fossils and cross-referencing their assessment of the bones, the scientists came to the same conclusion. The leg and spine bones and fragments of skull seemed to be those of a Spinosaurus. What was even more intriguing to Ibrahim was that, on closer inspection, these bones appeared remarkably similar in colour, texture, and shape to those in that box he'd been sold a year earlier in Morocco. It seemed to be too much of a coincidence, but the evidence in front of him suggested that, together, these two collections of bones might be leading him towards the most complete Spinosaurus skeleton in existence.

To prove his hunch, Ibrahim had to find the dig site — and that meant tracking down the fossil dealer who'd sold him the box of bones. No easy task when they'd only met for a few minutes, and in a region where the fossil trade was a huge business — at the time, there were 50,000 fossil-hunters operating in Morocco alone.

▲ **Fossil trade**
The Moroccan oasis town of Erfoud is a hub for tourists who come to tour dig sites and visit the town's many fossil museums and exhibitions, one of which is shown here.

In 2009, the chase for this fossil dealer began in earnest. The only clue to his identity was the prominent moustache that adorned his face (not the most distinguishing facial feature in Morocco, it must be said). It seemed, a few weeks into the search, that Ibrahim's quest was doomed to failure. Despite having spoken to dozens of fossil-hunters (many of them with impressive moustaches) in a string of far-flung locations across Morocco, the mysterious man behind the box of bones remained elusive. Despondently sipping tea in a café, Ibrahim and his team were on the verge of giving up. The great hope of finding a complete Spinosaurus skeleton was fading once again. But as if the script had already been written, or as the story is now told, just at that very moment a moustached man walked past their table, with just enough of a hint of familiarity to suggest to Ibrahim that it might just be worth one more "Excuse me?" conversation.

The rest is, or will be one day, part of palaeontological history. This was the man they'd been looking for. And yes, the bones in the box and the bones in the Milan museum did come from the same site — a site that Ibrahim would win permission, after quite a lot of wrangling, to begin to dig, in search of the rest of this extraordinary creature.

Where there had once been, in the Cretaceous, the riverways and scrub forests of the Kem Kem, there was now only rock, sand, and dust. But when Ibrahim and his team finally arrived on site, they knew with some certainty that the remains of an extraordinary monster lay somewhere beneath their feet. Now all they had to do was find it.

Ibrahim had been dreaming of an opportunity like this since he was five years old, growing up in Berlin with an imagination that transported him to endless ancient worlds; an imagination fuelled by his precious book of dinosaurs, which included an account of Stromer's Spinosaurus. But finding

▲ **Kem Kem fieldwork**
Ibrahim and his team conducted extensive surveys of the area, to identify the most promising digs sites.

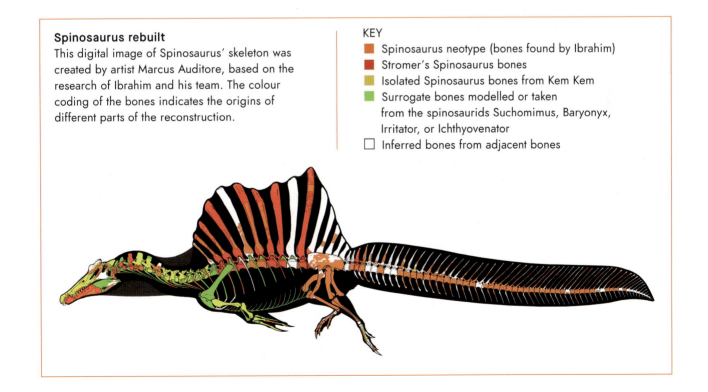

Spinosaurus rebuilt
This digital image of Spinosaurus' skeleton was created by artist Marcus Auditore, based on the research of Ibrahim and his team. The colour coding of the bones indicates the origins of different parts of the reconstruction.

KEY
- Spinosaurus neotype (bones found by Ibrahim)
- Stromer's Spinosaurus bones
- Isolated Spinosaurus bones from Kem Kem
- Surrogate bones modelled or taken from the spinosaurids Suchomimus, Baryonyx, Irritator, or Ichthyovenator
- ☐ Inferred bones from adjacent bones

THE BIGGEST KILLER

▶ **Stromer's spines**
These replicas of the neural spines, found by Stromer and destroyed in 1944, are on display at the Natural History Museum in Berlin.

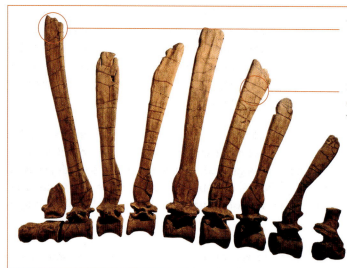

The longest spine was 1.65 m (5.4 ft) in length.

Spines are long extensions of the vertebrae.

▶ **New model**
This life-size reconstruction, informed by Ibrahim's research, was unveiled at the National Geographic Museum of Exploration in Washington D.C., in 2014.

52   CHAPTER ONE

the fossil layer in which the giant predator lay hidden would not prove to be easy; the first few visits to the dig site, in brutal conditions, returned nothing but aching bones (those of the team), broken tools, and tonne after tonne of empty sandstone rock. But by 2018, more than 15 tonnes (16.5 tons) of rock had been cleared from the site and under the sweltering heat of the Saharan sun, the team finally began to uncover the fossilized bones of the animal they had come to find.

Their first find was a single caudal vertebra, but before long they were uncovering bone after bone, sometimes just minutes and centimetres apart. A whole skeleton of a Spinosaurus tail was emerging from the ground. By the end of the 2018 dig season, the team had uncovered a total of 36 tail vertebrae and 131 bone fragments. And without a single duplicate bone, this strongly suggested that all the fossils belonged to a single animal.

A year later, the team returned to the site once again and pulled, amongst other things, foot bones from the prehistoric burial site. This specimen is the most complete skeleton of a predatory dinosaur from the Cretaceous Period ever found in mainland Africa, but the value of what Ibrahim and his team discovered goes far beyond even that. The combination of their excavated fossils and the two boxes of bones that had instigated their search added up to the most complete Spinosaurus specimen in existence and the first that scientists could study since that destructive day in Munich in 1944. With their discovery, Ibrahim and his team had opened a whole new realm

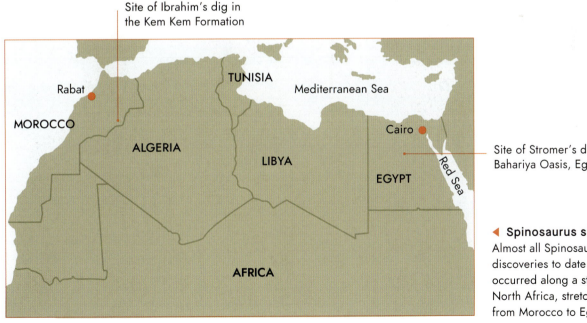

◀ **Spinosaurus sites**
Almost all Spinosaurus discoveries to date have occurred along a strip of North Africa, stretching from Morocco to Egypt.

THE BIGGEST KILLER

of research; the chance to understand these creatures in more detail than ever before, and to gain new insights into how Spinosaurus was able to live so successfully amongst the waterways of the Kem Kem.

Comparing the remains of this Spinosaurus with the illustrations of the Spinosaurus tail vertebrae that Stromer had published in 1934, most scientists now believe with some certainty that at least one spinosaurid species thrived in Cretaceous North Africa, between 100–94 million years ago, spread out across the continent from what is now Morocco all the way east to Egypt.

WALKING WITH SPINOSAURUS

At 14 m (46 ft) long, Ibrahim's Spinosaurus is the longest terrestrial carnivore ever discovered and, as far as we know, the biggest predator ever to have walked the Earth — even longer than the longest T.rex discovered so far. With a tooth-filled, crocodilian-like skull and powerful forearms, topped off with a giant claw on the first of three digits, this was an animal equipped with a fearsome arsenal to take down prey. Combined with short, powerful legs and a distinctive sail structure running along its back leading to a long, whip-like tail, there is nothing about this creature that doesn't appear menacing to the human eye.

But the remains of this dinosaur have not just helped to rewrite our understanding of spinosaurid anatomy and behaviour, they have also transformed our wider knowledge of how dinosaurs lived. In particular, this find has challenged our understanding of how adaptable some dinosaurs were to a range of different environments.

▼ **Tail bones**
During filming of *Walking With Dinosaurs*, the team inspects some of the more than 40 tail vertebrae so far uncovered at the site.

It has long been thought that despite the dinosaurs' impressive versatility, there was one environment that they never conquered — water. There were, of course, plenty of marine creatures during the age of the dinosaurs; prehistoric sharks, ichthyosaurs, and fish such as

◀ **Built to fish**
This scene from *Walking With Dinosaurs* showcases Spinosaurus' long skull and conical teeth, perfectly adapted for grabbing and gripping slippery prey.

coelacanths, to name a few. But as far as our understanding of the clade of dinosaurs was concerned, they were most certainly not aquatic creatures. This find has changed all that, fleshing out the early finders' hunch that Spinosaurus was piscivorous (fish-eating) into a fully-fledged description of not just a fish-eater, but an animal that was built for the water. This body of evidence is opening up a whole new world of possibilities, making us look again at other dinosaur skeletons to see if we've missed evidence that might point to the existence of other water-dwelling dinosaurs. The evidence that links Spinosaurus so strongly with a watery lifestyle appears in almost every detail of its fossilized skeleton — quite literally from head to tail.

Let's start our exploration of this evidence by imagining this creature slipping in and out the myriad waterways that criss-crossed the Cretaceous Kem Kem. As we've already seen, the Spinosaurus skull was very similar in shape to that of a modern-day crocodile; it was flat, long, low, and narrow — and crucially, with two small nostrils located in the middle of the skull. The small size and placement of these nostrils so far back on the head suggests that, just like a crocodile, Spinosaurus was still able to breathe whilst part of the head was submerged in water. The skull was also full of large, straight, conical teeth (with no serrations), which interlocked at the front of the snout. This dental configuration, combined with the dinosaur's powerful forelimbs and curved, blade-like claws, suggested to Ibrahim's team that this was an animal well suited for catching a slippery fish for supper rather than land-based prey.

▼ **Making a moving model**
The team scanned each bone they found (top). These were then used to create a digital skeleton (bottom) to test theories about how Spinosaurus might have moved and hunted.

The researchers also discovered that the skull had intriguing neurovascular openings at the end of the snout. Similar openings are found in the snouts of crocodiles and alligators, containing pressure receptors that sense movement in water. So it's reasonable to imagine these openings contained similar receptors in Spinosaurus, allowing it to sense movement and gain the upper hand when pursuing its most challenging but valuable prey, the 4 m (13 ft) Onchopristis, or sawskate.

Moving further down the body, we find a long neck and trunk — gait analysis has revealed that this conformation shifted the dinosaur's centre of mass forwards. This would have made walking on two legs challenging for these creatures, reducing their agility on land but potentially facilitating their movement in water.

All of this is circumstantial evidence that points towards a watery lifestyle, but it was when the team looked inside their dinosaur's bones that Ibrahim thought he had found the most compelling evidence for his aquatic hypothesis. Analysis of the fine microstructure of Spinosaurus' bones revealed that they are surprisingly dense and compact. This is something we see in modern animals that spend a lot of time in the water; it is a useful quality that helps them control their buoyancy. Known as osteosclerosis,

56   CHAPTER ONE

Bone density

The team studied the femurs (thigh bones) of a range of terrestrial and aquatic animals. Spinosaurus' bone density was comparable to that of other fully aquatic predatory animals.

ARAMUS
Extinct, semi-aquatic bird

CAIMAN
Semi-aquatic reptile

SPINOSAURUS
Semi-aquatic/aquatic dinosaur

this process results in the filling in of the centre of bones, increasing their density and leaving them without the marrow cavities usually seen in predatory dinosaurs. Similar adaptations are seen in aquatic animals such as king penguins, hippos, and alligators, allowing these animals to efficiently submerge themselves in water. In effect, bone density is a powerful indicator of whether an animal is able to sink beneath the surface and swim underwater.

◀ **Live animal studies**
Ibrahim studied alligators as part of his research into the aquatic locomotion of Spinosaurus.

> The findings provided the most compelling evidence yet that Spinosaurus could have been an underwater hunter.

THE BIGGEST KILLER

To test their hypothesis, Ibrahim and his research team examined a large range of leg and rib bone cross-sections from 250 species of extinct and living animals, from a wide range of different habitats. These included seals, crocodiles, whales, elephants, mice, and even hummingbirds, as well as extinct marine reptiles such as mosasaurs and plesiosaurs. Once collated, the researchers were able to compare the bone cross-sections of all these creatures to those of Spinosaurus and its relatives, Baryonyx and Suchomimus.

The correlation was clear to the team; animals that hunt underwater have bones that are almost completely solid, whereas hunters based on land have more hollow, lighter bones. And Spinosaurus and Baryonyx most certainly fitted into the dense-bone category. Published in *Nature* in 2022, the team's findings provided the most compelling evidence yet that these gigantic killers hunted underwater. As Ibrahim said on the paper's publication: "The bones don't lie, and now we know that even the internal architecture of the bones is entirely consistent with our interpretation of this animal as a giant predator hunting fish in vast rivers."

▼ **Water babies**
In *Walking With Dinosaurs*, a young Spinosaurus hitches a ride to the riverbank on its father's back.

58　　　　　　　　　　　　　　　　　　　　　　　　　　　　　　　　　　　　　　　CHAPTER ONE

◀ **Digging for clues**
While being filmed at the dig site, Ibrahim and his team made a number of finds that would provide significant clues to Spinosaurus' lifestyle.

But the evidence does not end there. When some of the Kem Kem Spinosaurus' foot bones were excavated during the 2019 season, it became clear to Ibrahim that, unlike other predator dinosaurs, Spinosaurus feet were not adapted for perching, but for moving across soft surfaces, much like a modern shorebird. In fact, the evidence suggests that Spinosaurus may even have had webbed feet for walking on soft mud or helping to propel it through the water. A giant, predatory dinosaur with duck feet is something palaeontologists could have barely imagined just a few years ago.

And so, finally, this brings us to the tail end of this extraordinary story. Exactly how this Spinosaurus and its relatives lived and hunted in the waters of the Kem Kem and beyond is, like so many things in palaeontology, still hotly debated. Was Spinosaurus a semi-aquatic feeder, paddling on the banks of the waterways, peering into the water for the next meal? Or was it a pursuit predator, capable of complete submersion in its hunt for prey?

> Was Spinosaurus a pursuit predator, capable of complete submersion in pursuit of prey?

THE BIGGEST KILLER

▲ **Mighty tail**
Although the huge tail is unwieldy on land, loosely connected bones enabled it to move in a wave-like motion, helping to power Spinosaurus through the water.

When you are looking back across 100 million years, certainty does not come easily. But the work of Ibrahim and his team does seem to be pointing in the direction of the latter hypothesis; an animal much like a modern crocodile or alligator, not just at home in the water but an agile and active underwater hunter. And now, with the painstaking compilation, across a series of digs, of every bone in the Spinosaurus tail, this picture has been painted perhaps more convincingly than ever. It wasn't until the team had the full tail that they could begin to realize the true nature and purpose of this appendage.

As more and more tail bones emerged from the ground, it became apparent that this dinosaur's tail was similar to that of a newt; a newt's tail not only steadies the creature in the water, but propels it at speed. Loosely connected bones enable such a tail to bend in a wave-like fashion. To measure the potential propulsive capability of the tail, Ibrahim teamed up with a group of scientists at Harvard University, who specialized in aquatic locomotion.

The Spinosaurus remains provided the basis of an innovative piece of research, enabling the creation of a computer-based model that could reveal in detail how the Spinosaurus tail might have functioned. With 100-million-year-old data points driving a 21st-century animation engine, this work generated the data that, for some, provides the decisive evidence that places spinosaurids very firmly in the water. What the Harvard model suggests is that, in the water, the tail of Spinosaurus would have clearly outperformed all other known dinosaurs, making it comparable to the tails we see in fully or largely aquatic animals alive today.

It's a tantalizing final piece of evidence which, combined with other new data provided by the remains, makes Ibrahim and others now believe that Spinosaurus may have spent as much as 80 per cent of its time in a swimming position in the water.

"We battled sandstorms, flooding, snakes, scorpions, and more to excavate the most enigmatic dinosaur in the world," Ibrahim recently said in an online lecture. "And now we have multiple lines of evidence all pointing in the same direction — the skeleton really does have 'water-loving dinosaur' written all over it."

> "The Spinosaurus skeleton really does have 'water-loving dinosaur' written all over it."

There is no doubt that our understanding of these astonishing creatures will continue to deepen as new technology and new discoveries open up ever-bigger windows into the past. But for now, this spectacular find has provided us with the best chance to piece together the lives of these extraordinary giants, so that they can, once more, walk again.

◀ **Putting it together**
This anatomically-precise skeleton, built and assembled under the supervision of Ibrahim, represents the most up-to-date knowledge we have about Spinosaurus.

THE BIGGEST KILLER

CHAPTER TWO
TERRESTRIAL TITAN

SEARCHING FOR SAUROPODS

Sauropods, the group to which Lusotitan belonged, were the giants of the dinosaur world and also distinctive-looking, with a relatively tiny head, huge torso, and unfeasibly long neck and tail. When you look at the numbers, they seem too big to be believable. How did creatures weighing up to 80 tonnes (88 tons) manage to walk on land? At 35 m (115 ft) long and 18 m (60 ft) tall, how could they support themselves? These are some of the questions scientists are still addressing as more fossil evidence is uncovered and analysed.

> Fossil skeletons don't lie — sauropods were the largest animals ever to walk on Earth.

But their fossilized skeletons don't lie — these were the largest animals ever to walk on Earth. Sauropods existed from the Early Jurassic Period, 201–174 million years ago; in that time they spread across much of the planet becoming ever more gigantic. They survived right up to the end of the Cretaceous, 66 million years ago, when they were wiped out along with all other non-avian dinosaurs.

The landmasses that made up Jurassic Earth looked very different to today's continents. Some areas of the planet were too cold for sauropods, who appear to have avoided habitats in which the temperature dropped close to freezing. From the fossil records, it seems that sauropods gravitated towards warmer, drier habitats than other dinosaurs at the time.

▼ **Earth's giants**
Sauropods were much larger than the largest living land animal, the African elephant. The modern blue whale is heavier, but has the advantage of being supported by water.

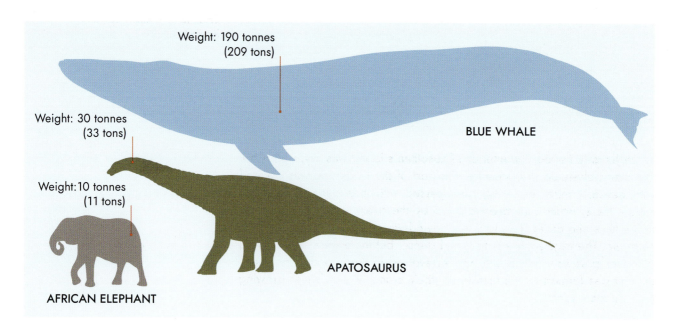

Weight: 190 tonnes (209 tons)

BLUE WHALE

Weight: 30 tonnes (33 tons)

Weight: 10 tonnes (11 tons)

APATOSAURUS

AFRICAN ELEPHANT

Nevertheless, sauropods were widespread and their fossils have been found in all parts of the world, including North and South America, Europe, and, more recently, China, Africa, and Australia.

In *Walking With Dinosaurs,* we charted the unearthing of a Lusotitan in Portugal. This sauropod was found in an area known as the Lourinhã Formation. During the Jurassic Period when this dinosaur lived, Portugal, along with the rest of what is now the Iberian Peninsula, was not part of a continental landmass, but an island in a shallow ocean. At its western end a giant mountain range known as the Berlengas Horst pierced the skyline — today it forms the Berlengas island chain.

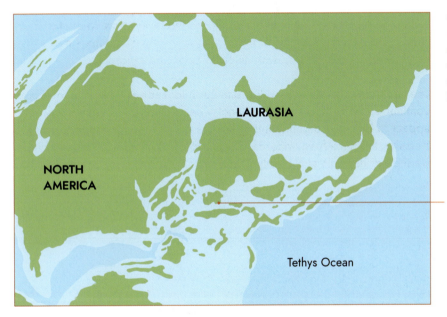

◀ **Jurassic Europe**
150 million years ago, Pangaea had split to form the embryonic continents of North America and Asia. Shallow seas covered much of what would become Europe.

Small islands made up the future Southern Europe.

In the Jurassic Period, the interior of Lusotitan's island was dry, with a few mountains clustered in the centre. The rest of the landscape was covered with dense, coniferous forest, interspersed with meandering rivers and oxbow lakes, which had been created by the rivers as they aged. River floodplains and deltas gave way to the windswept beaches that fringed the coastline. The vegetation was lush and dense, but there were no flowering plants or grasses — these had not yet evolved in the Jurassic. The forest canopy was formed by very tall trees, their branches and leaves growing high on their trunks.

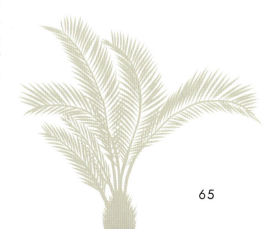

TERRESTRIAL TITAN

Evergreen coniferous trees flourished, alongside less common ginkgo trees. At ground level, the scene would have looked more familiar to us with mosses, cycads, and a few ferns. There were no grasses or palms at this time – these would not appear for millions of years.

The climate of the Lourinhã Formation at this time was subtropical; warm and wet all year round, with an average air temperature of 27–34°C (80–93°F). Alongside Lusotitan, a range of other herbivorous dinosaurs thrived in the area, as well as predatory carnivores including Allosaurus. Filling the skies were pterosaurs with wingspans of up to 4 m (13 ft), such as the fish-eating Rhamphorhynchus. Mammals such as Drescheratherium scurried in the undergrowth. In wetter areas, snakes (some with small limbs), frogs, and lizards flourished.

Lourinhã dinosaurs
This region was home to predatory dinosaurs such as Torvosaurus, Allosaurus, and Ceratosaurus, as well as the armoured plant-eater Miragaia. The Portuguese site contains remains of animals similar to those found at the Morrison Formation in North America. The eggs and embryos that have been found here are among the oldest sauropod nests found so far.

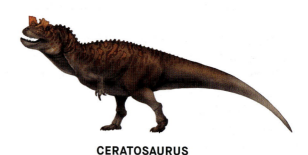

CERATOSAURUS
A medium-sized, three-horned predator

TORVOSAURUS
Theropod, the largest predator in the region

ALLOSAURUS
Theropod specialized for attacking large prey

MIRAGAIA
A plated herbivore

UNEARTHING A GIANT

Sauropods were plant-eaters, and most sported a distinctively long neck and tail. They stood on four legs but despite their huge bulk, some species could rear up on their hind legs. They may have done this to reach high tree branches, as a show of aggression towards rivals, or as part of a courtship ritual. A typical sauropod's head was small relative to the rest of the body, with a correspondingly small brain. Nonetheless, despite existing alongside ferocious carnivores, sauropods were very successful — by the time they reached adulthood they were pretty much too large to kill, unless the predators hunted in packs. Only an injured or elderly sauropod would have been easy prey. In the past, scientists thought that, to have enough time to grow so huge, sauropods must have lived for a century or even longer. They now believe that these animals grew comparatively quickly, typically reaching full size at around 20–30 years old, and living to the age of 60 or so.

When the Lusotitan featured in *Walking With Dinosaurs* was unearthed, the scale of the bones left everyone astonished; the ribs alone were up to 3 m (10 ft) long and this was thought to be one of the largest dinosaur specimens ever discovered in Europe. Lusotitan was a giant by any standards; however, it would still have been dwarfed by some of its sauropod relatives.

The crown for tallest sauropod would have been claimed by Sauroposeidon, which roamed central North America during the Early Cretaceous and measured 18 m (60 ft) from head to toe — twice as tall as a typical two-storey house. It would have peered down at the tallest animal alive today — the giraffe, which stands at "just" 5 m (16 ft) tall.

> Despite their bulk, many sauropods could rear up on their hind legs to towering heights.

▼ **Rearing Barosaurus**
This exhibit at the American Museum of Natural History is the world's tallest freestanding dinosaur mount. It's made from casts of the real bone fossils.

TERRESTRIAL TITAN

Comparatively small head made it easier for the neck to support it.

Long, flexible neck, up to 7 m (23 ft)

Unlike most sauropods, Lusotitan held its neck at a 45 degree angle.

LUSOTITAN

This colossal creature roamed the land we now know as Portugal. Like other sauropods, Lusotitan had a long neck and tail, huge, barrel-shaped body, and four sturdy legs. Its long, strong, flexible neck allowed it to reach leaves and branches at all levels, including heights other herbivores couldn't reach. This advantage over the competition helps to explain how these giants grew so supersized.

Elephant-like legs and feet

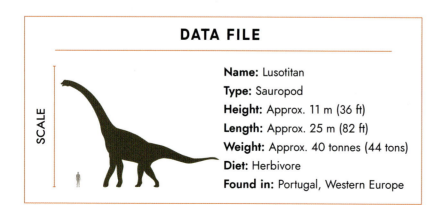

DATA FILE

SCALE

Name: Lusotitan
Type: Sauropod
Height: Approx. 11 m (36 ft)
Length: Approx. 25 m (82 ft)
Weight: Approx. 40 tonnes (44 tons)
Diet: Herbivore
Found in: Portugal, Western Europe

TRIASSIC	JURASSIC	CRETACEOUS
252 MYA	201 MYA	145 MYA

LUSOTITAN TIMELINE: 158–145 MYA

LONGER LEGS, HIGHER REACH

When first discovered in the 1950s, Lusotitan was thought to be a species of Brachiosaurus; it wasn't recognized as a genus in its own right until 2003. The error was understandable: Brachiosaurus and Lusotitan share characteristics that were unusual in sauropods — long front legs and the ability to hold the head and neck upright.

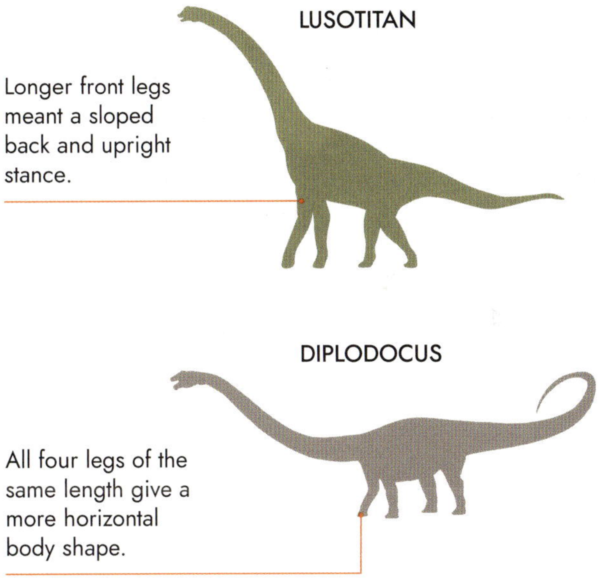

LUSOTITAN

Longer front legs meant a sloped back and upright stance.

DIPLODOCUS

All four legs of the same length give a more horizontal body shape.

Enormous gut for digesting low-nutrition plant matter.

Long, whip-like tail counterbalanced the weight of the neck.

69

▼ **Argentinosaurus**
This colossal herbivore was one of the titanosaur group of sauropods, which included the largest-ever land animals.

The "longest dinosaur" title is currently being contested between *Argentinosaurus huinculensis* and Supersaurus, both thought to have been up to about 35 m (115 ft) long. Both would put today's longest land animal, the African elephant, to shame — it reaches a length of only 7.3 m (24 ft). The sauropods also probably outdid the world's largest living animal, the blue whale, in both length and height. If you think, however, that sauropods were the longest animals ever, think again. The bootlace worm (*Lineus longissimus*), a water-based ribbon worm, has reached a length of 55 m (180 ft). However, while the worm may technically be the winner, an encounter with one would definitely not have the same impact as meeting a giant sauropod of almost the same length!

The championship contenders in the heavyweight class, according to the fossil evidence, are Patagotitan, Puertasaurus, and Argentinosaurus: all three have been found in South America and weighed in at around 80 tonnes (88 tons). By comparison, the heaviest African elephant is a paltry 10 tonnes (11 tons). However, with its huge mass supported by seawater, the modern blue whale can weigh up to 135 tonnes (149 tons), making it the heaviest animal ever to have lived on Earth. Sorry, sauropods.

The word "sauropod" derives from ancient Greek and means lizard foot.

FIRST FINDS
The first recorded sauropod fossil finds were made in England; at the time of these early discoveries, no one knew they were dinosaurs, far less the group they might belong to. The group we now recognize as sauropods was first identified and named by American palaeontologist Othniel Charles Marsh — he coined the name from two Greek words, and it means "lizard foot". Marsh, Professor of Palaeontology at Yale University and President of the National Academy of Sciences, was one of the foremost fossil-hunters of his age; by the late 1870s, he and others across the USA had found enough sauropod bones to

70   CHAPTER TWO

be able to assemble partial skeletons of these giant creatures. In 1884, Marsh had a bumper year. He unearthed the most complete Brontosaurus skeleton found to date and also the most complete sauropod skull so far, which he named Diplodocus; this dinosaur would become one of the most recognizable of all. Not that Marsh allowed himself time to dwell on his success — he was much too busy trying to find more specimens to add to his tally. As well as his desire to add to our knowledge of these ancient animals, Marsh was driven by another motive: the need to win out against his nemesis, fellow palaeontologist Edward Drinker Cope. The pair's intense rivalry, which resulted in accusations, counter-accusations, and even legal action, become widely known as the Bone Wars.

The Bone Wars began during a period in which knowledge of dinosaurs was increasing at an unprecedented rate. One of the most antagonistic, jealous feuds in the history of science, it involved spying, sabotage, and ultimately financial and professional ruin. The conflict started out as a fairly low-key disagreement but, as insult piled on insult and spat upon spat, it escalated into a bitter, lifelong vendetta between Cope and Marsh.

It was in 1863, at a scientific meeting in Berlin, that 32-year-old Marsh and Cope, aged 23, first met. Both were studying natural sciences at the University of Berlin, but Cope may have had another, more pressing reason to be in Germany — to avoid being drafted into the army to fight in the American Civil War. The two men were quite different characters; Cope was as gregarious as Marsh was reticent. Marsh had the upper hand academically; while Cope had a few scientific papers to his name, Marsh already had two degrees behind him, with a third on the way. Cope was born into a prominent Quaker family in Philadelphia whereas Marsh grew up poor, on a farm in Lockport, New York. What they did share, however, was an unquenchable thirst for palaeontology.

The two men initially got on well and after that first meeting, they exchanged a few friendly letters. In 1868, they even went on an expedition together to a site in New Jersey, which Cope knew of because his mentor, Joseph Leidy, had dug there 10 years earlier. During that season, they managed to find three new dinosaurs. However, when Cope later returned there alone, he found out that Marsh had secretly bribed the site managers to have any future fossil discoveries sent straight to him. Understandably, Cope was not happy. This, perhaps, kickstarted the enmity that would ramp up over following decades.

DIG DEEPER

Othniel Marsh
Marsh and Yale University were inextricably linked. After graduating from there in 1860, he went on to become its first Professor of Palaeontology. On his death, he left his vast fossil collection to the university, as well as his house and grounds, now part of Yale's Botanical Gardens.

TERRESTRIAL TITAN

DIG DEEPER

Cope's club
Edward Cope belonged to the Megatherium Club, based at the Smithsonian Institution. Named after an extinct sloth, its members were young naturalists, reportedly as keen on partying as on furthering their understanding of the natural world.

Then, in 1868, Cope made an error which was to haunt him for the rest of his life. He was sent a large skeleton that had been unearthed in western Kansas. It was around 12 m (39 ft) long and Cope reckoned it was a marine reptile from the Cretaceous, related to the plesiosaur. He named the specimen *Elasmosaurus platyurus*. So far so good. He also reported that there was sediment around the head and neck, which made it difficult to see that area clearly. But this fact did not excuse the major mistake he was about to make...

When Cope assembled the skeleton, he mixed up the neck and tail vertebrae. This gave his reconstructed dinosaur a very long tail and a short neck when it should have been the other way around, with the neck more than 7 m (23 ft) long. To compound the error, he positioned the head on the end of its tail. When Marsh came to take a look at the reconstructed skeleton, Cope's mistake did not go unnoticed. Cope published a correction, and reportedly tried to buy up all the copies of the American Philosophical Society Journal, in which the paper containing the error had been published. But the story was already out there and Marsh certainly made the most of it, bringing it up in public whenever he got the chance.

However, Marsh himself wasn't immune to playing fast and loose with dinosaur anatomy. In 1877, he uncovered a new dinosaur he called Apatosaurus, which was missing its skull. In his haste to publish the findings,

Back to front Elasmosaurus
Cope's error in reassambling the skeleton may have been partly due to the fact that bones had been jumbled up during the fossilization process, with the skull lying close to the tail vertebrae.

As well as the misplaced head, flippers also faced the wrong direction.

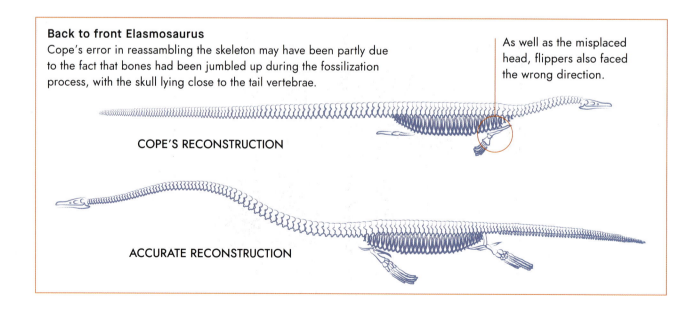

COPE'S RECONSTRUCTION

ACCURATE RECONSTRUCTION

72 CHAPTER TWO

Marsh simply used the head of another dinosaur (probably a Camarasaurus) to complete his reconstruction. Palaeontologists at this time were working fast, scrabbling to claim discoveries and name as many new species as possible — and none were more competitive than Marsh and Cope. This excessive haste didn't do Cope, in particular, any favours. His output was prolific and in one year alone, he published more than 75 papers. It is perhaps not surprising, therefore, that the quality and accuracy of some of these papers reflected the lack of care and attention taken in their preparation. Cope's reputation as an academic suffered accordingly, and this may have contributed to the difficulties he would later face in securing funding for his expeditions. Marsh, on the other hand, was less prodigious and much more careful in his output, tending to target only the more reputable scientific journals; in contrast to Cope, his academic standing at this time steadily grew.

▼ **Yale Peabody Museum**
The Peabody, founded in 1866, houses one of the world's oldest and largest natural history collections.

With family wealth to fall back on, Cope was able to self-fund his explorations. When his father died in 1875, he used his $250,000 inheritance to finance multiple expeditions. But Marsh also had a useful advantage in the shape of a rich uncle — the financier George Peabody. Uncle George funded the building of the Peabody Museum at Yale University and Marsh became its first Professor of Palaeontology. This, along with his appointment as Vertebrate Palaeontologist of the US Geological Survey allowed Marsh to employ a large team over 10 years, which turbo-charged his chances of making new discoveries. Both Cope and Marsh used their resources to head to the bone-rich areas of Colorado, Nebraska, and Wyoming each summer and then spend the winter investigating and publishing their discoveries.

In Como Bluff, Wyoming, Marsh found a 27-m- (88.5-ft-) long Diplodocus skeleton, as well as the remains of a Stegosaurus. Cope, meanwhile, was accusing Marsh of trespassing on his territory. Between them, the two men and their crews collected so many fossils that some, such as the skeleton of an Allosaurus, languished in sealed boxes until long after their deaths.

◀ **Bone battleground**
Como Bluff, Wyoming was a fossil-rich ridge where Cope and Marsh organized rival digs. Here, vertebrae from a Brontosaurus are being encased in plaster for transportation.

TERRESTRIAL TITAN

AN ISLAND HABITAT

Lusotitan and other dinosaurs flourished in the Lourinhã Formation, part of an area that is now western Portugal. 150 million years ago, the region formed part of an island that nestled in a shallow ocean, and which consisted of sandy beaches, rivers, lakes, and forested mountains.

CONIFER TREE
The Jurassic conifers on which Lusotitan fed would have looked similar to this modern relative, the Canary Island pine.

CLASSOPOLLIS POLLEN
Fossilized pollen of the extinct conifer family Cheirolepidiaceae, a conifer Lusotitan would likely have eaten.

DIVERSE BIOMES

The interior of Lusotitan's huge island was scrubby and dry, with the Berlengas Horst mountain range to the west. Towards the exterior, forests and coastal floodplains could be found, with long beaches fringing the ocean. The subtropical climate provided a perfect environment for dense coniferous forests to thrive as well as cycads and ferns — all ensuring a plentiful food supply for plant-eating Lusotitan.

THEN AND NOW

The subtropical climate was warm and wet, with much more rain in summer than winter. The wet season brought monsoon rains and violent storms. To experience what this Jurassic ecosystem might have been like, you could look to New Caledonia in the Pacific Ocean, or the Atlantic islands of Fuerteventura or Gran Canaria.

CHAPTER TWO

The interior of the island of Gran Canaria is thickly forested with pine trees adapted to the hot, dry climate.

The Berlengas Islands, a rocky archipelago off Portugal, are thought to be the remains of the Berlengas Horst.

TERRESTRIAL TITAN

> Cope and Marsh accused each other of bribery, theft of fossils, and even of spying.

Marsh and Cope's competitiveness led the pair to engage in what can at best be described as ungentlemanly behaviour. A discovery by one would be met by the other with accusations of bribery, stealing workers and fossils, and even of spying. The rivalry became so intense that stopping the other man from getting his hands on new specimens seemed to matter to them at least as much as finding fossils themselves. The two men were so protective of their respective dig sites that they reportedly filled in the excavations with rocks to prevent any remaining fossils from falling into their rival's clutches. On one occasion, it is said that members of the two teams actually threw stones and rocks at each other. Cope even accused Marsh of ordering his crew to smash any fossils they couldn't take away with them, although Marsh denied this.

The feud escalated when, in 1889, Marsh asked John Wesley Powell, director of the US Geological Survey, to audit Cope's fossil collection. As a result of Marsh's findings, Cope was asked to give up to the Smithsonian Institution any fossils he had found on digs that had been financed by federal funds. Cope was absolutely furious – he had spent a great deal of his own money on these expeditions, and felt that the order was extremely unfair. He fought back hard, producing records and receipts that he claimed proved he had personally paid for, and therefore owned, the fossils in question. Although he won the argument and was allowed to keep his collection, his fury with Marsh increased. This incident moved their vendetta from the relatively closeted world of academia into the public domain. In January 1890, the *New York Herald* published an article with the sensational headline: "Scientists Wage Bitter Warfare". Cope was quoted in the story, accusing Marsh of plagiarism and fraud, and claiming that Powell was corrupt and had misappropriated government funds. The newspaper, eager to generate more column inches, happily published Marsh and Powell's counterclaims against Cope. This public war of words didn't run out of steam until the following January – by which time the

▶ **Smoky Hill River**
In 1871, Marsh and his Yale students returned to this site in western Kansas and successfully recovered a pterosaur found the year before.

CHAPTER TWO

reputations of both Cope and Marsh were in tatters, and the public's respect for the field of palaeontology had taken a serious hit.

The Bone Wars also proved financially disastrous for both men. Cope's campaign led to criticism of the expense of Marsh's expeditions and he was forced to resign his position at the US Geological Survey. At the same time, economic recession in the USA led his uncle's Peabody Estate to reduce its funding of Marsh's projects, so he had to mortgage his huge house to finance his work. Cope's finances also suffered. He had tried to generate funds for expeditions by investing his fortune in mining – and when that didn't work out, Cope was forced to rent out a floor of his fabulous house to make ends meet.

Even when both men were facing financial ruin, they didn't stop. The bitter rivalry lasted until Cope died, aged just 56, in 1897. Even on his deathbed, Cope couldn't help firing one final salvo; he announced that after his death he would donate his brain to science to be measured for size – and he challenged Marsh to do the same. At that time, brain size was thought of be a measure of intelligence and Cope claimed that this would prove him to have been the cleverer man. Perhaps finally laying their rivalry to rest – or maybe as the ultimate snub – Marsh did not accept the challenge.

In their haste to outdo each other on the number of new dinosaur species they could claim to have discovered, some of Marsh and Cope's descriptions led to confusion that took years for palaeontologists to unravel. But whilst some of their ideas have not stood up in the light of new discoveries, others, such as Marsh's argument that birds are descended from dinosaurs, are now widely accepted. Both were prolific; Marsh discovered 80 new dinosaur species while Cope found 56. They found or identified some of the best-known dinosaurs including Triceratops, Diplodocus, Stegosaurus, and Allosaurus. Despite (or perhaps propelled by) all the drama, controversy, and competition, Othniel Marsh and Edward Cope each made an immeasurable contribution to our knowledge and understanding of dinosaurs today.

▼ **Imagining the past**
Cope made sketches of what his finds might have looked like when alive: this image of *Naosaurus cruciger*, Dimetrodon, and Edaphosaurus was first published in 1886.

TERRESTRIAL TITAN

77

THE BIG QUESTION

When we see the skeleton of a sauropod, the first question that springs to mind is probably, "How on earth could any animal be that big?"

> When the first sauropods were discovered, it was thought they must be aquatic animals.

In fact, when the first sauropods were found in the 1840s, it was assumed that they were aquatic because no one could imagine animals that huge could possibly support their own body weight on land. After all, the only modern animals of comparable size are whales; in the water their bulk is supported but if beached on land, their own body weight would quickly crush the whales' internal organs. However, as early as 1871, people started to suggest that the evidence pointed more towards sauropods being land animals — and by the early 20th century, this was generally accepted by most palaeontologists.

Once the experts agreed that these animals were terrestrial, there were plenty of questions: How — and why — did they grow so large? How did they move and support their own weight? And how could they possibly eat enough to support their growth and fuel such enormous adult bodies?

The question of how they managed to support their own weight, especially those long, long necks, which reached 17 m (56 ft) in some species (six times longer than a giraffe's), became easier to answer when experts realized that some bones were hollow. Most of the vertebrae contained cavities that would have been filled with air sacs; in some sauropods, air made up 60 per cent of their necks, reducing the weight of the neck considerably. These air pouches also played a key role in the sauropods' breathing; in a similar way to how modern birds breathe, the sacs inflated and deflated with every breath, constantly pushing oxygen through the lungs even as the animal breathed out.

The number of neck vertebrae — up to 19 in some species — and the way the ligaments, tendons, and muscles connected them, also helped sauropods to support the still considerable weight of their necks. Relatively small heads were an added bonus; a sauropod with a T.rex-sized skull would never have been able to lift its head off the ground.

Intriguingly, it appears that sauropods didn't get big just once. An analysis of 250 sauropod species found that they independently evolved to become enormous at least 36 times

▼ **Diplodocus**
The long neck of Diplodocus contained 15 elongated vertebrae and made up a considerable proportion of the sauropod's length.

CHAPTER TWO

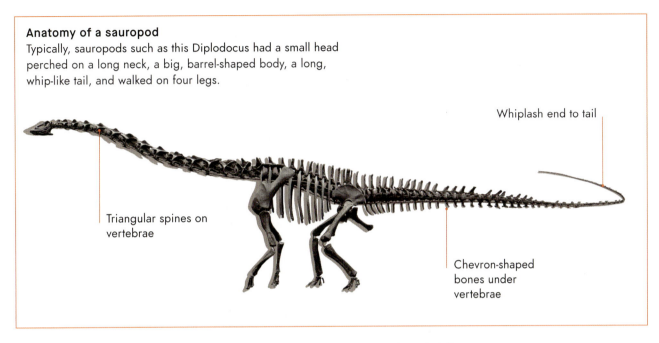

Anatomy of a sauropod
Typically, sauropods such as this Diplodocus had a small head perched on a long neck, a big, barrel-shaped body, a long, whip-like tail, and walked on four legs.

Whiplash end to tail

Triangular spines on vertebrae

Chevron-shaped bones under vertebrae

over 100 million years. This implies that in different habitats, sauropods took different evolutionary routes to the same destination — becoming unimaginably large.

So, how could a sauropod eat enough to grow a body from the size of an egg into an 80-tonne (88-ton) monster? First of all, it had to have access to enough food. The long neck was a huge help, as it allowed a sauropod to sweep its head from side to side without having to move the rest of its body, so it was able to reach and devour a huge area of foliage. The tallest species could reach up more than 20 m (65 ft) — and even higher when rearing up on their hind legs — to graze on foliage inaccessible to other animals. Sauropods did not waste time chewing — they simply raked leaves off branches and swallowed them straight down, taking in the maximum amount of food in shortest time. This was essential — even an average-sized sauropod such as Camarasaurus needed to consume vast amounts of vegetation and could spend up to 18 hours a day eating.

Some of the plants that sauropods ate still grow today, including species of *Equisetum*, commonly known as horsetail. These plants' tough stems make them very challenging to digest, so how did sauropods get the nutrition they needed from their fibrous, leafy diet? One theory is that the dinosaurs fermented the food in their huge guts over many days, to extract the maximum amount of nutrients. Herbivorous dinosaurs also

▼ **Prehistoric plant**
Horsetail is one of Earth's oldest plants, pre-dating the age of the dinosaurs.

TERRESTRIAL TITAN

had a way of supplementing a diet that could lack essential minerals such as calcium and phosphorous — gnawing on animal bones. Osteophagia (from the Latin for "eating bones") is a behaviour that sauropods may have shared with some modern herbivores, including giraffes. In the bush, giraffes, particularly pregnant females, can often be seen chewing and licking on scavenged bones, in order to supplement their leafy diet.

▼ **Aiming high**
In this scene from the BBC series *Secrets of the Jurassic Dinosaurs*, a sauropod uses its height to feed on leaves other herbivores can't access.

There is evidence that sauropods often lived in herds — so when each adult in a herd needs to get through hundreds of kilos of plant matter every day, the group would be able to strip a large area of vegetation in no time. How did these animals find enough to eat? The answer may come by looking at a present-day reptile — the giant tortoise. Together with birds and crocodiles, tortoises form a group of animals that are the closest living relatives to dinosaurs. Biologist Dr Stephen Blake and wildlife vet Dr Sharon Deem have been researching giant tortoises for more than a decade, at St Louis Zoo in the U.S. and in their natural habitat on the Galápagos Islands. In the zoo, the tortoises are treated to a daily diet of nutritious carrots and greens, but in the wild they often only have access to food of lower nutritional value, such as native grasses. This means the wild tortoises must find and eat a large volume of plants every day.

Just like Jurassic sauropods, these tortoises extract precious nutrients by fermenting the food they eat. But this does not solve the bigger problem: like sauropods, they need to consume such a huge volume that a group can quickly strip a landscape bare. In the dry season, which runs from May to December on the Galápagos Islands, there is not enough food for the tortoises living on the lowlands. To find out how they survive this period, the researchers fitted one group of tortoises with GPS trackers.

What they discovered confounded their expectations — the giant tortoises were migrating long distances. The GPS data showed that the huge, slow-moving tortoises were travelling up to 2 km (1.2 miles) a day, covering up to 9.5 km (6 miles) in less than a week, through volcanic boulder fields, to get from their dry lowland habitat to the highlands, where vegetation still flourished in the moist atmosphere at altitude. This journey would be the human equivalent of walking from London to Bristol.

If their long distant tortoise relatives are anything to go by, Jurassic sauropods may have migrated hundreds of kilometres between lowland watering holes, where food ran out in the dry season, and upland areas, where food was sparser but grew all year round due to more rain and cooler temperatures. But were these heavyweights mobile and agile enough to migrate such vast distances?

◀ **Field study**
In *Secrets of the Jurassic Dinosaurs*, Drs. Blake and Deem study and record the feeding habits of giant tortoises.

Professor Bill Sellers of The University of Manchester, UK, has spent years researching how these behemoths moved and has noted a particular challenge faced by bulky sauropods: "As you get bigger, your weight goes up by the cube of your height, but the force your muscles can generate only goes up by the square, so your strength-to-weight ratio gets much worse."

Professor Sellers has created a digital Diplodocus skeleton, based on a real specimen, to which he added virtual muscles to make the model walk. To see how fast sauropods might have moved, he first had to know the length of their stride. He was able to measure this for himself thanks to one dig site in the weatherbeaten badlands of the Bighorn Basin in Wyoming, USA.

At the Jurassic Mile site, the remains of more than 15 dinosaurs have been found; these include the predatory Allosaurus and various sauropods, including Diplodocus. Close to the remains lies evidence of their movements in the form of trackways — fossilized footprints. These prints allowed Sellers to measure the stride length (distance between footsteps) of an individual Diplodocus. Then, by programming his computer model to follow in the footprints found at the dig site, it was revealed that Diplodocus would have had a stately stride with a top speed of up to 25.2 kph (15.6 mph), covering 100 metres (109 yards) in about 15 seconds.

"It looks as if sauropods could easily cover long distances in search of food and water."

It looks, therefore, as if sauropods could fairly easily cover long distances across the Jurassic landscape in search of food and water. It must have been an awe-inspiring sight — a huge herd of the largest creatures ever to walk the Earth, sweeping majestically across the vast landscape. The power of

TERRESTRIAL TITAN

▲ **Diplodocus herd**
This illustration by Dr Mark Witton shows some of the group drinking while others keep watch for predators.

the sauropod to inspire awe and wonder continues to this day – and one the most striking examples of this is the massive bronze Diplodocus skeleton that greets visitors to London's Natural History Museum. This cast is the latest iteration of a figure familiar to countless people who have visited the museum over more than a century. The first version arrived in 1905, courtesy of a Scottish-born steel magnate.

Andrew Carnegie emigrated from Scotland to the U.S. in 1848, aged 12. He started work as a telegraph operator, but after seizing every business opportunity that came his way, he had amassed a vast fortune. He built up the Carnegie Steel Company which, when he sold it, made him America's richest person. In today's currency, his fortune has been estimated at the equivalent of over $300 billion.

Carnegie was a keen philanthropist and during his lifetime he gave away more than $350 million, which equates to more than $6 billion today. Carnegie sponsored the building of four museums in the city of Pittsburgh, including the Carnegie Museum of Natural History. In 1898, he reportedly read a story in the *New York Post* about the discovery of a huge dinosaur in the Wyoming badlands. He asked the director of the Museum of Natural History to buy the dinosaur skeleton. Unfortunately, director William Holland wasn't able to acquire that particular skeleton but undeterred, he arranged for a team of palaeontologists to search the area for another one. Seven months later, on the Fourth of July 1899, they found their specimen. Estimated to be around 153 million years old, the 20 m (65.6 ft) skeleton was retrieved, cleaned, and assembled — and it stands in the Hall of Dinosaurs at the Museum of Natural History in Pittsburgh to this day. Once experts had examined the specimen, it was declared a new species and named in Carnegie's honour: *Diplodocus carnegii*.

Carnegie had a poster made of the Diplodocus skeleton and hung it proudly in his castle in Scotland, where Britain's King Edward VII saw it and reportedly expressed the desire to have a Diplodocus in a British museum. Carnegie obliged the king by having a replica made of his skeleton — but he didn't stop at just one. Several plaster copies were created, which he then donated to museums across Europe and South America. Carnegie hoped that, by celebrating a shared interest in scientific discoveries, nations would acknowledge that they had more in common than that which separated them. His Diplodocus casts had become dinosaur diplomats.

Carnegie's replicas were admired by influential figures around the world, from Kaiser Wilhelm II of Germany to Grand Duke Vladimir Alexandrovich of Russia, as well as by millions of members of the public. Diplodocus quickly became one of the world's first celebrity dinosaurs and in 1914,

◀ **Andrew Carnegie**
Carnegie is pictured here at his home in Westchester, New York in 1911, the year he launched his philanthropic foundation, the Carnegie Corporation of New York.

◀ **Diplodocus diaspora**
In 1913, Queen María Cristina of Spain officially opened the Diplodocus exhibition at The National Museum of Natural Sciences in Madrid.

TERRESTRIAL TITAN

▶ **Star sauropod**
Pioneering animator Winsor McCay began by making short films of his dinosaur creation, Gertie, and using them as part of his Vaudeville act.

starred in one of the earliest animated films, *Gertie the Dinosaur*. The film is often cited as an inspiration to a whole generation of early animators, including Walt Disney.

The UK's version, nicknamed Dippy, was unveiled in London's Natural History Museum in 1905 and immediately created a buzz. After being displayed in different parts of the museum, it was moved in 1979 to the museum's huge Hintze Hall. Dippy became the highlight of thousands of school trips, inspiring dino-mania in children from all over Britain and further afield. In 1993, Dippy's pose was updated to reflect the improved understanding of what these majestic creatures looked like. It stood in the Hintze Hall welcoming visitors until 2017, when it was painstakingly dismantled and packed up, ready to start a tour of the UK before heading to Coventry for a three-year residency. In the seven years that followed, visitors to the London museum continued to bemoan the loss of their beloved dinosaur.

Then, in 2024, the Natural History Museum rekindled its relationship with Dippy; a huge skeleton, now transformed into a gleaming bronze cast, took pride of place in the museum's impressive new Evolution Garden. Dippy, albeit with a new look and a new name, Fern, was finally back where it belonged. Thanks to some cunning invisible engineering — internal post-tensioned cables threaded through the vertebrae — the neck and tail of this diplodocus seem to float without support. Fern has proved every bit as big a hit with museum visitors as its venerable plaster ancestor.

EUROPE'S SAUROPOD

How thrilling it must be to unearth bones that have been buried in the ground,

▼ **Dippy's return in 2024**
The bronze cast was created for the Natural History Museum, London, using digital 3D images of each of the original plaster cast's 292 bones.

84   CHAPTER TWO

undisturbed, for millions of years; to be the first human being to see the remains bathed in sunlight after eons of darkness. Now imagine if this happened to you completely by chance: that is precisely what happened to one resident of Pombal, Portugal and his family in 2017.

Pombal is a small, picturesque city a couple of hours' drive north of Lisbon, nestling in foothills below an impressive Moorish castle. The city merits only a brief entry in most travel guides, which mention the castle and a museum dedicated the Marquis of Pombal, one of Portugal's most famous and influential politicians. But if you scroll down Pombal's Wikipedia page, you will eventually come across this intriguing sentence: "In 2017, an 82-foot-long skeleton of a possible sauropod dinosaur was uncovered in a Pombal property owner's backyard."

The backyard in question was owned by Rogerio Alvarez, a local resident for over 50 years. He had decided to do a bit of home improvement and put up a new garage. He and his son-in-law were hard at work preparing the ground when suddenly, the younger man called out — something unexpected had appeared in the bucket of his mechanical digger. There, amongst the rocks and soil, were bones. Alvarez knew this was something out of the ordinary. "These were not the bones of normal, domestic animals — it was something much more interesting. That's when I called the experts."

When the researchers arrived, the scale of the discovery soon became apparent. This was the skeleton of a sauropod. The discovery put the town on the palaeontological map and changed Alvarez's life forever. "Now everyone knows me ... as the dinosaur man," he has said. This unexpected find of Lusotitan bones may have ruined his plans for a new garage, but his loss was science's gain. His discovery, literally in his own backyard, has turned out to be one of the most significant so far this century.

The father and son-in-law team had not unearthed just any sauropod. As more bones began to emerge, it became apparent that this creature — a Lusotitan — was seriously huge. In 2022, the research team uncovered a section of massive ribs, some 3 m (10 ft) long. They also found parts of the spine and limb bones, which led to an estimation that this animal could have been 12 m (39 ft) tall and 25 m (82 ft) long. That made it one of the largest specimens ever found in Europe.

> In 2017, the skeleton of a sauropod was uncovered during building works in a backyard in Pombal, Portugal.

▲ **Huge discovery**
Palaeontologists from the University of Lisbon take a break from uncovering giant sauropod bones.

TERRESTRIAL TITAN

Western Portugal
No longer the lush Jurassic world through which Lusotitan strode, western Portugal retains records of the distant past in the rocks that line its beaches.

▲ **Dig sites**
This map shows the locations of the Pombal and Cabo Espichel digs, about 170 km (100 miles) from each other.

The other exciting aspect of this find was that many of the Lusotitan's bones were articulated, which means that they were still in the same position as when the creature was newly dead. Often, buried bones are pulled apart and moved around by natural events such as floods, erosion, or movements of tectonic plates. As Dr Elisabete Malafaia from the University of Lisbon observed of the Pombal find; "It is not usual to find all the ribs of an animal like this, let alone in this position, maintaining their original anatomical position." Then, in 2023, Dr Malafaia and the team found something even more extraordinary.

At another site, about 5 km (3 miles) from Rogerio's backyard, the team discovered more bones — including another rib of a similar size to those at the first find. At that distance from the original site, the team felt that this rib was unlikely to have come from the same animal. Was this another Lusotitan? Finding two in such close proximity had never happened before, and the team set to work in the lab to prepare the bones to see what they could reveal.

CLIFFSIDE DISCOVERY
Revelations about dinosaurs don't always come from their bones. In another part of Portugal, astonishing evidence of the resilience of these big beasts can be seen near Cabo Espichel, a stunning section of Atlantic coastline. Here, dramatic cliffs rise 130 m (426.5 ft) above the pounding surf, yet this wild world is just a short drive south from the suburbs of Lisbon, Portugal's capital.

The prehistoric evidence is on the cliff face and can only be reached on a fine day without too strong a prevailing wind. During the *Walking With Dinosaurs* filming, that task fell to Francisco Ortega, Professor at the Faculty of Sciences at Universidad Nacional de Educación a Distancia (UNED) in Madrid, who abseiled down 100 m (328 ft), on a near-vertical section of bluff. His target was a row of almost circular depressions etched into the cliff face, each over 50 cm (19.5 in) diameter — a trackway of incredibly well-preserved fossilized sauropod footprints.

So, what is a trail of dinosaur footprints doing halfway up this almost sheer cliff face? The answer is that the ground has shifted in the 150 million years or so since the tracks were made. Back when the trackway was laid down, this cliffside would have been flat ground; in the intervening millennia, the ground has been subjected to enormous, sustained pressure from both north and south. This has squeezed and folded the rock strata, pushing them upwards and creating a break in the earth's crust. Older layers of rock were then pushed up over more recently formed layers. This has left the cliffs of Cabo Espichel exposed, showcasing the prehistoric footprints etched on them.

Finding a trackway is an even rarer occurrence than finding bones. This seems the wrong way round, as a dinosaur can obviously only leave behind one skeleton, whereas it could potentially create many thousands of footprints in a lifetime. However, in order for a footprint to fossilize, the conditions have to be absolutely perfect. The first factor is the consistency of the ground — you can't make any kind of print on hard rock; whereas on too-soft ground, an impression could be erased by wind or rain, get stamped on by other dinosaurs, or simply collapse in on itself. A surviving print then needed to last long enough to bake hard in the sun, a process that could take anything from days to months. Even if tracks did successfully harden, they would only survive if they were covered by a layer of protective soil, to stop erosion. Only if all the conditions were just right would a footprint become a fossil, ready to give up its secrets hundreds of millions of years later to a team of information-hungry researchers.

Once Professor Ortega reached the trackway, he measured the distance between each footprint and found something intriguing. The gap between prints on the right side was around 207 cm (81.5 in), whereas the on the left side, the interval was only about 197 cm (77.5 in). Ortega and his team came to a fascinating conclusion to explain this pronounced difference: the creature that made these tracks must have walked with a limp!

"Finding a trackway of dinosaur footprints is even rarer than finding bones."

◀ **Spot the palaeontologist**
Francisco Ortega abseils down the cliff at Cabo Espichel to examine the dinosaur trackway.

TERRESTRIAL TITAN

▲ **Chapel of Memory**
Panels inside the tiny clifftop chapel depict the legend of how the Virgin Mary ("Lady of the Cape") created the trackway in the rock.

We can infer so much more from a trackway than the simple fact that an animal once walked along that route. This fossilized track told the researchers that even though this animal was injured, perhaps by predators or as the result of a fall, it didn't just lie down and die. It was still able to walk, perhaps even covering long distances, even in its weakened state.

In 1410, long before people had heard of dinosaurs, local people came up with a different explanation for the strange tracks in the rock face at Cape Espichel. The story goes that two elderly fishermen reported seeing a vision of the Virgin Mary riding a giant mule up the steep cliff. This was taken seriously by locals and news of this miraculous vision spread far and wide. Soon, so many pilgrims were making the journey to the remote site that a church was built, which, along with other buildings, including a hostel to shelter pilgrims, still stands today.

One wonders what kind of creatures the men might have seen in their vision had a different dinosaur left its tracks on the cliffside. Theropods, the group of dinosaurs that included T.rex, would have produced a very different looking trackway to the large, saucer-like prints of a giant like a sauropod. The three-toed theropods would have left tracks resembling oversized versions of a bird's footprints. Although it's almost impossible to narrow down a species from just a footprint, the age of the rocks in which they were found and their location can also provide good clues to help palaeontologists with identification.

SAUROPOD STOMPING

When it is not possible to learn any more from studying the evidence left by dinosaurs, it's reasonable to look at their modern counterparts to try to understand more about them. At Whipsnade Zoo in Bedfordshire, UK, biologist Dr Beth Mortimer and geophysicist Professor Tarje Nissen-Meyer have been studying the sensory systems of elephants, to work out how the largest land animals alive today detect predators approaching from afar — specifically, the ways in which they sense and interpret seismic vibrations travelling through the ground.

Although elephants are nowhere near as large as sauropods, when they walk they still generate micro-earthquakes in the form of small seismic vibrations. In the field in Kenya, Dr Mortimer tested how well these vibrations could be picked up by other elephants some distance away. She and her team created their own vibrations using different methods, including hitting a stake into the ground with a mallet. When recordings were played back to elephants, they interpreted them as evidence of potential danger and quickly retreated.

But how did the elephants detect the tremors? The answer is that mammals, including humans, have nerve sensors embedded in the skin that can register even the slightest vibration. As Dr Mortimer notes; "Elephants have a large number of these types of sensors on their feet. Another possibility is the vibrations could be going through their feet into their leg bones, and then it's bone conduction all the way to their middle and inner ear."

▼ **Sound vibes**
Mortimer's team studied elephants' ability to detect and interpret vibrations.

Professor Nissen-Meyer thinks that dinosaurs could also have tuned into this seismic world: "What I can say as a geophysicist is these signals propagate really fast and if you have the corresponding physiology to detect them, there's nothing to say that you shouldn't be using them. Dinosaurs should have evolved to make the best use of any communication senses. And as such, it's not a far stretch to assume that if they produce seismic signals, they could have used them."

So, as a sauropod rumbled its way around a watering hole, it may have been able to detect seismic signals from a distant predator such as the ferocious Allosaurus, and been able to work out if the danger was getting closer.

TAIL-WHIPPING
From the metre-wide base to the pencil-thin tip, the extraordinarily long tail of the sauropod has puzzled scientists for decades. Why was it so long? What was it used for? These were questions that Dr Nathan Myhrvold in Seattle, USA, sought to answer. But he didn't look to a modern-day animal for a solution — he turned to technology.

Dr Myhrvold made his mark as Chief Technical Officer at Microsoft, but I.T. wasn't his first passion — he had been fascinated by dinosaurs since his childhood. When he came across a book by zoologist Robert McNeill Alexander in which the author speculated that sauropods might have "cracked" their tails like a whip in order to make a sound, Nathan was intrigued. Could this have been a method that dinosaurs used to communicate?

Nathan began to correspond on the topic with the Canadian palaeontologist Professor Philip Currie; together they batted around ideas, studied bones and created computer models and simulations. It has to be said that their published work on the topic was

TERRESTRIAL TITAN

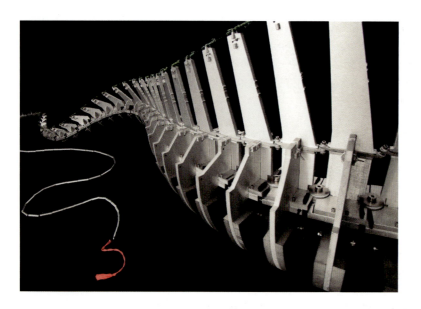

▲ **Whiplash tail**
At the end of the scale model of the tail was a "popper" — a strip of leather to simulate the tip of a bullwhip.

> "[The crack of the sauropod's tail] would have been as loud as the guns on a big battleship going off!"

received with a certain degree of scepticism, so Dr Myhrvold and his colleagues decided the best way to put their theory to the test was to create something physical — a working model of the tail of a sauropod.

The team based their model on an Apatosaurus skeleton in the American Museum of Natural History. They took the dimensions of each of the 82 tail bones, but to make the model more manageable they built to one-quarter scale. The model was around 3.5 m (11.4 ft) long and accurate to within 1 per cent, although without any soft tissue or the fine control that the creature would have had in life. The model was made of aluminium, stainless steel, neoprene, and Teflon, with weights added to each vertebra to simulate the weight of the soft tissue.

At the end where the tail would have attached to the body, it was suspended on a tripod, so it could be pulled quickly from side to side. Dr Myhrvold thinks that this action would have produced a whip crack at the tail's far end: "In the same way that a human can pick up a bull whip, and with a very ordinary arm [action] can make it crack, I think this would require a negligible amount of energy on the sauropod's part."

Dr Myhrvold set about investigating whether it was possible to whip the tail with enough energy to make the tip break the sound barrier, thus creating a cracking sound. He captured the test on high-speed cameras. Then, using the footage, he calculated that the tip of the tail exceeded 360 m/s (805 mph) when it was being "whipped", faster than the speed of sound at 343 m/s (767 mph). Scaled up to sauropod size, Dr Myhrvold reckoned the sound would have been very loud: "… as loud as the guns on a big battleship going off, an enormous canon *Kaboom*!"

Dr Myhrvold appreciated that his investigations and simulations could not be taken as proof and indeed later research, carried out using computer simulations by a team in Portugal, disagreed with his conclusion. Using the latest modelling with simulations of soft-tissue resistance, the Portuguese team found that while the tip of the tail could theoretically reach supersonic speeds, it would not have been able to cope with the stress of moving so fast without sustaining injuries. But a whip-cracking tail is such an audacious and attractive idea that perhaps Dr Myhrvold will upgrade his model and try to prove the Portuguese team wrong!

Either way, the question remains: why would sauropods make a loud noise with their tails? Dr Myhrvold wonders if it was used as a signal of reproductive fitness. "I think it's a good chance that they used this amazingly loud noise … as a form of communication. '*Kaboom*! See? I can really crack my tail.' And the next guy says, 'Oh yeah, you heard that? *Kaboom*!'"

COURTSHIP DISPLAYS

In addition to the ear-splitting tail cracking, sauropods may have employed an attention-grabbing sexual signalling technique that was designed to be seen rather than heard. Some scientists speculate that sauropods may have been able to rhythmically inflate and deflate an exterior air sac on their head to attract the attention of the opposite sex. Imagine looking up at that long neck with its tiny head, and watching a bulge repeatedly appear and grow above the nose, then gradually disappear again … the effect would have been mesmerizing.

Evidence to back up this theory lies in the anatomy of a brachiosaur's skull. As with many dinosaurs, the nostrils are positioned at the front of the snout, but there is also a large cavity in the area around them.

Could this cavity have been used for something more than just breathing? Perhaps by inhaling a huge amount of air, then exhaling while closing their nostrils, a male brachiosaur could inflate the soft tissue around this area to create an appealing (at least to a sauropod of the opposite sex) bump. A number of modern animals in different groups, including camels, frogs, and pufferfish, sport similar inflatable pouches. During its courtship ritual, the male frigatebird inflates a sac in its chest and drums its beak against the stretched skin.

◀ **Brachiosaurus skull**
The large nasal cavities are clearly visible on this skull at Berlin's Natural History Museum.

▲ **Frigatebird display**
The throat pouch is inflated for courtship displays: scientists think some sauropods may have used a similar technique.

In the Arctic, male hooded seals use their huge, red, inflatable noses to attract females, and to amplify their threatening calls to rival males. It is more likely than not that animals in the prehistoric world would also have made use of this eye-catching adaptation.

As well as using facial air sacs whilst courting, sauropods may also have engaged in elaborate displays using their long necks. Many long-necked animals today, including giraffes and ostriches, sway their necks and intertwine them during courtship rituals. After all, while the neck may have evolved primarily for feeding, if you've got it there's absolutely no reason not to flaunt it!

BRIDGING CONTINENTS

As palaeontology progresses, answers have been found to many queries, but there are always new hypotheses to be explored. Sometimes, it takes the discovery of fresh evidence – a bone, footprint, or a complete skeleton – to prompt the next step forward in understanding.

When scientists were examining the Pombal Lusotitan, they noted that it bore a striking resemblance to Brachiosaurus which, during the Jurassic, roamed the region that is now the western United States. They wondered how two animals could live thousands of miles apart on opposite sides of a vast ocean, and yet be so similar. It turns out the Lusotitan may not have been the only European dinosaur with a North American counterpart – and the evidence for this has come from another skeleton found in Portugal. This time it was not the remains of a sauropod, but of a ferocious predator – Allosaurus, the lion of the Jurassic.

At the National Museum of Natural History and Science in Lisbon, there are rooms full of carefully labelled drawers. One of them contains the fossilized bones of a carnivorous dinosaur that was discovered near Pombal. On reinspection at the end of the 20th century, the remains were found to belong to Allosaurus. When this was discovered, experts were baffled that this dinosaur, one of the most common theropods of North America, had been found on another, distant continent. This was the first evidence of an Allosaurus ever found outside North America – and it was the first time a single species of dinosaur had ever been found on two separate continents. How could this be?

Palaeontologists had to rethink much of what they thought they knew. They began to re-examine other fossils that had been found in Portugal, looking for further evidence of intercontinental dinosaurs. They soon began to realise their Allosaurus wasn't the only outlier. Armoured dinosaurs such as Stegosaurus and other large predators, including Ceratosaurus and Torvosaurus, all seemed to have been living on both sides of the Atlantic during the same time period. We know that not long after the start of the Jurassic 200 million years ago, the continents started to split up, with the newly forming Atlantic Ocean separating Europe from North America. But if the ocean had formed quickly, that would have isolated the dinosaur populations on the landmasses on either side of the water – which means they would have evolved separately and differences would have developed. The new fossil evidence makes this look unlikely, so what could have happened?

Dr Malafaia notes: "For theropods, we have almost the same dinosaurs in North America and Europe. This suggests that during the Late Jurassic, the land masses were still connected – there were land bridges between both continents along which the dinosaurs could travel."

It looks as though the two continents must have taken many millions of years to fully separate – there may still have been land bridges connecting the continents deep into the late Jurassic. This could help to explain why Portugal ended up as the final resting place of our Lusotitan – perhaps the dinosaur was an American export before the Atlantic Ocean expanded and the last land bridge sank beneath the waves for ever. The final separation of the continents spelled the end for the dinosaur intercontinental highways. It would be another 150 million years before a new set of explorers would once again find a way to bridge the gap between the two landmasses.

◀ **Shoreline showdown**
In this scene from *Walking With Dinosaurs,* Lusotitan faces off against a pair of Torvosaurus on the hunt.

TERRESTRIAL TITAN

CHAPTER THREE
THE CREATURES OF GRAND COUNTY

THE BIGGEST RAPTOR

Moab is the county seat of Grand County in southeast Utah, USA. It lies between Salt Lake City to the northwest, Denver to the northeast and, if you're happy to drive 744 km (462 miles) to the southwest, you could be rolling dice on the Las Vegas Strip in just over six hours. Moab may only have a population of 5,000, but if you're partial to fossil-hunting it is a very special place — a veritable Dinosaur Central.

Over 100 species of dinosaur have been found in the rock formations of Utah, most of them in the last 30 years or so — and around half of those discoveries have been within Grand County. This region was home to some of the most bizarre-looking creatures of all time, from the spikiest armoured dinosaurs to perhaps the most fearsome raptor — Utahraptor.

▶ **Sandstone formations**
Thousands of natural arches adorn Arches National Park near Moab. Several Utahraptor skeletons have been found in sandstone to the north of the Arches region.

98   CHAPTER THREE

▲ **Giant among raptors**
A hunter on the plains of the Early Cretaceous, Utahraptor, seen here in *Walking With Dinosaurs*, is the largest known raptor.

Utahraptor was truly ferocious. About the height of a human adult at around 1.75 m (5.7 ft) tall, but about 5 m (16.4 ft) in length, and weighing in at about 250 kg (551 lb), this was a bipedal killing machine. The body was covered with feathers, including a long tail fan of complex feathers, which the dinosaur used to help keep its balance. The arms were also covered in complex feathers, which may have been used for display or as a distraction technique when hunting.

Utahraptor's box-shaped head was about 60 cm (23.5 in) long and held sharp, serrated teeth, while its hands and feet sported fearsome claws. On each foot was an extra-long claw, which was held aloft— a sickle-like weapon that could easily rip open the hide of prey. This predator must have been a truly terrifying sight for the creatures it was eyeing up for its next meal.

THE CREATURES OF GRAND COUNTY

UTAHRAPTOR

The largest of the dromaeosaurs, Utahraptor would have dwarfed its more famous relative, Velociraptor. Neither as fast or agile as its cousin, it favoured a surprise ambush to chasing down prey.

Robust, stocky build suited to ambushing and overpowering prey.

Long skull housed a large brain, relative to body size.

Claws on the hands specialized for piercing

Small, serrated teeth easily cut through flesh.

DATA FILE

SCALE

Name: Utahraptor
Type: Dromaeosaur
Height: 1.75 m (5.7 ft)
Length: 5 m (16.4 ft)
Weight: 250 kg (551 lb)
Diet: Carnivore
Found in: North America

TRIASSIC	JURASSIC	CRETACEOUS
252 MYA	201 MYA	145 MYA

UTAHRAPTOR TIMELINE: 140–133 MYA

All dromaeosaurs are believed to have been covered in feathers.

Although long and broad, arm feathers did not enable flight.

KILLER CLAW

Flexible joints in Utahraptor's feet allowed the second toe, with its elongated, curved claw, to lift away from the rest of the foot. In motion, Utahraptor created a distinctive two-toed footprint.

The raised claw was up to 25 cm (10 in) long, sickle-shaped and razor-sharp.

▶ **Middle Cretaceous North America**
Around 125 million years ago, the Western Interior Seaway was not yet fully formed and the continent was a single landmass.

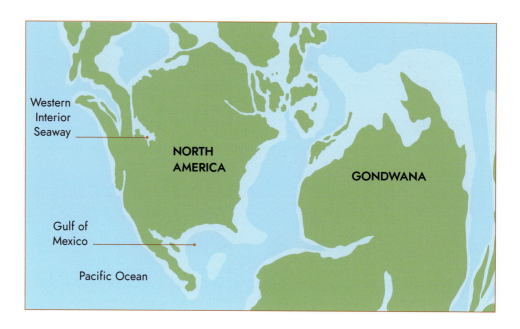

A LAND SHAPED BY SALT

You may wonder why so many fossils of Utahraptor and other dinosaurs have been found in Grand County. One possibility is that the makeup of Earth's crust in this region was especially good for preserving bones — and the geology of prehistoric Utah bears that out.

It's all to do with a mineral we need to exist, and what makes a dish like fish and chips so irresistible. A big "no" to any of you thinking of vinegar — the hero of Utah's fossil preservation is salt. As you will be aware if you've ever swum in the sea and licked your skin after you've dried off in the sunshine, salt is deposited from seawater as it evaporates. Imagine that effect multiplied millions upon millions of times, and this will take you to what Utah was like long before dinosaurs roamed its lands.

Back then, a deep basin formed on what is now the border between Colorado and Utah. Shallow seas flowed into this basin and then evaporated, leaving a deposit of salt behind each time. This happened repeatedly over millions of years, until the salt deposits were hundreds of metres thick. Gradually, these salt beds were covered by dirt and rocks, and the weight of this debris started to make the salt layer beneath the rock shift and subside. The reason is that salt and rock respond differently to a force: salt is far less dense and not as strong as rock and when it is subjected to pressure, it acts more like a viscous fluid than a solid. The result of this was that, while some areas of what would become Grand County rose in height, others fell, in a process geologists call salt tectonics. Dips and channels formed in the landscape and, by the

102   CHAPTER THREE

time of the Early Cretaceous, many had filled with freshwater and become lakes and ponds that could support life. And the water in these lakes was exactly what was needed to help turn the bones of dinosaurs into well-preserved fossils.

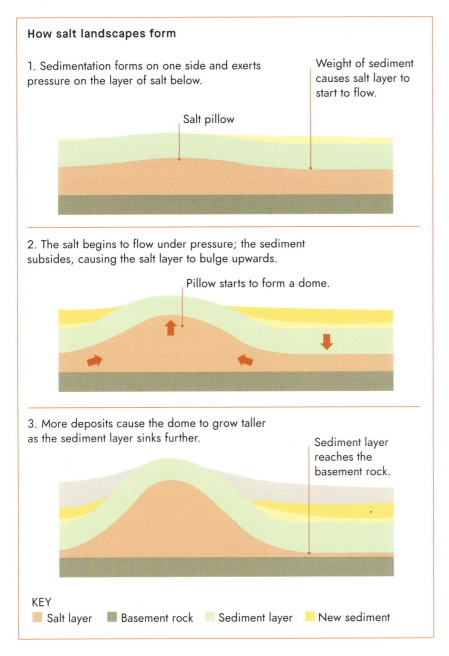

How salt landscapes form

1. Sedimentation forms on one side and exerts pressure on the layer of salt below.

Weight of sediment causes salt layer to start to flow.

Salt pillow

2. The salt begins to flow under pressure; the sediment subsides, causing the salt layer to bulge upwards.

Pillow starts to form a dome.

3. More deposits cause the dome to grow taller as the sediment layer sinks further.

Sediment layer reaches the basement rock.

KEY: Salt layer | Basement rock | Sediment layer | New sediment

▼ **Bonneville Salt Flats**
This is the remnant of a vast ancient lake that once covered most of western Utah.

THE CREATURES OF GRAND COUNTY

103

> The landscape of Cretaceous Utah was a perfect hunting ground for Utahraptor.

LIFE IN CRETACEOUS UTAH

The landscape of Utah during the Early Cretaceous, shaped by the movements of salt and sediment, was a perfect hunting ground for Utahraptor, the region's apex predator of the period. Over the 20 million years Utahraptor existed, many different herbivores would have been on its menu. Planicoxa, one of the so-called "cows of the Cretaceous", was a plant-eater that stood about 2 m (6.5 ft) tall and 4.5 m (14.7 ft) long, with very strong jaws for chewing tough, fibrous plants. Another herbivore that lived in the locality was long-necked Cedarosaurus. It is thought that sauropods like this adapted to the tough vegetation by swallowing stones, known as gastroliths, which helped to grind down plant matter as it passed through the digestive system. Some of these pebbles are thought to have lodged in the muscly gizzard, while others passed through the whole digestive tract.

Utahraptor was a theropod — a bird-like, bipedal carnivorous dinosaur — and there were also other theropods in the vicinity, including sickle-clawed predators Geminiraptor and Yurgovuchia. Therizinosaurs, the long-clawed plant-eating "scythe lizards", also roamed the region, including Falcarius and Martharaptor.

▶ **Planicoxa**
Discovered in the Cedar Mountain Formation in 2001, Planicoxa's name means "flat hip", referring to its distinctively shaped pelvic bones.

Nedcolbertia justinhofmanni, a relatively small, feathered theropod and contemporary of Utahraptor, was named after American palaeontologist, Edwin "Ned" Colbert, with its species name coming from 6-year-old Justin Hofmann, who won a competition to have a dinosaur named after him.

◀ **Falcarius**
A mass graveyard of these previously unknown feathered dinosaurs was unearthed in Utah by Dr Jim Kirkland and his team in the early 2000s.

THE "NON-EXISTENT" DINOSAUR

In 1991, no one was actively looking for the Utahraptor because no one imagined it could exist. The term "raptor" is commonly used to refer to smallish, bird-like dinosaurs. But in strict scientific terms, "raptor" is only ever used as part of a longer name, such as Velociraptor. The family name that encompasses raptor-like dinosaurs is dromaeosauridae, meaning "running lizards" — and until the dromaeosaur Utahraptor was found, almost nobody imagined that a so-called raptor could be that huge.

"Almost nobody" is the right way to put it, because it's now pretty much impossible for most of us to think of raptors without a certain movie franchise springing to mind — and the raptors in *Jurassic Park*

▼ **Rampant raptors**
The *Jurassic Park* team supersized their Velociraptors, not knowing then that a different raptor of a similar size really had existed.

THE CREATURES OF GRAND COUNTY

105

▲ **In the field**
Jim Kirkland at the Yellow Cat Quarry in 1993. The Utahraptor claw he found is set out on the rock in front of him.

were very large indeed. But when Michael Crichton, author of the 1990 novel of the same name, and film director Steven Spielberg started visualizing the Velociraptors that would feature in the film, there was no evidence at all to back up their imagined versions of large raptors. In fact, (spoiler alert!) it was thought that no raptor species grew any larger than a big dog!

However, in 1991 there was a seismic shift in the world of raptor research — and it had nothing to do with the movies. In October of that year, geologist Dr Jim Kirkland, along with colleagues including Robert Gaston and Donald Burge, were taking part in a dig in Grand County that would change everything.

The team was actually searching for armoured dinosaurs and had already unearthed a jawbone and some teeth when another member of the team found what he thought was a rib bone. Jim took a look at the thin, blade-like bone, shaped like a sickle, and realized that it looked more like the core bone of a claw. It resembled the slashing claw of two dromaeosaurs, Velociraptor and Deinonychus, except for one crucial thing; it was far too big. A bone this long would have supported a claw over 24 cm (9 in) long. This would mean that it belonged to a creature *much* bigger than any raptor yet found — and that was an incredibly exciting idea. The possibility that they had found evidence of a huge raptor would be backed up by later finds, as well as

▶ **Weapons in waiting**
This image from *Walking with Dinosaurs* clearly shows Utahraptor's two oversized, upward-pointing claws.

106   CHAPTER THREE

some remains that had been discovered back in 1975 but not identified at the time. Perhaps, the team wondered, a raptor the size of a grizzly bear really could have existed?

News of the huge claw and its potentially massive raptor owner broke out of the scientific community and made news headlines in 1992 – the year before the movie *Jurassic Park* was released. What timing! Kirkland's discovery helped not only to build anticipation around the film, but to justify the use of supersized raptors in the film. And as the film went on make more than a billion dollars at the box office, the producers never had cause to regret Spielberg's decision to upsize the movie's raptor stars.

By the time Utahraptor was discovered, it was too late to change the name of the raptors in the movie, so Utahraptor lost out on its chance of movie superstardom.

▲ **State dinosaur**
A poster featuring Utahraptor greets drivers crossing the state line from Colorado into Utah.

However, the giant raptor did manage to attain a different kind of recognition. In 2018, a 10-year-old dinosaur fan, Kenyon Roberts, proposed that Utahraptor should be adopted as the official symbol of the State of Utah. A bill to this effect was considered by the Senate and Kenyon was quizzed by the lawmakers to make sure he knew his stuff. He was asked to name a dinosaur beginning with X and immediately responded with the theropod Xenotarsosaurus. The bill was passed unanimously and Utahraptor is now the state dinosaur of Utah.

In 1993, Dr Kirkland and his colleagues published their paper describing *Utahraptor ostrommaysi,* a raptor over 5 m (16.4 ft) long and weighing up to 500 kg (1,100 lbs), although that figure has since been scaled back to 250 kg (550 lbs).

There had been an idea to name the species *Utahraptor spielbergi* after the film director, in exchange for him funding some palaeontology research. But the deal didn't materialise and instead the dinosaur was named after two people: John Ostrom, a scientist who researched the link between dinosaurs and birds, and Chris Mays, a former airline pilot who set up a robotics company that Jim Kirkland had worked for.

PLAINS AND FORESTS

When Utahraptor roamed its territory in Cretaceous North America around 130 million years ago, the environment was semi-arid, with conifer forests growing beside rivers that cut a swathe through the landscape. The region would have been dry for much of the year, with frequent forest fires, followed by a short wet season.

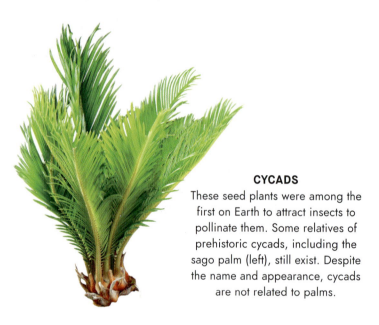

CYCADS
These seed plants were among the first on Earth to attract insects to pollinate them. Some relatives of prehistoric cycads, including the sago palm (left), still exist. Despite the name and appearance, cycads are not related to palms.

FLOURISHING FLORA

Alongside drought-tolerant conifers such as monkey puzzle trees, ferns were common, spreading out over the forest floor. Cone-bearing cycads also flourished. Although flowering plants, palm trees, and grasses had yet to develop, there was plenty of vegetation to attract grazing herbivores — and their predators.

THEN AND NOW

Pine forests and river plains, such as those found in North America today, would have looked familiar to Utahraptor. Look across the lonelier parts of Red River in Texas, and you'll be presented with similar views to those experienced by the inhabitants of Utah in the the Early Cretaceous.

CHAPTER THREE

The Red River in southern USA meanders through flat, open plains and forests that resemble prehistoric Grand County.

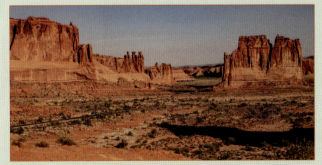
Grand County today is a dramatic landscape of sparse deserts and jagged red rock formations.

THE CREATURES OF GRAND COUNTY

109

A QUESTION OF SIZE

Jim Kirkland has had a distinguished career as a palaeontologist. He has been involved in discovering many species of dinosaur, and since 1999 has been Utah State Palaeontologist for the US Geological Survey. And he has never stopped investigating the Utahraptor. One of the questions he considered is this: how did Utahraptor get so big?

> Nature adapts and when one species goes extinct, this creates opportunities for the survivors.

Kirkland thinks the answer could be linked to a localized extinction event at the end of the Jurassic. According to him: "We lose three major groups of large predatory dinosaurs, the kings of their creation, they ALL go extinct. Other animals do survive elsewhere, but in this region we have nothing. It's almost a total wipeout."

For reasons no one fully understands, big carnivores like Torvosaurus and Allosaurus completely disappeared from this part of North America at the end of the Jurassic. But nature adapts and when one species goes extinct it creates opportunities for the survivors.

With the disappearance of the biggest predators from this region, a vacancy was created at the top of the food chain. As Dr Kirkland explains: "There's this niche open, and no one is filling it. Utahraptors got real big to take advantage of the hole in the landscape." So it's likely that, thanks to a near-extinction event in Jurassic Utah, Utahraptor evolved and transformed itself over millions of years into an apex predator — and became one of the biggest raptors that ever lived.

▶ **Jurassic wipeout**
The fossil record indicates that Utah's large predators, including this *Torvosaurus Tanneri*, perished in some form of local extinction event at the end of the Jurassic.

Stikes Quarry was the site of the initial Utahraptor find, in 2001.

◀ **Utahraptor Ridge**
This ridge, near Moab, was named Utahraptor Ridge in 2015. The U.S. Board on Geographic Names gave its approval because of the number of Utahraptor fossils recovered there.

MOVING THE MEGABLOCK

When you are studying dinosaurs, you can never have too much evidence. This is particularly true when the species you want to know more about can only be found in one small area of the globe and is a relatively recent discovery, as was the case with Utahraptor. If you have only a small number of bones to go on, your investigation is never going to be as full as you'd like, so every palaeontologist hopes that they might one day come across a treasure trove of beautifully preserved skeletons. For most, it remains an unfulfilled dream — the incentive that keeps them coming back to dig in fierce weather and remote locations year after year. But finding that once-in-a-lifetime cache of buried treasure is exactly what happened to Dr Kirkland in 2001.

Matt Stikes, a geology student who was working with Kirkland, came across something extraordinary halfway up a ridge in the Cedar Mountain Formation close to Moab. In what became known as Utahraptor Ridge, he found what he thought was a human arm bone sticking out of the sandstone rock — remember, he was a geology student, not a palaeontologist! Kirkland went up to investigate and realized that the bone was not human, but the remains of a member of the raptor family of dinosaurs. And that this discovery might just be the tip of a palaeontological iceberg.

"You couldn't put an ice-pick in without hitting something!"

THE CREATURES OF GRAND COUNTY

▲ **Moving the remains**
Jim Kirkland and his team pose by the megablock, which they have jacketed prior to being moved.

▼ **Moving the megablock**
The precious block of bones is slowly towed down the mountainside on a specially designed sled.

After more excavation works, he could barely believe the wealth of evidence the team was uncovering. As he put it: "You couldn't put an ice-pick in without hitting something."

Kirkland and his colleagues spent 12 dig seasons excavating this sandstone burial ground, but it was so densely packed with fossils that they ultimately decided they had to make a radical move — to take a whole slab of the mountainside out in a single "megablock" so they could move their investigations indoors, safe from Utah's winter weather.

They encased the 9-tonne (9.9-ton) block in a protective plaster jacket, then heavy machinery was deployed to move the block onto a specially made track down the precipitous mountainside. Once the block had been manoeuvred onto a low loader, the fossilized remains set off on their first journey in over a hundred million years to a rather unlikely location: a parking lot in Salt Lake City, Utah's state capital. Here, in a nondescript lock-up garage, the team began their work, painstakingly exhuming each bone from the rock. What they discovered surprised them all. As Dr Kirkland said of the block's contents: "There's a greater density of small, meat-eating dinosaurs than I've seen. This thing is at least 95 per cent meat-eating dinosaur."

In fact, they had found the remains of a group of dinosaurs. So far, they have uncovered seven adult and juvenile Utahraptors and one iguanodontid — the raptors' prey. The fossilized bones were beautifully preserved — as well as claws, they found hundreds of teeth, still in place in their jawbones. They also found something incredibly rare — a juvenile Utahraptor's braincase, which protected the dinosaur's brain while it was alive. This discovery meant that the team could calculate the size of Utahraptor's brain; they concluded it was of a similar size to that of a modern-day parrot. This would make it a relatively large brain

◀ **Releasing the fossils**
Scott Madsen of the Utah Geological Survey uses pneumatic air tools to reveal the fossils — a delicate task.

compared to other dinosaurs, so Utahraptor might have been capable of complex thought processes and behaviours, and been among the more intelligent animals of the time.

The condition of the bones led Dr Kirkland to wonder if the block had another secret to reveal. The fossils' position and pristine state told him that they had not been disturbed, which meant that the block also provided a record of the time the raptors died. The geology of the area also offered clues as to what could have happened to cause the untimely, simultaneous death of the animals. The block is made of sandstone — and although that sand is rock-solid today, Kirkland thinks that when the raptors met their deaths, this sand was far more liquid: "What killed them is [also] what buried them. Given the geology of the setting, most likely we're looking at a mass mortality tied to quicksand."

Kirkland's theory is that this block is the first example ever discovered of a group of dinosaurs that died together, trapped in quicksand. So what could have caused the mass fatality? Jim Kirkland thinks that the iguanodont remains found alongside the raptors might be the key to unlocking this mystery.

In the early Cretaceous, the fossil site would not have been halfway up a mountainside as it is now — it would likely have been flat ground, like most

___

Utahraptor's relatively large brain suggests it may have been among the more intelligent animals of its time.

THE CREATURES OF GRAND COUNTY   113

> A predator trap is a natural hazard, such as quicksand, in which both prey and predators become fatally trapped.

of the land around it. Perhaps the iguanodont was travelling across this prairie in search of food. Maybe it set off towards some tasty-looking vegetation. But the sandy surface wasn't as solid as it looked and the iguanodont started to sink. Struggling, it would have cried out as it was sucked further in. The cries of the creature would have attracted predators, and they in turn sank into the quicksand, too. More predators would have headed towards the trapped creatures in search of an easy meal, but they too might have become stuck. This is what is known as a predator trap — a naturally occurring hazard that can lure both prey and predators to their death. For many days

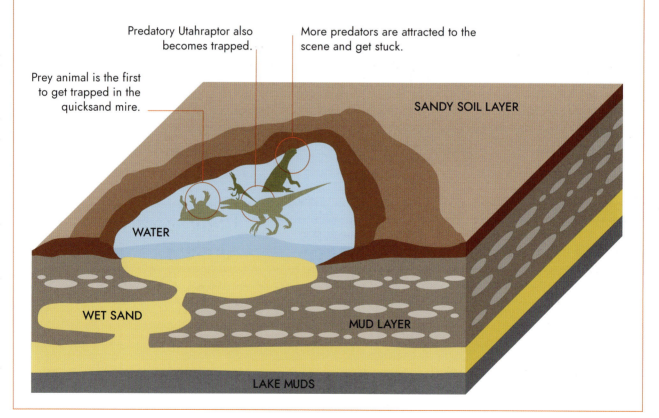

Anatomy of a death trap

In a 2016 paper, Dr Kirkland and colleagues set out their theory, based on geological observation, that quicksand killed the dinosaurs in the Stikes Quarry site. Eruptions from underwater springs breached the mud layer to mix with the sandy soil layer above and form mires of unstable, semi-liquid quicksand.

Predatory Utahraptor also becomes trapped.

More predators are attracted to the scene and get stuck.

Prey animal is the first to get trapped in the quicksand mire.

SANDY SOIL LAYER

WATER

WET SAND

MUD LAYER

LAKE MUDS

◀ **Pack attack**
In *Walking with Dinosaurs,* the Utahraptors hunt Gastonia as a team. While one creates a diversion, the others attack from all sides, heading off escape attempts.

after the event, the smell of death would have continued to attract carnivores, each of them hoping for a free lunch — only to end up stuck for eternity in the killing sands.

BORN TO HUNT
Utahraptors were prolific predators and may even have hunted in groups. Dr Kirkland reckons they would have been ruthless, efficient hunters: "Utahraptor liked to stalk in the brush; prey had no clue it was there until it was within striking distance. And as soon as it was, it would flex open its arms and leap, screaming at its prey. But it would happen so quick. When you look at a leopard or a lion attack — BAM! They're on it. That's how Utahraptor would have been, too."

Utahraptor had powerful legs, enabling it to leap onto prey. Once there, it could restrain the captured animal by gripping with its feet as it flapped its wings and swung its tail up and down and from side to side to keep it balanced as it made the kill. At this point, Utahraptor's key weapon could

> Utahraptor was a ruthless, efficient predator that may have hunted in groups.

THE CREATURES OF GRAND COUNTY   115

then come into play – the 25 cm- (10in-) long, super-stabbing claws projecting from its back feet. This was such an important weapon that when the dinosaur ran, it held this claw aloft so the sharp tips would not be blunted by rubbing along the ground.

Dr Kirkland thinks that Utahraptor used the sharp point on its claw like a can-opener to slit open the soft underbelly of prey, or to target areas where an animal would bleed out quickest, such as the arteries. After a large kill, Utahraptor could eat up to 70 kg (159 lb) of meat in one sitting. The killing claw could also be used to pin down and immobilise smaller prey, while the raptor took off chunks of flesh with its teeth.

Utahraptor must have been a fearsome sight as it leapt on top of prey, slashing and stabbing, its feathered arms and tail swishing around to keep it stable. It brings to mind the image of a modern bird of prey – but on a much, much larger scale. But this image raises a further question – do we know for sure that Utahraptor had feathers, and if so, how do we know?

▼ **Modern-day raptor**
Feet first and powerful talons splayed, a golden eagle closes in on its prey. A strike by Utahraptor might have looked similar to this.

FINDING FEATHERS

If you take a look at this image of Utahraptor (right), created by the *Walking With Dinosaurs* VFX team, the complex feathers really stand out. They are visible on the tail and forelimbs, along with an all-over layer of feathers and fuzzy down. The team worked with a number of scientists to make as accurate a depiction as possible, given the current scientific knowledge. But there has never been any evidence found of a feather that came from a Utahraptor. So what makes scientists so confident that these were feathered creatures?

▲ **Plumage on display**
In this scene from *Walking With Dinosaurs*, Utahraptor displays its feathers to distract a prey animal.

When Kirkland first came across the Utahraptor claw, the idea of feathered dinosaurs had gone in and out of fashion as often as skinny jeans. In 1991, no one had found physical remains of feathers on any dinosaur. It wasn't until 1996 that a paper was published describing a dinosaur discovery two years earlier, in China. This changed everything. *Sinosauropteryx prima* was a 1.5-m- (5-ft-) long dinosaur, which was described as having short feathers on its head, back, and tail.

◀ **Sinosauropteryx site map**
China's Liaoning Province has been the site of some of the most important fossil finds of recent years.

THE CREATURES OF GRAND COUNTY

GASTONIA

In the Early Cretaceous, Gastonia would have been fair game for a hungry Utahraptor. Gastonia was smaller and slower, but it was by no means an easy target. Its extensive body armour and thrashing tail were intimidating deterrents.

Rows of curved, vertical spikes intimidated both hunters and rivals.

Bony rings covered the neck.

Extra-thick skull

Jaw lined with small teeth for grinding plants

Gastonia lumbered on four stout limbs.

DATA FILE

SCALE

Name: Gastonia
Type: Ankylosaur
Height: 1 m (3.3 ft)
Length: 5 m (16.5 ft)
Weight: 1 tonne (1.1 tons)
Diet: Herbivore
Found in: North America

TRIASSIC	JURASSIC	CRETACEOUS
252 MYA	201 MYA	145 MYA

GASTONIA TIMELINE: 140–133 MYA

A DEADLY DEFENCE

The horizontal spikes that lined either side of Gastonia's tail gradually decreased in size down to the tip. If positioned in an overlapping formation, they would have been capable of cutting through flesh like scissors, severely injuring or killing any would-be attackers.

Triangular tail spine

Large underbelly shielded by horizontal spikes

Unlike some ankylosaurs, Gastonia had no heavy tail club. However, the flexible, spiked tail was still a formidable weapon.

The writers of the paper on Sinosauropteryx posited the theory that the feathers did not make the dinosaur capable of flight, but were possibly useful for insulation.

> In Liaoning Province, dinosaurs buried by fast-moving lava flows have been preserved in breathtaking detail.

After this, evidence for feathered dinosaurs kept on emerging from China — and from one province in particular, which was exposed to a very different climate in the Early Cretaceous compared to now. Liaoning Province lies east of Beijing and next door to North Korea. During this time, continuous volcanic eruptions covered vast areas of this region. Animals that were killed by superheated lava or toxic gas were then totally encased in ash, preserving the bodies in exceptional detail.

We can see a similar effect today in the excavations of the area destroyed by the eruption of Mount Vesuvius in 79 CE. There, inhabitants of the Roman city of Pompeii have been preserved in harrowing detail; forever frozen at the moment of their death, curled up or crouched, trying to protect

▶ **Cast in time**
This cast shows a resident of Pompeii. Volcanic ash filled every space around them; then pyroclastic flow hardened it to create a perfect mould. Volcanic eruptions millions of years earlier preserved dinosaurs in the same way.

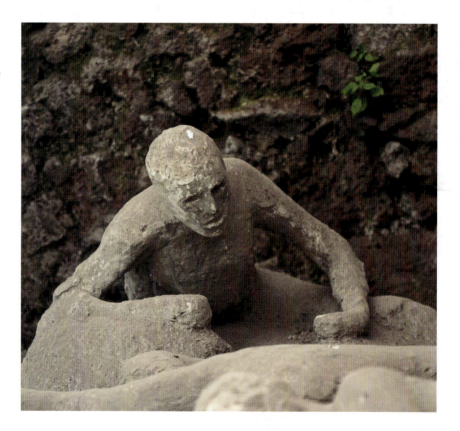

CHAPTER THREE

themselves from the lava flow. In some, even their final facial expressions are clearly visible. In Liaoning Province, the dinosaurs have been preserved in the same breathtaking detail.

Among the most exceptional Liaoning finds have been of dromaeosaurs, the dinosaur group of which Utahraptor is a member. A local farmer near Sihedang in Jianchang County found a skeleton that had been compacted onto a rock. The rock was taken to be studied by a preparator at the local museum, after whom it was named Zhenyuanlong (Zhenyuan's Dragon).

▲ **Zhenyuan's Dragon**
Despite the long feathers (indicated by white outlines), Zhenyuanlong had small arms and probably quite a weighty body.

▼ **On the wing**
In this detail, 30 covert feathers (indicated by white outline) can be counted on the right forearm.

The remarkable thing about this dinosaur was that some soft tissue was preserved, suggesting that the skin was covered by down. But as well as the soft tissue, there was evidence that it had the largest feathered "wings" that have been found on any dinosaur to date. Lü Junchang of the Chinese Academy of Geological Sciences in Beijing and Steve Brusatte of The University of Edinburgh described the find, noting three different types of feathers: primary, secondary, and covert. The primaries were attached to the hand, the secondaries to the forearm and both were covered by the coverts, so air could flow smoothly across them. The arm feathers were long — around twice the length of the upper arm bone. Long feathers also covered what was found of the tail. In the images on this page, the feathers can be made out with the naked eye.

In other locations where there has been no soft tissue preservation, clues have still been found pointing to the existence of feathers. This is because where feathers attach to bones, there are sometimes bumps

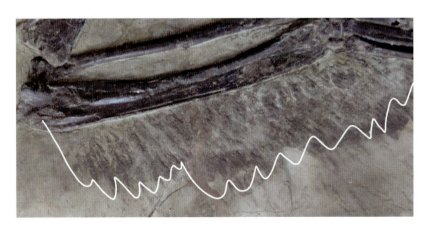

THE CREATURES OF GRAND COUNTY

▲ **Armoured ankylosaur**
Gastonia's array of armour included rows of triangular spikes pointing outwards along its sides.

Utahraptor existed at the same time as Gastonia, and would have been one of its deadliest foes.

called quill knobs. Raptors with quill knobs on their arms have been found in sites including Mongolia, Mexico, and South Dakota, USA.

ARMOURED GASTONIA

What kind of animals would be able to defend themselves against a large, agile predator like Utahraptor? Dinosaurs that were neither quick nor nimble enough to outrun Utahraptor would have had to rely on other attributes and skills to survive. One of the spikiest dinosaurs ever to exist was discovered in Utah's lower Cedar Mountain Formation in the 1990s and described by Dr Kirkland in 1998. It was from the clade of dinosaurs known as *ankylosauria* — the armoured lizards.

Ankylosaurs and their intriguing fossilized body parts were first written about by naturalists as far back as the early 19th century. But long before that, they cropped up in the stories and legends of Native American people. The Lenape or Delaware people spoke of magical rituals in which the bones of ancient monsters, possibly ankylosaur remains that could be found locally, were burned and smoked in clay pipes. In the southwest U.S., part of the Navajo people's creation story involves a huge, armoured beast called Yeitso — a creature that could well have been inspired by ankylosaur fossils found by Navajo hunters over the centuries.

Ankylosaurs have been found on every continent, but Utah is so far the only location in which Gastonia remains have been discovered. The dinosaur was first identified by Jim Kirkland, who named it Gastonia after amateur fossil-hunter and palaeo-artist Rob Gaston, who had found the site on which the remains were discovered. There are two known species of Gastonia and they were both first unearthed within 1,500 m (1,650 yards) of each other. Fascinatingly, Utahraptor remains were also found at both these sites and have been dated to the same time period as the Gastonia species. So we know that Utahraptor existed at the same time as Gastonia, and would undoubtedly have been one of the armoured dinosaur's deadliest foes.

Ankylosaurs were certainly some of the weirdest-looking plant-eaters. They walked on four legs and were heavily armoured — some even had clubs on the end of their tails. Gastonia was medium-sized for an ankylosaur, at about 5 m (16.5 ft) long and just over 1 m- (3.3 ft) tall, with a girth of about 1.2 m (4 ft), and weighing around 2 tonnes (2.2 tons).

Gastonia's teeth were small in relation to the size of its skull, but perfectly adapted for grazing on plants — as was its wide pelvis, allowing room for a really huge gut, so the long digestive tract could extract as much nutritional value as possible from the vegetation Gastonia consumed.

But the most stunning aspect of any ankylosaur is its armour — and Gastonia's bony spikes, spines, and plates are among the most impressive. It's now known that these bony defences sported an additional layer of protection. This layer was made of a substance that is an integral part of our body make-up, too: keratin. On humans, this protein is the structural material that makes up hair, eyelashes, fingernails, and toenails. In Gastonia, it covered the bony plates and spines, creating a shield many centimetres thick. In the same way that our fingernails can be sharp, these keratin coverings could have razor-sharp edges. Even Gastonia's soft underside had some defence against predators' claws, as it was dotted with osteoderms — pieces of bone the size of conkers that fused with the skin.

▲ **Gastonia skull**
A profile view of the Gastonia skull cast from the Museum of Moab, Utah, shows the small teeth typical of a herbivore. At the front is a toothless beak.

◀ **Osteoderms**
Many ankylosaurs had osteoderms; tiny, flat-bottomed bones embedded in the skin, which afforded an extra layer of defence.

THE CREATURES OF GRAND COUNTY

Grand County
The Colorado River — once known as the Grand River — winds through the county. Erosion has helped to create the dramatic rock forms for which the area is famous.

THE CREATURES OF GRAND COUNTY 125

DIG DEEPER

THE "URANIUM KING"
Geologist Charles Steen kicked off Utah's Glow Rush in 1952, when he hit a huge deposit of uranium ore near Moab. The find made him rich and very famous, but he lost his fortune following a serious mining accident from which he never fully recovered.

▶ **Mi Vida mine**
Charlie Steen's mine yielded more than a million tonnes of uranium ore during its peak years. During that time, uranium miners far outnumbered fossil-hunters in this part of Utah.

However, all this armour had a significant downside. A medieval knight in a suit of heavy chain-mail covered in plates of metal armour would have been unable to move quickly on foot, making him vulnerable to someone with weapons powerful enough to breach his defences. Exactly the same mobility issue would have applied to Gastonia — and as we will see later in this chapter, this may have led directly to the demise of one particular Gastonia group in prehistoric Utah.

UTAH'S "GLOW RUSH"

The amazing preservation of the remains in this region has already been noted, thanks to the geological conditions that deposited so much salt in the area. But apart from bones, something else of value is also found in large quantities in the ground. In 1952, a huge deposit of high-grade uraninite ore was discovered southeast of Moab. Word quickly spread and Moab soon became the uranium capital of the world. Much like the Gold Rush a century before, thousands of prospectors rushed to Utah to make their fortune in an era that became known as the Glow Rush. Uranium is a crucial ingredient in the manufacture of nuclear weapons — and that made it very hot property indeed in the Cold War era.

Uranium can be found in rocks all over the world, but only in certain geological conditions does it concentrate in amounts that make extracting it economically viable. One of those ways is by fossilization, in which bone is replaced by an inorganic replica that contains the minerals from the

◀ **Dalton Wells Quarry**
This exceptionally rich bone bed has yielded more than 4,200 bones over 11 field seasons.

surrounding sediment. In the case of the fossilization process around Moab, this means fossils can contain uranium and are sometimes found alongside uranium deposits.

As the Cold War waned and demand for uranium declined, prospectors gave way once more to palaeontologists in the area. Alongside their arsenal of rockhammers, chisels, and brushes, these fossil-hunters may still decide to throw in a Geiger counter so that the uranium can lead them, like a trail of radioactive breadcrumbs, to the bones they seek.

BAND OF BROTHERS
Since the first Gastonia remains were found in the Gaston quarry in the Cedar Mountain Formation, hundreds more bones have been discovered, both there and in the nearby Dalton Wells Quarry.

The fact that so many Gastonia remains have been found together here has prompted palaeontologists to theorise that Gastonia may have lived in groups. However, these may not have been stable, family groups — it's possible that the Gastonia in these gangs only joined together on a temporary basis.

During the time Dr Kirkland, Dr Josh Lively, and their team were being filmed by the *Walking With Dinosaurs* crew, they were investigating a

THE CREATURES OF GRAND COUNTY

discovery of the remains of a group of animals that appeared to have been the same age when they all died. Kirkland observed that the bones were not fully developed, so were likely to be those of teenage dinosaurs. This is significant because finding teenagers together could mean that Gastonia had developed an interesting survival adaptation.

> Young male Gastonia, banished from their group, may have teamed up to boost their chances of survival.

This grouping of adolescents has parallels in the behaviour of modern animals, for instance in the case of lions. Male lion cubs are nurtured in the family pride until they reach an age — and size — when they might threaten or challenge the group's dominant males. When that time comes, they are banished from the family and have to fend for themselves. These males often form coalitions with other young males, to boost their chances of establishing their own territory or winning mates.

It's possible that, in the same way, young male Gastonia, ejected from their groups and with their armour not yet fully developed, would have teamed up to help them survive in areas where the deadly Utahraptor was an ever-present threat.

How might a group have defended themselves if they came under attack? Gastonia's armour made the animals into walking tanks, but they were not

▶ **Family defence force**
In this scene from *Walking With Dinosaurs,* two grazing Gastonia are about to repel a Utahraptor attack by mounting a defence as part of a group.

128

CHAPTER THREE

◀ **Fossilized femur**
This well-preserved upper leg bone helped provide the team with evidence that Gastonia's sturdy legs were not built for speed.

invulnerable. A family group would have sought to protect the youngest or weakest members by forming a defensive ring around them. Unlike most other dinosaurs, Gastonia's most potent weapon was not its claws or teeth — it was the tail. The protective ring was formed by Gastonia parked on their stocky legs, tails facing outwards, confronting the enemy and ready to swing into action.

Gastonia's legs were perfectly adapted to stand firm and fight. During the time the *Walking With Dinosaurs* crew were filming Dr Kirkland and his team, they discovered a Gastonia femur (upper leg bone) and tibia (lower leg bone). The relative proportions of these bones were interesting. The tibia was short in relation to the femur, measuring only about half its length. Dr Kirkland noted that this is the opposite of what you expect to see in an animal that relies on its speed. The hind legs of Gastonia clearly were not adapted for running fast.

As Dr Kirkland explains: "These are not just simple bones; they have huge muscle attachment points, so [Gastonia had] developed their bodies for serious, strong manoeuvrability. You can just see these Gastonia holding their ground and swinging their tails with those big blades slashing across — probably reaching head height easily and slapping a Utahraptor right in the face."

"You can just see Gastonia swinging its tail, slapping Utahraptor right in the face..."

THE CREATURES OF GRAND COUNTY

Ordeal by fire
In this scene from *Walking With Dinosaurs* the young Gastonia, its escape blocked by predators, succumbs to smoke from the fire sweeping through the forest.

THE CREATURES OF GRAND COUNTY

▶ **Relics of an ancient fire**
Under the microscope, samples taken by Dr Carol Hotton showed grains of tree pollen mixed with scraps of black charcoal.

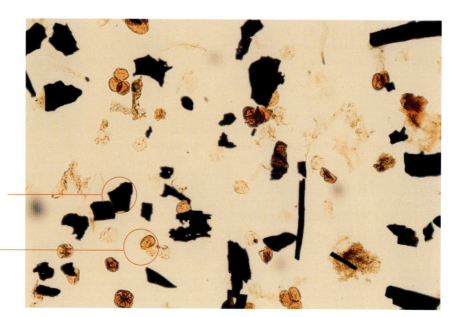

Charcoal

Pollen from a member of the cypress family, adapted to dry habitats

It's thought that when Gastonia's flexible tail was swinging side to side during combat, its spikes might have overlapped. If so, not only could it have bludgeoned a Utahraptor, but perhaps also sliced into it, using a pincer action. Gastonia's brain was the size of an egg, so it wasn't likely to win any dinosaur IQ contests, but ganging up together would have made them a seriously risky prey for Utahraptor to take on.

> Bones are not the only clues to prehistoric life; the whole ecosystem has a tale to tell.

Of course, it wasn't necessarily Utahraptors that killed the Gastonia whose remains were unearthed in *Walking With Dinosaurs*, or those found at other sites in the Cedar Mountain Formation. But if not predators, what might have caused their demise? The answer might by found by looking beyond Gastonia's remains. Bones are not the only clues to life in the prehistoric past — the whole ecosystem has a tale to tell.

Palaeobotanist Dr Carol Hotton of the Smithsonian National Museum of Natural History is an expert in interpreting the information contained in ancient pollen. She was investigating the evidence of the flora of the early Cretaceous whilst Kirkland and Lively were examining their Gastonia bones. Under the microscope, Dr Hotton was able to identify different ancient pollen grains by their distinctive shapes — for instance, a round grain that looked like a flat tyre came from an extinct conifer — and in the course of making these comparisons, she found something fascinating.

All these samples had something in common — they were adapted to live in dry conditions. This must have been a parched, arid environment back in Gastonia's time and during the long, dry summers, the forests would have turned into a tinderbox. Could this give a clue to what might have happened to those Gastonia that died together around 130 million years ago? Could there have been a drought? And if so, did the Gastonia die from dehydration, or even by poisoning, if their dwindling water source had become full of toxic algal blooms?

But there was yet more evidence to be found on Dr Hotton's microscope slides — she noted that the samples were flecked with lots of tiny black shards. As she explained: "In all probability, they represent charcoal. It's unlikely to be anything else and I see that in all my pollen samples."

Only one phenomenon could have produced that much charcoal: a forest fire. Once it takes hold, such a fire can spread at over 22 km/h (14 mph) — not fast enough to outpace a Utahraptor, but the same can't be said for Gastonia. With legs adapted for manoeuvrability rather than speed, and carrying the weight of its defensive armour, Gastonia's top speed was around 8 kph (5 mph) — definitely not speedy enough to outrun a wildfire.

So, the gang of teenage Gastonia that grouped together to try to survive their predator, Utahraptor, may have fallen victim to an equally deadly killer — the climate. Overcome by smoke or consumed by flames, they may have died, far too young, as they tried to find shelter from one of the regular wildfires that ravaged the region.

Once the drought was over and new life after the fire had begun to emerge, layers of ash and soil built up on the bodies of these dead youngsters, protecting their remains from scavengers and entombing them underground for over a hundred million years — until we started to uncover their bones and piece together their story.

Carrying the weight of its armour, Gastonia was not speedy enough to outrun a wildfire.

▼ **No escape**
In this scene from *Walking With Dinosaurs*, Utahraptor tries to flee the forest fire, only to find itself fatally trapped in another deadly hazard — quicksand.

THE CREATURES OF GRAND COUNTY

CHAPTER FOUR

THE DEADLIEST PACK

> Albertosaurus was nimbler and faster than T.rex, and may have hunted in packs.

If you ever find yourself in Drumheller, Alberta, deep in the Canadian badlands, you'll be left in no doubt that you've reached the portal into a world where ancient monsters once roamed. It is the self-proclaimed "Dinosaur Capital of the World" and it backs up this audacious statement with a series of dinosaur-related attractions including the "World's Largest Dinosaur" — a model T.rex moulded from steel and fibreglass that stands over 26 m- (85 ft-) tall and 46 m (150 ft) long, much larger than the original version!

But the hero of Alberta's prehistoric world is not T.rex, but the dinosaur that is named after the province itself — Albertosaurus, the "lizard of Alberta". This was a predatory, carnivorous tyrannosaur that lived 73–70 million years ago, relatively shortly before its more famous relative arrived on the scene. Albertosaurus was nimbler and much faster than T.rex, and it's thought it may have hunted in deadly, flesh-ripping packs.

HORSESHOE CANYON

Albertosaurus lived in an area that is now known as the Horseshoe Canyon Formation. Its stomping ground was sandwiched between the Western Interior Seaway, a body of water that ran through the middle of two of the

▶ **Towering T.rex**
The world's largest dinosaur isn't in a museum, and she isn't prehistoric. Tyra the model T.rex has loomed over the Visitor Information Centre in Drumheller for a mere quarter-century.

CHAPTER FOUR

landmasses that would eventually join up to form North America, and the forested uplands of the still-forming Rocky Mountains to the west.

The Rockies began to form around 80 million years ago and, by the time Albertosaurus was the apex predator in the region, the peaks would have been visible from the coast of the Western Interior Seaway. At the time, they were more jagged — rockier, in fact — and not as tall as they are today. The different elevations of the young mountain range created distinct environments for diverse species to evolve. Many herbivores flourished, such as ceratopsians — horned dinosaurs including Triceratops and Pachyrhinosaurus — and hadrosaurs, the duck-billed dinosaurs. This proliferation of plant-eaters afforded Albertosaurus plenty of choice of prey animals to hunt.

COASTAL HABITAT

Evidence from plant fossils suggests that around 71 million years ago, Albertosaurus' Alberta home had a warm-to-temperate climate. This was actually an ecotone — a transition area between two climates, so both subtropical and warm-temperate plants were found here.

▲ **Alberta Badlands**
A UNESCO World Heritage Site, the Dinosaur Provincial Park in Drumheller is one of the richest dinosaur fossil sites in the world.

▼ **Pillars of rock**
Millions of years of erosion have formed these eerie sandstone columns, called hoodoos.

THE DEADLIEST PACK

137

Bone crests protruded in front of the eyes.

Banana-shaped, serrated teeth

Small, two-clawed arms typical of tyrannosaurs

ALBERTOSAURUS

Imagine Albertosaurus charging towards you. The ground would shake as massive, three-toed feet pounded the ground. The thick tail would move from side to side in coordination with the stomping feet. If you caught even a glimpse of that toothy snarl, it would already be too late.

DATA FILE

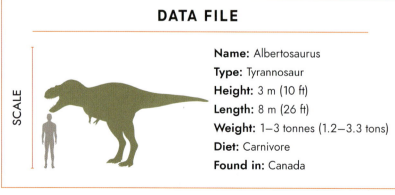

SCALE

Name: Albertosaurus
Type: Tyrannosaur
Height: 3 m (10 ft)
Length: 8 m (26 ft)
Weight: 1–3 tonnes (1.2–3.3 tons)
Diet: Carnivore
Found in: Canada

TRIASSIC	JURASSIC	CRETACEOUS
252 MYA	201 MYA	145 MYA

ALBERTOSAURUS TIMELINE: 73–70 MYA

Muscular tail held off the ground for balance

Long, strong legs could travel considerable distances.

LIGHTENING THE LOAD

An adult Albertosaurus skull was as long as 1 m (3.3 ft) in length and featured holes between bones known as fenestrae (Latin for "windows"). These gaps reduced the weight of the huge head, making the tyrannosaur more mobile. The largest hole, the antorbital fenestra, is unique to archosaurs, the ancient reptile group to which dinosaurs belonged.

ALBERTOSAURUS SKULL

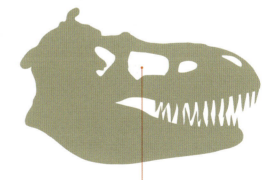

Wide antorbital fenestra sits next to the eye socket.

139

▶ **Late Cretaceous North America**
Albertosaurus prowled the forests of Laramidia on the shores of the Western Interior Seaway.

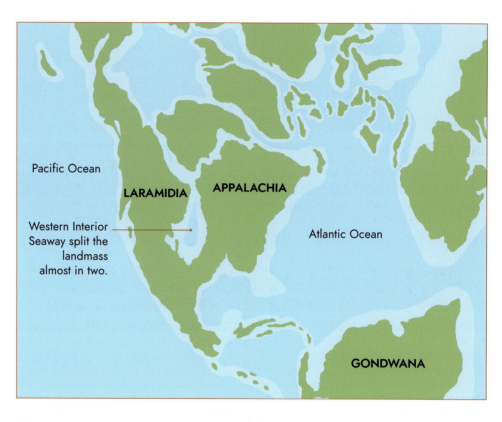

▼ **Snowdonia**
This part of Wales resembles the prehistoric Rockies, but with added grass cover.

The average temperature was warmer and less extreme than today. There was a lot more rain, with an average annual rainfall of about 1500 mm (60 in). These levels are roughly comparable to Scotland nowadays and more than three times the average rainfall in Drumheller today. To imagine how the young Rockies might have looked, picture Snowdonia in North Wales — except that you need to see it in your mind's eye bare of any grass. There were hardly any grasses on Earth 71 million years ago.

Albertosaurus would have shared this rich habitat with a range of other predators and prey dinosaurs, as well as non-dinosaur reptiles, like snapping turtles, and amphibians including frogs and salamanders.

Albertosaurus was a terrifyingly effective carnivore. It's tricky to estimate, but adults may have needed to consume an average of 60 kg (132 lb) of meat a day to stay alive. Although not as large as T.rex, this meant it was faster and more agile than its celebrated relative, and more able to chase down prey with its long, athletic legs. The long, muscular tail acted as a counterweight to help the huge animal keep its balance while running. The eyes were forward facing, giving it excellent binocular vision for hunting, and it had very powerful jaws with around 60 long, serrated, banana-shaped teeth, which helped it grab and grip prey. Then there were those tiny arms with just two fingers on the end … what were they for? Well, one scientist has an interesting theory about that — more of which later.

UNEARTHING ALBERTOSAURUS

In 1884, 25-year-old geologist Joseph Tyrrell was prospecting for coal deposits in the badlands of the Horseshoe Canyon Formation. As he searched the banks of the Red Deer River, he came upon an almost complete skull. It turned out to be the first carnivorous dinosaur discovery in Canada, although at the time, no one was quite sure what the remains were.

Five years later, another skull was found by one of Tyrrell's colleagues. The two geologists assumed that both skulls must belong to a previously discovered theropod and it wasn't until 1905 that they were recognized as the skulls of a newly discovered genus. Alberta was established as a province of Canada that same year, so the dinosaur was named Albertosaurus in honour of the new province.

In 1910, Barnum Brown, the palaeontologist who had discovered T.rex, led an expedition along the Red Deer River for the American Museum of Natural

DIG DEEPER

Joseph Burr Tyrrell
Discovering dinosaurs was not Joseph Tyrrell's only claim to fame. After years of hardship exploring the wild Canadian landscape, Tyrrell went on to become a successful gold miner. He died a very wealthy man at the age of 98.

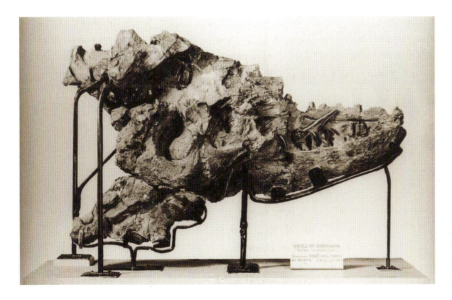

◀ **First Albertosaurus**
Tyrrell admitted to getting "a fright" when he saw this Albertosaurus skull leering at him from a rock!

THE DEADLIEST PACK   141

▼ **Red Deer River**
The river follows a scenic route from the Rockies through prairies and the fossil-rich badlands of Alberta.

▼ **Gang of three**
This scene from *Walking With Dinosaurs* illustrates Currie's theory that Albertosaurus lived and hunted in groups.

History. He found the remains of nine individual Albertosaurus skeletons jumbled together in a bonebed (see page 169 for more on bonebeds). Time was short so Brown excavated as many bones as he could, and left the rest in the ground. As was often the case at the time, he was so preoccupied with making more discoveries that he didn't study in detail the remains he took away from the site. Astonishingly, Brown never returned to retrieve the rest of the bones and the precise location of this extraordinary site was subsequently forgotten.

However, in 1997 Philip J. Currie, a renowned palaeontologist working at the Royal Tyrrell Museum of Palaeontology in Drumheller, undertook some impressive dinosaur detective work. He remembered reading an old article in *National Geographic* magazine by Barnum Brown, which mentioned a site with lots of tyrannosaur remains. Inspired by this claim, Currie combed the archives for mentions of Brown's Red Deer River expedition. Eventually, he came across four photographs taken by Brown of the dig site. Brown hadn't left any written details about the site, so the photos were all Currie had to go on. The reason for Brown's secrecy? He probably didn't want to leak the site's position to a rival who might find better specimens than his own. In the fiercely competitive world of 19th century palaeontology, helping competitors was absolutely not an option.

Currie set off for the badlands around the Red Deer River with copies of the photos and a whole lot of optimism that he would be able to identify Brown's original site. On the first day, they found absolutely nothing. Towards the end of the long second day, hunting in scorching heat that would have deterred all but the most determined, the team members headed back to base.

But Currie kept going, looking for a distinctive tree-dotted ridge line that he had seen in one of the photos. And finally, his persistence paid off. At the crest of the very last hill he'd resolved to climb, he spotted the ridge and the trees! From this, he was able to pinpoint the site itself. He and his team started excavating in 1998 and found hundreds of bones of different sizes from 13 individual Albertosaurus skeletons.

The range of sizes of these bones meant that the dinosaurs were at different stages of development and therefore of different ages. Finding a multi-generational group of Albertosaurus, close together in the same geological formation, suggested to Currie that Albertosaurus may have been a social creature – these dinosaurs might even have all been from the same pack. If so, imagine what a formidable team these massive predators would have made, working together to hunt down prey and make a kill. Currie's discovery was potentially so significant to the understanding of these animals' behaviour that he published a paper about the discovery.

At Brown's dig site, Currie's team found bones from 13 different Albertosaurus skeletons.

PACK LIFE

Currie was the first person to publish the theory that Albertosaurus might have spent at least some time living in groups. So what would life have been like in the most ferocious gang on the planet? Living in a group of apex predators was likely to have been a brutal affair and evidence of this is carved into the bones.

The jawbone of one of the largest skeletons found in the mass grave is scored with deep gouges, each of which tells a gruesome story. Mark Powers, one of the dig leaders filmed for *Walking With Dinosaurs*, noted of one of the gouges; "It looks like [a] tooth came down from the top... it would have required some kind of force from this diving angle to actually remove that piece of bone."

What could have inflicted this kind of injury on an apex predator? The answer is that it's likely to have been one if its peers – one Albertosaurus attacking another. As Powers' colleague Dr Greg Funston remarks; "... the biggest predator in its ecosystem and it's still getting beaten up, day to day."

In fact, more than half the Albertosaurus skulls unearthed from the site have teeth marks on them. We can't be sure why the dinosaurs were in-fighting;

▲ **Written in bone**
This jawbone, from one of the largest Albertosaurus found at the site, is scarred with bite marks.

DIG DEEPER

Philip J. Currie
Professor Currie's lifelong fascination with dinosaurs began with a toy found in a cereal box. He played a key role in founding the Royal Tyrrell Museum of Palaeontology and has undertaken outstanding fieldwork in Cretaceous localities all over the world.

> The main reason for Albertosaurus to live together would have been to improve their chances of survival.

possible causes include competition for a mate or disputes over food. It's likely that the pack had a hierarchy, perhaps headed by a patriarch or a matriarch, and those higher up the food chain would expect to eat first. A pack member attempting to jump the queue would have been dealt with swiftly and harshly.

Despite all the scarring on the bones, it's probably not the case that pack members behaved aggressively all the time. The position of Albertosaurus' tiny arms gave Mark Powers the idea that they might have used these limbs to interact with each other. He says: "If you're going to live in a group, you've got to have ways of communicating with one another that go beyond just grunting and staring. So maybe they're using their hands, side by side on the flank, reassuring one another — a morale boost."

The main reason for these dinosaurs to live together would have been to improve their chances of survival. For instance, forming a pack may have helped Albertosaurus rear their young. This behaviour is seen in one of Albertosaurus' modern relatives, the carrion crow. In 2008, biologist Daniela Canestrari and her team published a paper showing that crows benefited from living in a bigger family. Adult birds in the group helped those parents caring for and guarding their young by protecting the nests and collecting food for them. This communal approach gave the young a better shot at surviving to adulthood.

Another key reason to band together would be to gain an advantage over prey. The huge size of some prey animals would have made them very challenging for a single Albertosaurus to overpower and kill. Edmontosaurus was a herbivore that migrated north through Albertosaurus territory every spring. Adults stood 3 m (10 ft) tall, were 11 m (37 ft) long, and weighed in at 6 tonnes (6.6 tons), so a healthy Edmontosaurus would have presented a tough target for an Albertosaurus hunting alone.

At a site close to the Dry Island bonebed, Mark Powers and Henry Sharpe found an Edmontosaurus jaw bone — and buried alongside it was the serrated tooth of a tyrannosaur, probably an Albertosaurus. For the two scientists, this provided compelling evidence that Albertosaurus did, in fact, manage to bring down these huge "cows of the Cretaceous", and there is no doubt that the odds of a successful kill would have been tipped in the predators' favour if they had been working together.

HOW TO FIND A FOSSIL

So how exactly do palaeontologists like Powers and Sharpe search for evidence in the 21st century? Barnum Brown's bonebed has so far given up 26 Albertosaurus, ranging from one specimen under 2 m (6 ft) long and aged around 18 months, to an adult that measured an impressive 9 m (30 ft), and which survived for about 26 years before meeting its death. The fact that so many bones were jumbled together at this site suggests that what scientists call a "high-energy event' took place, such as a hurricane, flood, or fire. The team looked for any evidence that could provide clues — for instance, the presence of tree trunks might suggest a hurricane, and charcoal would suggest a fire.

Of course, before you get started, you have to find a great dig site — and how do you do that? Relying on detective work in the way that Phil Currie did isn't exactly the norm, but when you're on the lookout for a dinosaur skeleton, you will have to do a certain amount of hunting for clues. Some palaeontologists employ sophisticated kit, from ground-penetrating radar to Geiger counters — and the use of GPS pretty much goes without saying these days. However, a lot of fossil hunting is still a very low-tech affair. Knowing where to start looking is critical and there are geological formations that are known to produce a lot of dinosaur bones, so these are good places to begin to search. But palaeontologists also get help from a less predictable source — the weather.

If you prospect for bones in an area where the weather is eroding the soil, it's doing your work for you and may reveal bones close to the surface. Many important discoveries have been made by people spotting a bone that had just become visible by being eroded out of the rock and soil around it. That's exactly what happened to Mark Powers and Henry Sharpe as they walked the hills around the Red Deer River in 2021. As Henry remarked: "The thing is about the Badlands is everything can be found here. You've just got to spend enough time looking."

This was the same area where the very first Albertosaurus skull was found back in 1884, so Powers and Sharpe knew it was a promising area to look. But they didn't bring hi-tech equipment with them. More than 200 years after the first-ever dinosaur remains were discovered, the chief tools of the trade are still

▼ **On the radar**
Ground-penetrating radar enables researchers to detect objects buried up to 10 metres (33 ft) underground.

▼ **Photographic survey**
Some evidence on a dig site is best seen from the air. The camera drone is an invaluable tool that comes into its own in less accessible locations.

THE DEADLIEST PACK

▲ **Uncovering Rose**
Painstakingly, the team unearth the bones of Albertosaurus, the dominant predator in this region for more than 3 million years.

curiosity and a trained eye. Even if a bone has been partially eroded from the ground, what's visible may be just the tip and that may be broken or at an odd angle. Also, it could be the same colour as the surrounding rock and soil, making it almost invisible. All this makes finding anything incredibly challenging. It takes a lot of knowledge and experience, and sometimes, of course, a little luck.

Powers and Sharpe were at the end of a long day of prospecting and hadn't found a single thing when their luck suddenly changed. As Sharpe describes the find; "Eventually we got to one layer where we spotted some bones just kind of eroding out of the hillside. As Mark was standing up to see how far it went in either direction, I happened to look down at his boots and he's standing on Rose's femur." The pair had stumbled upon the leg bone of an Albertosaurus.

Mark Powers adds: "We found the tibia was still connected to the femur, and when we explored that, the foot was still there. So everything was just together and more and more bones were popping up."

They hadn't just found a leg, but an articulated leg — this meant that the bones were still in the same place they had been in life. Powers brought a team out to take a look and they soon realized that lying just below the surface was the remarkably complete skeleton of a young Albertosaurus that they called Rose.

In Rose's case, there were many large bones at the site, but sometimes pieces of evidence can be really tiny. Even the smallest bone fragment has an intriguing tale to tell, so every piece has value. However, a small fossil can look just like a lump of rock, so how can you tell the difference? Palaeontologists have a few tried and tested methods, some of which are more surprising than others. If there's a break in the bone, you can look to see if the inner texture looks the same as the outer surface. If that's the case, it's likely to be rock; the structure of rock tends to be uniform — bone much less so. But even if there's no convenient break to allow a glimpse of the

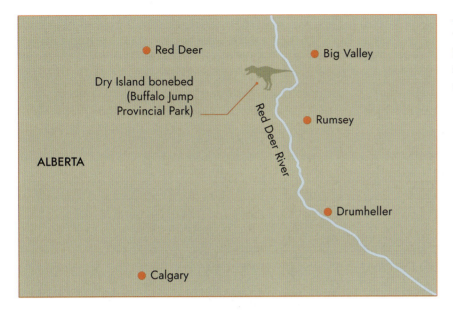

◀ **Dry Island**
The Albertosaurus bonebed lies within Dry Island Buffalo Jump Provincial Park, about 80 km (50 miles) northwest of the Alberta city of Drumheller.

inside of the fossil, there are other ingenious ways of working out exactly what you've found.

One technique is definitely not something anyone should try at home. It's called the "lick and stick" test, because the palaeontologists actually do lick the specimen. The reason they do this is because a fossil will stick to the tongue and a rock will not. This is because fossilized bone is porous, and the tiny tubes inside it draw in water from the tongue thanks to capillary action and surface tension. That will make the bone stick to the tongue — and show that it is a fossil and not a stone.

The size and shape of Rose's bones meant that it was immediately clear to the team that they had found a fossil. And from these bones, they were also able to determine that Rose was a sub-adult — a teenager. How did they come to that conclusion? The growth pattern of an Albertosaurus is similar to that of other tyrannosaurs — at certain stages of life, they undergo growth spurts. Tyrannosaurs had a growth spurt between 10 and 15 years old, much as humans do during puberty. Tyrannosaurs finished growing by their early twenties and had a life expectancy of 25–30 years in their harsh environment. Scientists have deduced this by studying the pattern of growth rings in long bones such as the femur, the thigh bone. Similar to growth rings on a tree, these patterns allow scientists to determine the approximate age of the dinosaur.

> Albertosaurus had a growth spurt in its early teens, much as we humans do at puberty.

THE DEADLIEST PACK

COASTAL FORESTS

Fossils excavated from the Horseshoe Canyon Formation have interesting tales to tell because the dinosaurs there were adapting to constant change. The Western Interior Seaway moved in and out, altering the ecosystems around it. In Albertosaurus' time, the landscape consisted of flat, temperate forests and low-lying coastal plains.

Tightly packed follicles contained seeds

Broad, U-shaped leaves

ARCHAEANTHUS
The large flowers of this magnolia-like plant would have attracted pollen-feeding beetles.

FIRST FLOWERS

At the start of the Cretaceous, angiosperms (flowering plants) began to appear. The blooms of the earliest flowering plants were far smaller than those of the flowers we know today, but they quickly diversified alongside the later dinosaurs. By the time of Albertosaurus, many had developed large, vibrant blooms.

THEN AND NOW

The coastal areas in which Albertosaurus made its home would have looked somewhat similar to the gentle slopes of the west coast of Scotland (but without grass). There were no sea-cliffs back then, and nearby marshes were dotted with large trees.

Island beaches such as West Beach on the outer Hebridean island of Berneray in Scotland, resemble Western Interior Seaway coasts during the Cretaceous.

Today, the Drumheller area in the Alberta Badlands has evolved from a forest by the sea to a landscape of rocky canyons containing prehistoric fossil beds.

THE DEADLIEST PACK

▶ **Formidable foe**
In this scene from *Walking With Dinosaurs*, Rose the young Albertosaurus is outmatched in size and strength by an adult Arrhinoceratops.

▼ **Counting the rings**
Palaeontologist Michael D'Emic took this image of growth rings in a Majungasaurus bone, which shows evidence of its age and growth spurts.

The thickness of Rose's bones also told a tale. Powers and a colleague, Christiana Garros, examined the metatarsal bones in Rose's mid-foot. Garros noted that at 3.5 cm (1.4 in) in diameter, these bones were "quite narrow and compact for an animal that people usually envision as being huge."

For comparison, Mark studied the metatarsals of a fully grown adult Albertosaurus. Although they were about the same length, the adult's foot bones were much thicker, with a diameter of about 6 cm (2.4 in). So an adolescent like Rose may have been almost as tall as an adult, but was likely to be about half the weight and definitely not as powerful. In a pack of Albertosaurus with different strengths and abilities, it's likely that dinosaurs of different sizes and ages would have taken on different roles when it came to hunting.

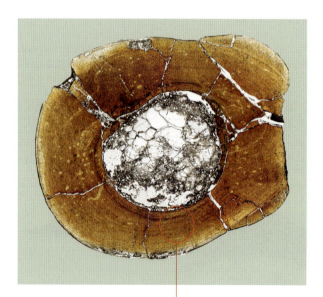

Growth rings are more widely spaced during phases of rapid growth.

Theropods may employ two different killing techniques — they can either pursue their prey over a long distance, or they can ambush them. Albertosaurus is thought to have used both styles of hunting.

A teenage Albertosaurus like Rose would not have had the power to kill large prey but, as the maximum speed of a ceratopsian such as Pachyrhinosaurus was around 25 kph (15 mph), Rose could easily outrun it in a pursuit. Her role in the hunting pack may well have been to go into a herd of prey animals to cause disruption and spread panic. She might then hone in on an individual, split it from the main herd and chase it towards the older, more powerful members of the pack. These stronger adults could use their muscular jaws to take down the prey with a bite to the throat, then rip off chunks of flesh and swallow them whole. This cooperative approach to hunting may have been an especially important strategy in times when prey was travelling in herds and had strength in numbers.

Albertosaurus didn't necessarily live in packs the whole time. When large herds of huge dinosaurs such as Edmontosaurus passed through on seasonal migrations, hunting together would give Albertosaurus an advantage. But at other times, they are likely to have hunted alone and they almost certainly ate different types of prey at different stages of their life. Fully grown Albertosaurus hunted larger prey such as ceratopsians for most of the year, but smaller, younger animals hunted prey such as little raptors, before teaming up when it was likely to benefit them all. Modern Komodo dragons do the same thing, although a group of these giant monitor lizards is known as a mob rather than a pack.

> Albertosaurus of different ages and sizes may have taken on different roles in a hunting pack.

We know the kind of prey that tyrannosaurs might eat because of an extraordinary discovery made by palaeontologists at Alberta's Royal Tyrrell Museum. In 2009, a fossil was unearthed at Dinosaur Provincial Park and taken back to the museum to be cleaned up. It turned out to be the bones of a juvenile Gorgosaurus, but it took years to separate them from the surrounding rock. As the researchers prepared the tyrannosaur's skeleton, they discovered toe bones protruding from its rib cage. These did not belong to the Gorgosaurus itself, but to the prey it had eaten not long before it met its death.

◀ **Dragons' dinner**
The bigger the mob, the bigger the meal! Komodo dragons are unusual among modern reptiles in hunting as a pack.

The scientists were able to work out which prey animal it was by comparing these toe bones with those of other species they held at the museum. They decided that the bones came from the legs of two small bird-like dinosaurs called Citipes. But the

▲ **Final meal**
Curators at the Royal Tyrrell Museum pose with the impressive skeleton of *Gorgosaurus libratus*, complete with preserved prey where the stomach would have been.

toe bones were all they found — there were no other Citipes body parts present. This kind of finding is rare, because two events must have happened at exactly the right time for the legs to have been preserved well enough to identify. Firstly, because dinosaurs digest their food very fast, the Gorgosaurus must have died very soon after it swallowed the Citipes. Secondly, the dead Gorgosaurus must have been covered by sediment immediately after death, otherwise the remains would have been scavenged and eaten.

From this specimen, it looks as though the young Gorgosaurus was a picky eater, as it appears only to have eaten the meaty legs of its prey. An adult would likely have chomped through the whole animal, so this might well be evidence that a tyrannosaur's eating habits changed with age.

WEATHERING THE STORM

We know that Albertosaurus' home territory was prone to storms and today, the exposed area around the dig site where they were working on unearthing Rose is still at the mercy of extreme weather — what helps palaeontologists to find dinosaur bones in the first place can also destroy their precious evidence. As soon as the bones are exposed to the elements for the first time in millions of years, they start to degrade, so must be protected. The dig team wanted to take Rose's bones back to the safety of the University of

▶ **On the hunt**
In *Walking With Dinosaurs*, a trio of Gorgosaurus track a herd of Pachyrhinosaurus into thick forest.

152 CHAPTER FOUR

Alberta in Edmonton where they could be stored in stable conditions, before being catalogued and studied. But at the "Rose" dig site, a storm was brewing. The team could see it barrelling towards them across the flat plains, and weather warnings were coming thick and fast over the radio, so team co-leader Annie McIntosh decided they needed to retreat. McIntosh told the team: "Winds up to 90 kph [are] strong enough to take shingles off of roofs. I think it's safer to vacate."

All the team could do to protect Rose's skeleton was cover the exposed bones with tarpaulins weighed down with rocks. As they headed to the shelter of base camp, they just had to hope that Rose would survive the stormy night on the mountain. Back at camp, the storm hit and was so fierce that the tents were in danger of being blown down — something that had never happened before. The team had to abandon the camp to spend the night in the safety of a cabin.

By next morning, the skies had cleared and the team headed back up the mountain with trepidation to see whether Rose's leg had survived the overnight battering. They were all relieved to see that their tarps had done the job and Rose was just as they'd left her. But they still had another problem to solve — how to get her huge leg down the mountainside. Because the limb was articulated, it was very valuable to scientists as they would be able to study its anatomy and biomechanics in much greater detail. But it also meant they had to get the huge leg down in one piece. And that took a serious amount of planning...

A COAT FOR ROSE
The first step in the procedure was to put a protective "jacket" around the leg. A jacket for dinosaur bones is very similar to the plaster-of-Paris cast that in the past, was often used to set human broken limbs — but on a far, far bigger scale.

Firstly, the team dug a channel around and beneath the enormous limb. Then they coated the top side of the bone with an adhesive that is easy to remove but which ensures any little bits of bone stay in place during transit. For a large fossil the size of Rose's leg, they added hessian as a cushion, before wrapping it all in aluminium foil to keep the bone separate from the next, messy part of the process — the final coat. They mixed up a big bucket of plaster of Paris, soaked strips of hessian in this white gunk, then laid these strips onto the fossil, making sure there were no gaps and the bones

During the storm, Rose's exposed skeleton was protected by tarpaulins weighed down with rocks.

were completely supported. They then left it for the plaster to set and harden before the really hair-raising part of the operation…

The team then had to dig underneath the bones and flip the encased leg over to free it from the soil. Palaeontologists get understandably nervous at this point, as they don't want any harm to come to the precious bones. The manoeuvre has to be carefully choreographed and there's sometimes a countdown so that everyone flips the jacket at precisely the same time. Once Rose's leg was turned, the other side was jacketed following the same procedure as before. The ancient limb was then ready to get moving again for the first time in millions of years.

HITCHING A RIDE

But this was not the end of the saga of Rose's big move. The jacketed leg now weighed more than 200 kg (441 lb). It was far too heavy for people to be able to carry it safely down the mountainside and there was no way a road vehicle could get anywhere near the site. There was only one solution — the team called for the support of a helicopter. The chopper hovered overhead as the jacketed leg was manoeuvred into a sling that had been attached to the aircraft. The signal was then given and the helicopter gained height. With Rose's leg swinging gently below it, the chopper whirled

▶ **Flying reptile**
Rose's leg is loaded into the helicopter's sling. For the first time in millions of years, Rose leaves her rocky bed, swinging high over the badlands.

154   CHAPTER FOUR

◀ **Safe landing**
At the foot of the mountain, the precious package is removed from the sling and securely strapped into a waiting pickup truck.

through the sky towards a truck waiting at the bottom of the mountain, ready to transport the leg back to the lab.

The Alberta weather means that the dig season here only lasts for about three months of the year. For the rest of the year, the palaeontologists are back at base, cataloguing what they've found, writing up their findings and publishing papers on their research, adding ever more to our understanding of this part of the world as it existed so many millions of years ago, and the extraordinary variety of creatures that inhabited it.

Our fascination with these prehistoric creatures is fuelled and fired by the quest for more knowledge. Amateur and professional palaeontologists piece together and share information, in order to understand better how dinosaurs lived their lives — from the moment they pecked their way out of an egg to the harsh realities of their everyday struggle for survival. Those comparatively few dinosaurs that met an untimely end and ended up preserved in the rock continue to provide us with tantalizing clues to their existence. In spite of dying before their time, these extraordinary animals have, in one sense, gained a kind of immortality.

CHAPTER FOUR

Red Deer River
The river, down which Barnum Brown sailed in 1910, snakes through Alberta. Since 1970, the bonebed he discovered has been part of Dry Island Buffalo Jump Provincial Park.

CHAPTER FIVE
THE EPIC MIGRATION

INTO THE LIMELIGHT

Let's start by acknowledging that Pachyrhinosaurus — a ceratopsian (horn-faced), herbivorous dinosaur that was quadrupedal (walked on all fours) — is not the most well-known of dinosaurs. Certainly it has a much better known (and some might say better-looking) cousin in the same clade: Triceratops. While Triceratops has certainly captured the public imagination, Pachyrhinosaurus has missed its place in the spotlight — until now.

However, as we will see, this dinosaur actually had a lot going for it: it evolved to live and communicate in enormous herds, embarked upon epic migrations, nurtured and kept its young safe, and could pick a mean fight using its characteristic facial feature, a big lump of keratin-covered bone on its nose called a nasal boss. In fact, it's that boss that gives the dinosaur its name — Pachyrhinosaurus translates as "thick-nosed lizard". And what's more, we know that Pachyrhinosaurus survived at least one epic, catastrophic event. This is a dinosaur with a tale to tell.

▼ **Who's the boss?**
The eye-catching nasal boss would make it easy to pick out Pachyrhinosaurus from a lineup of other horned dinosaurs.

160

CHAPTER FIVE

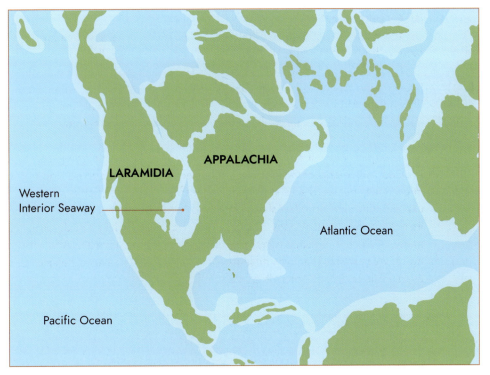

◀ **Cretaceous North America**
At the time of Pachyrhinosaurus, the shallow sea that had divided the two landmasses of North America was gradually shrinking.

THE WORLD OF PACHYRHINOSAURUS

Pachyrhinosaurus lived about 71–67 million years ago during the Late Cretaceous, in what would become North America, at that time part of the western landmass, called Laramidia. Three species of this dinosaur are known to have existed, and they were thought to roam in three separate areas between what is now Alberta and Alaska. *Pachyrhinosaurus lakustai* remains have been found in the Wapiti Formation in Canada, which stretches from the Edmonton region of Alberta to the far east of British Columbia. *P. canadensis* has been found in the lower Horseshoe Canyon Formation in southwestern Alberta. Remains of *P. perotorum*, the youngest of the three species, have been found further north in the Prince Creek Formation in Alaska.

▼ **Major finds**
All Pachyrhinosaurus remains have been found at three sites in Canada and one in Alaska, USA.

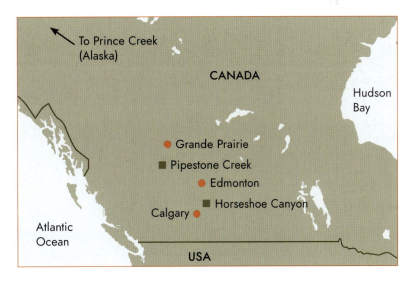

THE EPIC MIGRATION

PACHYRHINOSAURUS

This heavyweight quadrupedal herbivore consumed masses of low-lying vegetation daily, ripping up fibrous plants with its beak and grinding them down with its cheek teeth. The distinctive nasal boss came into play in confrontations with rivals or predators.

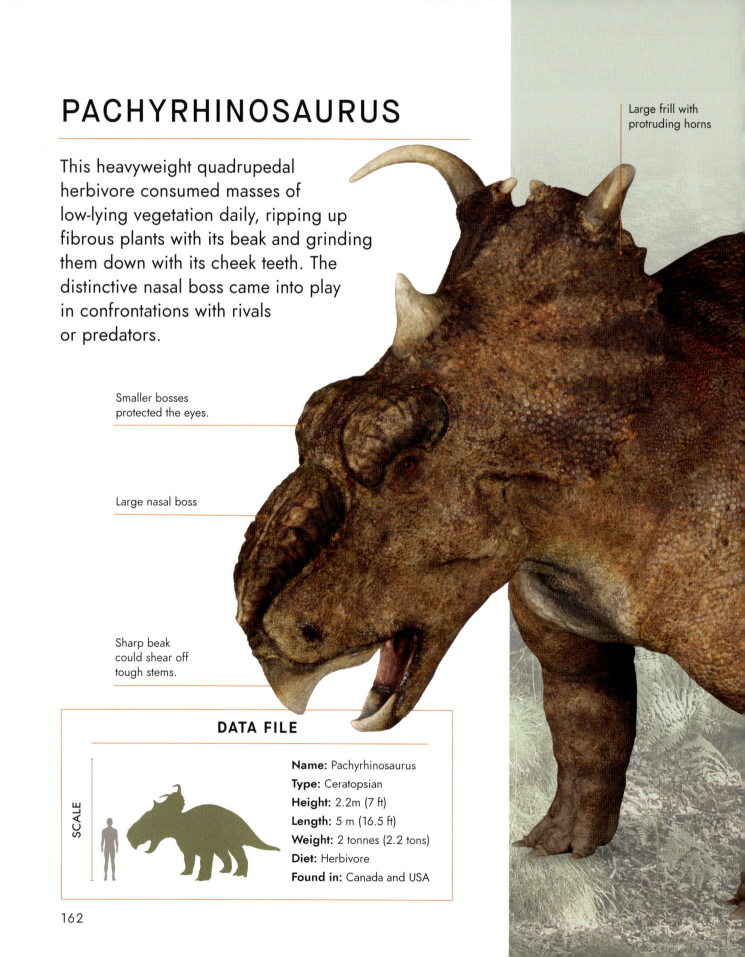

Large frill with protruding horns

Smaller bosses protected the eyes.

Large nasal boss

Sharp beak could shear off tough stems.

DATA FILE

Name: Pachyrhinosaurus
Type: Ceratopsian
Height: 2.2m (7 ft)
Length: 5 m (16.5 ft)
Weight: 2 tonnes (2.2 tons)
Diet: Herbivore
Found in: Canada and USA

TRIASSIC	JURASSIC	CRETACEOUS
252 MYA	201 MYA	145 MYA

PACHYRHINOSAURUS TIMELINE: 71–67 MYA

Thick ribcage protected the large gut.

FAMILIAR FACES

Fossil findings so far suggest that on every Pachyrhinosaurus, the neck frill, facial bosses, and horns were all arranged slightly differently. This may have helped them identify different species, or even individual members of the herd.

Every frill had a unique arrangement of horns.

Short, muscular legs

▲ **Fossilized leaves**
Analysing fossils is easier if they are from a plant with a living relative, like the plane tree leaf (right). The Nilssonia leaf (left) is from a long-extinct plant.

▼ **Rooted in the past**
Cathedral Grove, an ancient forest on Vancouver Island, provides a glimpse of how Pachyrhinosaurus' habitat on lower ground might have looked.

The *Walking With Dinosaurs* film crew followed palaeontologists as they excavated an area of the Wapiti Formation near Grande Prairie, Alberta. Here in the Late Cretaceous, vast mountain ranges extended for thousands of miles, towering over an untamed wilderness of dense, forested valleys. The Rocky mountains were in the process of forming and uplands were densely covered with conifers. At the base of the mountains the forest thinned; nearer the coast, the landscape turned to low-lying plains, dotted with rivers and swamps.

The local climate then was not as extreme as that of modern North America. Temperatures varied from a subtropical 15–25°C (59–77°F) in spring and summer down to a winter chill of 0–10°C (32–50°F), and snow was rare. One way scientists use to work out the temperature in a given period is by analysing leaf fossils. They take into account 38 different factors, including the leaf's size and number of veins. They then compare the fossilized leaves with those growing now in different habitats worldwide. By doing this, researchers are able to locate current environments that are most similar to that of the Late Cretaceous, allowing access to a range of information about the prehistoric climate in which the fossilized leaves flourished, such as temperature, precipitation and the number of daylight hours.

The modern ecosystems in which Pachyrhinosaurus would have felt most at home can be found in places that are not very far from where it roamed 70 million years ago: the USA's Pacific Northwest and the temperate rainforests on the west coast of British Columbia and Vancouver Island in Canada.

However, a major difference between the landscapes then and now is the presence of grass: grasslands are prevalent in all these locations today, but in the Late Cretaceous, grasses were a relatively recent addition in the region, and still rare.

▶ **Shared space**
This scene from *Walking With Dinosaurs* shows Pachyrhinosaurus grazing peacefully alongside other herbivores in the area known as the St. Mary River Formation.

SHARING THE HABITAT

As the Rocky Mountains formed and the Western Interior Seaway grew larger, many areas of land became islands, effectively cut off from each other. Land animals, including dinosaurs, could no longer travel easily and this isolation meant animals developed different adaptations specific to their particular environments. This led to animals of the same species evolving in different ways in their respective locations, eventually becoming different species altogether. Ceratopsians diverged relatively quickly during this time; Pachyrhinosaurus, for example, diverged into three distinct species.

Pachyrhinosaurus lived alongside many other dinosaurs. Apex predators such as Gorgosaurus and Nanuqsaurus would have been around at different times and places. In 2015, the remains of another predator from the period, the turkey-sized dromaeosaur Boreonykus, were confirmed in the area and, after analysis, deemed to be a close relative of Velociraptor. Troodontids, thought by some to be amongst the most intelligent dinosaurs on account of their relatively large braincase, were also likely to have lived alongside Pachyrhinosaurus. But the most numerous neighbours were duck-billed hadrosaurs such as Edmontosaurus – which, like Pachyrhinosaurus, formed vast herds.

> The bulk of Pachyrhinosaurus' neighbours were duck-billed hadrosaurs, such as Edmontosaurus.

THE EPIC MIGRATION

GIANT BROWSER

An adult *P. canadensis* was around 6–8 m (19–22 ft) long and weighed 3–4 tonnes (3.3–5.5 tons). The other two species were smaller at around 5 m (16.4 ft) long and weighing 2 tonnes (2.2 tons). All grew rapidly in their early years, reaching almost half their adult weight in their first decade. The growth rate then slowed and it wasn't until they were out of their teens that they reached their fully developed adult size, just under halfway through their estimated lifespan of 45 years.

Much of the plant matter consumed by Pachyrhinosaurus was low in nutrients, which meant it had to munch vast quantities of vegetation every day to survive. Its parrot-like beak was used to slice through leaves and twigs, then the strong cheek teeth shredded and ground down the plant matter. All that grinding quickly wore down the teeth, which were then replaced by new teeth growing behind them. If you'd had the opportunity to stare into the mouth of a live Pachyrhinosaurus, you would have observed teeth stacked in columns at different levels, depending on how much each crown had been worn down.

Whilst Pachyrhinosaurus' body was largely similar to that of other ceratopsids, the head was unique. In contrast to the three curved horns of Triceratops, Pachyrhinosaurus had a huge, bony boss over its nose – very useful in battle – and a smaller one above each of its eyes. Like Triceratops, it had a defensive bony neck frill, but in Pachyrhinosaurus' case the frill also sported horns in various arrangements. These horns, like the bosses, were made of bone with a reinforcing layer of keratin. It's thought that every set of horns was unique – the Pachyrhinosaurus version of a fingerprint!

EARLY DISCOVERIES

The first Pachyrhinosaurus remains were discovered in Alberta, Canada, in 1946 and named four years later by the American-Canadian Palaeontologist Charles M. Sternberg. The Sternberg family was practically royalty in

---

Pachyrhinosaurus grew rapidly in its early years, reaching half its adult weight within a decade.

▼ **Stacked teeth**
The teeth of some herbivores, including Pachyrhinosaurus, had teeth arranged in interlocking rows, or batteries. This example is from the hadrosaur Edmontosaurus.

CHAPTER FIVE

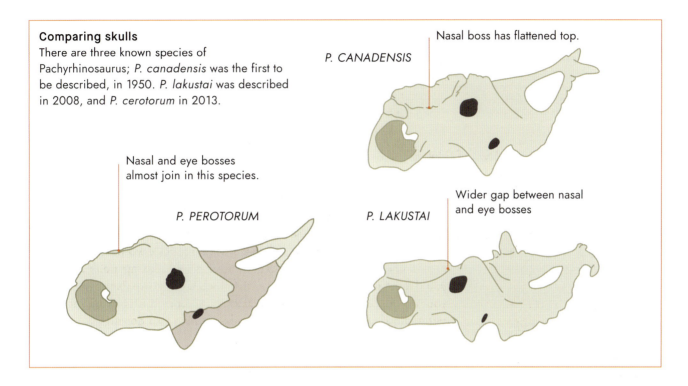

Comparing skulls
There are three known species of Pachyrhinosaurus; *P. canadensis* was the first to be described, in 1950. *P. lakustai* was described in 2008, and *P. cerotorum* in 2013.

P. CANADENSIS — Nasal boss has flattened top.

P. PEROTORUM — Nasal and eye bosses almost join in this species.

P. LAKUSTAI — Wider gap between nasal and eye bosses

palaeontology circles; George M. Sternberg was a high-profile military surgeon who first became immersed in fossil hunting after finding remains on his ranch in Kansas. His enthusiasm was evidently infectious because his brother, Charles H., became a professional fossil collector, too. They say the apple doesn't fall far from the tree — and all three of Charles' sons, including Charles M., also went into the family business of fossils. The eldest son, George F., amassed a huge fossil collection, part of which is now on display in the Sternberg Museum of Natural History in the town of Hays, northwest Kansas.

P. lakustai is the Pachyrhinosaurus species that the *Walking With Dinosaurs* team filmed being unearthed. The first specimen of this species was not discovered until the 1970s when Al Lakusta, a high-school science teacher in Grande Prairie, Alberta, took some of his friends to Pipestone Creek. The creek is a tributary of the Wapiti River, which runs a winding course through eastern British Columbia and western Alberta, before merging with the Smoky River.

▲ **George F. Sternberg**
Assisted by Harold Riggs, George Sternberg excavates a bone from a duck-billed hadrosaur in 1922.

THE EPIC MIGRATION
167

Al Lakusta was hoping to show his chums some fossilized remains, but they got much more than they bargained for. Exploring further upstream than he normally ventured, Lakusta saw what he thought might be dinosaur remains on the creek bed. As he went closer, he spotted a ledge of rock about 10 m (33 ft) above him on the bank. Wondering if the fossils might have fallen onto the bed from there, he decided to climb up and take a closer look. Great decision! It would turn out that he had just discovered an incredibly rich and important dinosaur bonebed.

▼ **Patched together**
This Pachyrhinosaurus, on display at the Royal Tyrrell Museum, Alberta, is a composite made up of bones from various incomplete specimens.

Lakusta returned to the site many times and accumulated a large array of different bones. He donated them to the nearest museum where they languished, unexamined, for six years. Eventually, the remains were taken out and analyzed and identified as those of Pachyrhinosaurus, and palaeontologists set up a dig to explore the site of Al Lakusta's find further. By the 1980s, after four summers of digging, the remains of at least 27 dinosaurs had been uncovered. By then, everyone had realized that this was just the tip of the iceberg — the seam was absolutely huge, packed with thousands of bones.

In 2008, when a description of the new species of Pachyrhinosaurus was finally published, it was named *P. lakustai* after Al Lakusta. To date, Pipestone Creek is the only place in the world where this species has been found.

▶ **A skull named Cybill**
Cybill is the *P. lakustai* holotype (specimen that establishes the defining features of a new species). It's named after the discoverer's TV crush, the actress Cybill Shepherd.

RECENT DISCOVERIES
The Pipestone Creek dig continues to this day. Every year, a six-strong team gets together to work on the site whenever the weather allows — usually, this is between the last snowfall of spring and the first of autumn, with most of the action on the site taking place in July and August. The dig team is now led by

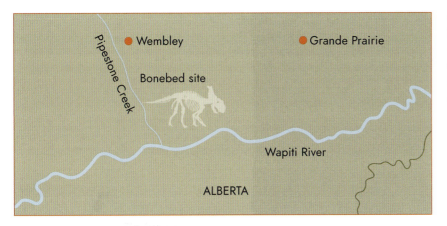

◀ **Bone bonanza**
The Pipestone Creek bonebed in Alberta, where *P. lakustai* was discovered, lies about 20 km (12.4 miles) from Grande Prairie and 10 km (6.2 miles) from Wembley.

Dr Emily Bamforth, Curator at the Philip J. Currie Dinosaur Museum in Wembley, Alberta. Dr Bamforth has been leading the dig since 2022 and she reckons this is one of the densest dinosaur finds in the world, with an average of around 200 bones per square metre. So far, the team has uncovered an impressive 4,000 bones. By drilling into the cliffside and examining core samples of rock, they have found that the bones extend at least 1 km (0.6 miles) into the hillside.

As Dr Bamforth says: "It could literally be hundreds of thousands, maybe millions of bones. And so we estimate the size of the Pipestone Creek [Pachyrhinosaurus] herd at 40,000 animals."

MASS GRAVE
An estimated 40,000 animals is an extraordinary number to excavate, especially as the team has so far only exposed an area about the size of a tennis court. Only about 2–3 sq. m (2.2–3.2 sq. yards) or so can be excavated each year, because it is such painstaking work. The other factor that makes unearthing these bones so complex is that they lie in a bonebed. This is defined as a layer of sediment that contains large quantities of fossilized animal remains, but — and it's a big but — those remains are unlikely to be articulated; in other words, the bones are not in the same place as when the animal died. Since the animal's death, external influences have acted upon the remains and the soil surrounding them to separate and scatter the bones. The resulting muddle of body parts is hard to unearth and investigate. As Dr Bamforth has put it: "It's a gigantic dinosaur bone omelette!" However, although the bones are somewhat jumbled up, they are not so displaced that she and her team can't identify groups of bones belonging to individuals.

DIG DEEPER

Emily Bamforth
Interested in fossil plants, dinosaurs, and mass extinctions, Dr Bamforth believes creativity is a critical quality for a palaeontologist. In her words; "You have to be able to look at a fossil in the ground and imagine that in the real world."

THE EPIC MIGRATION

MOUNTAINS AND FORESTS

In the Late Cretaceous, ice at the North and South Poles had melted, creating a waterway — the Western Interior Seaway — that ran right through what is now North America. The area around Pipestone Creek was relatively wet and warm. Rivers wound through mountainous forests down to flood plains and swamps near the sea.

GINKGO
The ginkgo genus, a non-flowering tree-sized seed plant with fan-shaped leaves, appeared in the Middle Jurassic. One ginkgo species survives today.

PLANT DIVERSITY

Where the Rocky Mountains were forming, ginkgos and monkey puzzle trees dotted the landscape, breaking up the swathes of conifers. On lower ground, redwoods and early elms, beech, and birches flourished, while horsetails thrived by the coast.

THEN AND NOW

The modern environments that most resemble Pachyrhinosaurus' world include the USA's Pacific Northwest and the temperate rainforests on the west coast of British Columbia, Canada.

170   CHAPTER FIVE

The climate and ecosystem of the Great Bear Rainforest, British Columbia, would be familiar to Pachyrhinosaurus.

Today Pipestone Creek, near the city of Grande Prairie, is an area of dense forest cut through by the Wapiti River.

THE EPIC MIGRATION

▼ **BIRD'S EYE VIEW**
This aerial view shows digging at Pipestone. Palaeontologists have nicknamed the site the "River of Death", as so many dinosaurs met their untimely ends there.

As well as the bones and skulls of Pachyrhinosaurus, the team has unearthed remains of a variety of other animals in the bonebed. These include the teeth of a tyrannosaur – possibly Albertosaurus – and the bones of Boreonykus, a small raptor; plus various mammal teeth, fish and lizard bones, and even osteoderms – conker-sized bones that grew within the skin of armoured dinosaurs.

> Perhaps the number of individuals buried together indicates that they were living in a large group at the time of their death.

The team has been investigating what might have caused so many remains to be found together in such a jumbled-up state. What does this say about how the dinosaurs died? This is an immense number of creatures to be found together. Was it a sudden, catastrophic event that caused their simultaneous death? It's a palaeontological mass-murder mystery!

In addition, there are many other questions that such an extraordinary dig site might be able to answer. For instance, does this site have anything to tell us about the way the dinosaurs lived? Perhaps the large number of individuals found buried together is an indication that, before death, these animals were living, moving, and feeding together in a herd. If so, how did they manage to live in such large groups and why would they have developed such behaviour?

HERD BEHAVIOUR
Trying to work out how an extinct animal lived and behaved is a real challenge when all you have to go on is a few fossilized bones – so we have to search hard for information about how an animal lived its daily life. One valuable source of evidence can be the skull. If palaeontologists are lucky

enough to unearth a skull, which is very rare, it can be scanned using medical imaging techniques to provide information about the structure of the creature's brain.

Professor Lawrence Witmer, a palaeontologist at Ohio University, was amongst the first people to scan dinosaur skulls using a CT medical scanner. CT (computed tomography) scanners use a combination of x-rays and digital technology to build up a detailed image of the inside of a body or other 3D object. These x-rays penetrate the dense skull bone and travel through to the centimetre-thick braincase. The inner contours of this layer of bone can reveal the shape of the Pachyrhinosaurus brain.

In his paper on the skull of *P. lakustai*, he reports that he found the brain to be "relatively small in size and basically rudimentary in structure"; he further noted that the brain structure was reptilian rather than having any bird-like characteristics. But don't write off *P. lakustai*'s brainpower just yet. Witmer also found that some other attributes of the brain "suggested considerable behavioural sophistication".

▲ **Palaeontology pioneer**
Lawrence Witmer's innovative techniques have led to important findings about dinosaur brain size and communication.

Dr Bamforth and her team followed up Witmer's research with their own CT scan of a Pachyrhinosaurus skull. Their aim was to see whether the brain of a herding animal was physically different to that of a solitary-living animal. Their hypothesis was that the demands of living in a group might cause certain parts of the brain to develop in different ways in order to enable behavioural traits or capabilities that would be helpful to survival.

The researchers used CT technology to compare the brain of a Pachyrhinosaurus with that of a non-herding dinosaur such as Triceratops and also with those of modern herding animals. They were looking for differences in the shape and size of comparable areas, because zones that are relatively larger are usually more important. For instance, in

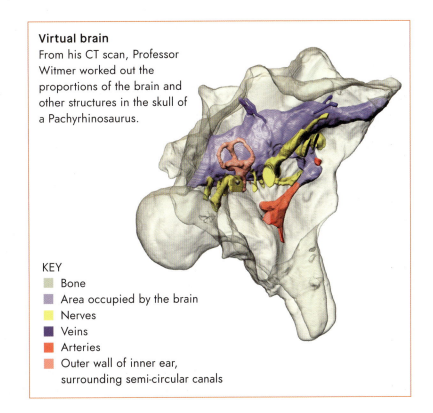

Virtual brain
From his CT scan, Professor Witmer worked out the proportions of the brain and other structures in the skull of a Pachyrhinosaurus.

KEY
▪ Bone
▪ Area occupied by the brain
▪ Nerves
▪ Veins
▪ Arteries
▪ Outer wall of inner ear, surrounding semi-circular canals

THE EPIC MIGRATION

a Pachyrhinosaurus brain, one structure closely associated with pattern recognition was found to be larger than in that of a non-herding animal. It's possible that the dinosaurs may have used this area of the brain to help them identify individuals in a crowd.

Which physical features would the creatures have looked at to help them identify their family members? One possible answer to this emerged when the *Walking With Dinosaurs* team was filming with Dr Bamforth. A rare find was unearthed — the bony frill of an adult Pachyrhinosaurus. One of the team, Max Scott, noticed something unusual about this frill; one of its horns was pointing in a completely different direction to the other.

They compared this frill with another found previously and Dr Bamforth noted; "On this individual, the horns that stick out of the side of the frill are straight, whereas this [other one is] asymmetrical … on this one, the horn is straight, while that one is curled."

▼ **Spot the difference**
At the dig, different neck frills are laid out for scientists to compare.

Remarkably, no two frills found so far on the Pipestone dig site have looked the same, leading Max Scott to remark that this variation perhaps served a purpose: "Based on the differences in these frill horns, it would be very easy for individuals to recognize each other."

Pachyrhinosaurus' brain may also have adapted to help it deal with one-on-one battles. Living in such large social groups, males were likely to have to fight for their pick of a mate, much like herd animals such as caribou do today. In the Pachyrhinosaurus brain as shown in the diagram on the previous page, the vestibular apparatus (part of the hearing system) appears to be enlarged, with an elongated rostral semi-circular canal — one of the three fluid-filled tubes that help an animal keep its balance and sense its body's position. Along with the muscles that control eye movement, this part of the brain ensures that Pachyrhinosaurus could keep its eyes fixed on a point even when the head was moving — an essential skill to enable the dinosaur to keep an opponent in its sights, even in the heat of battle.

The CT scans also reveal that the cerebral hemisphere — an area that indicates social intelligence — was relatively large. Taken together, these adaptations suggest that Pachyrhinosaurus might have been able to follow the micro movements of their other herd members. This is a form of communication unique to social animals, whose lives can depend on interaction with their group. If your neighbour is panicking it's probably for a reason, so it's important to be able track what's going on around you.

RIB DISCOVERY

As well as the exciting discoveries about the Pachyrhinosaurus brain, another find helped the team to understand a little more about this dinosaur's behaviour. Embedded in the rock, they found the tip of what appeared to be a rib. As they tried to free the bone from the sediment that had hidden it for more than 70 million years, they spotted something interesting: two sections of the rib were slightly offset. In a human, this would suggest that the rib had been broken. Could the same be true of the prehistoric Pachyrhinosaurus whose rib this was?

After some very gentle clearing away of the sediment using a small brush, a chisel, and a dental curette, they found that the rib was very thick — twice the thickness of a modern bear's. This suggested that it probably came from a bull — a huge adult male Pachyrhinosaurus. It also appeared as though one section of the rib had snapped and been pushed to one side. According to Dr Bamforth; "It would have to [have been] a considerable impact ... either the opponent striking it really hard or when it fell on its side. Whatever happened, it would be very painful. With an impact this size the rib could puncture a lung."

Was this rib damage the cause of death of this particular individual? As they continued to examine the bone, they noticed something else — a bulge had formed over the break in the bone. This was clear evidence that the animal hadn't died as a result of this injury. A bulge like this is highly likely to be a bone callus, which forms as part of the process by which the body repairs the broken bone, so the injury must have occurred some time before this individual died. As Dr Bamforth noted; "The bone has broken and shifted sideways while the animal was alive; then this bony lump has formed around it and set it. It would've been very painful for the animal, but they would've survived it".

▲ **Broken bone**
The bulge on the rib found during filming of *Walking With Dinosaurs* was clear evidence of a break that had since healed.

THE EPIC MIGRATION

It's something that her teammate Max Scott commented on too. "It's really quite an impressive feat. Shows just how tough he really was."

So what kind of animal could have done this sort of damage to a powerful Pachyrhinosaurus bull? The answer could certainly be another bull — especially if it happened during breeding season when males competed for the right to mate, much as buffalo, caribou, and musk oxen do today.

> "[The evidence] suggests that Pachyrhinosaurus bulls were capable of taking severe punishment and surviving."

P. lakustai's head was relatively long at about 1.35 m (4.4 ft), and quite slender if viewed from the front, much like a horse's head. The horns at the top of the frill were often asymmetrical and, as we have learned, probably unique to each individual. Either one or three much smaller horns, called the rostral comb, sat at the centre of the frill. Above the toothless beak were the nostrils and further up still were the three bony bosses, the largest of which was the nasal boss — and this is the weapon that could have caused considerable damage during combat with other males, for instance when fighting for a mate.

Dr Bamforth thinks the rivals might have fought by locking their bosses and shoving each other around, like an "epic sumo-wrestling battle" rather than running at each other at high speed and using their bosses as battering rams. She thinks that the structure of Pachyrhinosaurus' neck contradicts the idea of high-velocity ramming as the animal would have risked breaking its own neck. She also reckon that the boss was additionally used as a display structure.

MASS MIGRATIONS

These battles are likely to have taken place when the huge herds were on their annual migration. This was an epic 650 km- (450 mile-) journey that took around two months to complete. *P. lakustai* spent every winter as far south as the still-forming Rocky Mountains would allow but by the spring, with the lands in the south now almost completely bare, the herd needed to find new sources of food. So they headed north, where lush new vegetation was springing up as the summer sun began to warm the ground. Close to the northernmost end of their trek lay the place we now call Pipestone Creek.

▼ **Face to face**
It's possible that male Pachyrhinosaurus like these two developed a way to settle rivalries that carried less risk of serious or fatal injuries.

CHAPTER FIVE

Every discovery, however small, made at Pipestone Creek adds to the team's understanding of what might have caused the mass death of these Pachyrhinosaurus, but some finds have been particularly significant. Young animals were often eaten by predators — sometimes whole — so it's rare to find their preserved remains. When the bones of a juvenile Pachyrhinosaurus were uncovered at Pipestone Creek, Dr Bamforth and the team were understandably keen to investigate further.

One of the vertebrae was about 7 cm (2.7 in) long and from this the team was able to calculate that it was from a Pachyrhinosaurus of about 12 months old. It soon became clear that this youngster had not been alone. They found other juvenile bones close by and, intriguingly, all of them seemed to be from animals that were around a year old at the time of their death. This strongly suggested that the animals were likely to have been born at the same time, and therefore in the same place.

Dr Bamforth reckons this northern area must have been a nesting ground as well as a herd's summer food source. It's likely that the young animals were born on the previous summer migration, travelled south with the herd for winter, then back north again the following spring, in the same way as modern herbivores such as caribou and elk migrate each season. Such a long, arduous round trip would have been an epic journey for any member of the herd, but for those in their first year of life it must have been truly daunting.

▲ **Follow the herd**
A huge herd of herbivores required vast quantities of food. Migrating to where plants were plentiful was likely an annual necessity.

DISCOVERY OF A DUCK-BILLED DINOSAUR
Pachyrhinosaurus formed the biggest herds in the area around Pipestone Creek, but it was a key destination for other herds, too. One of the most common North American dinosaurs of the Late Cretaceous also migrated with the seasons.

In 2018, as a team of palaeontologists was prospecting for remains along the edge of Nose Creek, about 40 km (25 miles) from Pipestone, they spotted the tip of a bone that had been exposed by receding water. They had found the remains of a dinosaur

THE EPIC MIGRATION   177 often dubbed a "cow of the Cretaceous". Dr Bamforth and her team have excavated here on subsequent summers when the water level in the glacial-fed river is low enough to reveal the fossilized remains. In 2023, they made another discovery, aided by the river washing away sediment and exposing more bones. The bone they uncovered was from the same species of dinosaur – and this time it proved to be a huge hind-limb, more than a metre long. The team calculated that it must have belonged to an animal that measured at least 9 m (29.5 ft) in length; this was part of the leg of Edmontosaurus, a duck-billed hadrosaur.

A fully grown adult Edmontosaurus stood about 3m (10 ft) tall and around 11 m (36 ft) long from the tip of its tough bill to the end of its muscular tail, although evidence has been found that some exceptional individuals reached 15 metres in length.

▶ **Full-time feeder**
In *Walking With Dinosaurs*, a baby Pachyrhinosaurus falls in with a herd of Edmontosaurus. Near-constant grazing was a way of life for these large herbivores.

Herbivorous Edmontosaurus would have spent much of its life on all fours, its hind legs supporting most of its weight as it munched through the vast quantities of vegetation it required each day to sustain its 6-tonne (6.6-ton) bulk. However, if the dinosaur needed to reach foliage higher up on a tree, it is thought that it could rear up and stand on its hind legs, folding up its front limbs.

◀ **Two become one**
Zebra mingle with wildebeest in Serengeti National Park, Tanzania, Africa. Aside from their mutually beneficial feeding habits, the two species gain better defence against predators by combining numbers.

MIXED HERDS

Many experts believe that Pachyrhinosaurus and Edmontosaurus travelled together in mixed herds. As herbivores, neither was a threat to the other, and they probably weren't competing for the same food. A modern example of animals travelling in mixed herds like this is zebra and wildebeest: zebra normally feed on taller grasses, and this allows wildebeest better access to their preferred food, the shorter grasses growing underneath. Thus the two species live — and feed — in harmony.

A fossilized sample of stomach contents from Edmontosaurus, found in Wyoming, showed that it had been eating sequoia. This tall tree's branches would have been way above Pachyrhinosaurus' reach; it would not have been in competition with Edmontosaurus to eat the tree's foliage.

Being part of a mixed herd could have given the dinosaurs a useful advantage against predators. Pachyrhinosaurus had armour in the shape of bony frills, horns, and bosses to help defend itself, whilst the sheer size of Edmontosaurus was also an effective defence — a single predator would struggle to bring down a healthy adult. However, not all predators hunt alone. Some, including Albertosaurus, hunted in packs, so being in a large mixed herd was a good strategy for both Pachyrhinosaurus and Edmontosaurus as they could close ranks and protect one another.

> It's likely that Pachyrhinosaurus and Edmontosaurus travelled together in huge herds.

THE EPIC MIGRATION

Horsethief Canyon
The sun dips down to the horizon near Drumheller in Alberta, Canada. The canyon's many twists and turns, which once made it an ideal place to hide stolen horses, also conceal a wealth of fossils.

▼ **Looking forward**
In a head-on view of an adult Edmontosaurus, most of the eye socket can be seen — unusual for a herbivore.

Adult Edmontosaurus also boasted another defence feature that would have benefited the mixed herd: forward-facing eyes. Most plant-eating prey animals have eyes on the sides of their head, which gives them a wide view of their surroundings so they can spot potential predators. However, this positioning gives relatively poor judgement of distance. Edmontosaurus, had forward-facing eyes, which is more common in predators. The overlapping fields of vision of each eye gave the dinosaur excellent depth perception. This enabled it to judge the distance and speed of an oncoming predator pack, which would have given Edmontosaurus — and the rest of the herd — the maximum amount of time to take evasive action.

Hunter and hunted
A prey animal must be able to see what's coming from all angles, whereas a predator needs to focus with precision on its target. The diagrams below compare a typical visual field of a prey animal to that of a predator.

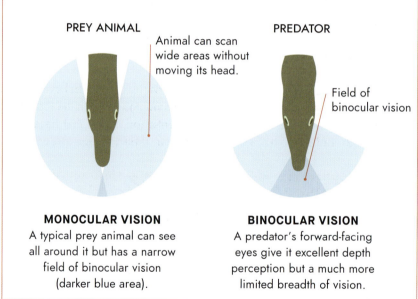

MONOCULAR VISION
A typical prey animal can see all around it but has a narrow field of binocular vision (darker blue area).

BINOCULAR VISION
A predator's forward-facing eyes give it excellent depth perception but a much more limited breadth of vision.

Curiously, Edmontosaurus was not born with binocular vision — in juveniles, the eye sockets faced to the side. As the animals developed into adults, the postorbital bone behind the eye enlarged, pushing the eye sockets so they rotated to face forwards. This has led some scientists to form an interesting hypothesis about the behaviour of some dinosaurs towards their young, particularly hadrosaurs.

A newly-hatched Edmontosaurus was about the size of a chihuahua dog, and almost defenceless. Being part of a huge herd would have been hazardous for the youngsters, as they could easily have been crushed under the feet of the adults. It could have made the herd more vulnerable too, as looking after their young could have diverted the adults' attention from the essential tasks of watching for predators or feeding. Some scientists have suggested that the adults may have left the babies to fend for themselves, perhaps in forest creches, well away from the open river plains where predators such as Albertosaurus roamed. This behaviour can be seen in modern grazing animals, such as antelope, who leave their young hidden while they go off to feed.

> Edmontosaurus may have hidden its babies in the forest, away from the open plains patrolled by predators.

The theory is backed up by the fact that the remains of young Edmontosaurus have very rarely been found close to those of adults. The young dinosaurs' size and lack of binocular vision may have made them a hindrance to the herd, but once they had grown and gained binocular vision, they were able to become a useful part of the group. Perhaps being "abandoned" in this way actually helped juvenile Edmontosaurus to reach an age when it would be safe to rejoin the herd.

The evidence seems to show that Pachyrhinosaurus herd behaviour was quite different to that of hadrosaurs such as Edmontosaurus. In the Pipestone Creek bonebed, the team has found different-sized bones that have been calculated as being from individuals of four different age groups; this

◀ **Impala fawn**
This day-old fawn in the Masai Mara, Kenya, has been left alone, hidden in long grass, while its mother grazes on open ground.

THE EPIC MIGRATION

▲ **Building a picture**
During filming of *Walking With Dinosaurs*, the team used scanners to create a full 3D model of the site.

▼ **Wave pattern**
In this section of rock taken from the Pipestone Creek dig site, swirls and waves are clearly visible, preserved in the mudstone.

suggests that Pachyrhinosaurus not only looked after their young within the herd but that those youngsters also stayed with the herd as they matured.

Teams of palaeontologists have been intensively investigating the Pipestone Creek bonebed for more than two decades, trying to discover why so many animals are buried here and what could have killed them. As well as their go-to trusty hand tools, the scientists have employed a range of hi-tech equipment and techniques to aid their studies. The teams have been using a hand-held photogrammetry scanner to create a high-resolution 3D model of the shape of the site. This can be combined with colour mapping to show where each of the bones was found, enabling the team to see how the bones are laid out. This has revealed that the bones are stacked on top of one another so densely that there is actually very little rock between them. It is this density that has led the team to estimate that there could be up to 40,000 Pachyrhinosaurus preserved at the site.

To investigate the mystery of what happened to these animals millions of years ago, the team cut into the rock to examine it in cross-section. This has revealed fascinating evidence. The type of rock, mudstone, is evidence that water was present when the bonebed formed, and black areas are the remains of shredded plant material. But the swirling pattern in the sample shows something extraordinary — preserved within this rock is a fossilized wave.

As Dr Bamforth says; "Something has picked up the mud and twisted it with enough energy to move that amount of material and shred the plants up like that. And that's right in with the bones. And all the swirls mean something dramatic has happened that involved water. This was a huge energy event."

This evidence points towards a flood of some kind, possibly a flash flood. Let's imagine what might have happened. The Pachyrhinosaurus are almost at the end of their migration, perhaps

◀ **Panic stations**
Every year, thousands of migrating wildebeest drown in flash floods — could our Pachyrhinosaurus herd have suffered a similar fate?

following a river bank. The weather ahead is stormy, with rain clouds over the mountains and rumbles of thunder. Suddenly, the ground starts to tremble. An enormous volume of water comes crashing down through mountain waterways, overwhelming rivers and devastating everything in its path. With a safe route to higher ground blocked by packs of predators shadowing the migrating herd, there is no escape for the Pachyrhinosaurus. Torrents of water sweep the animals to their death. A catastrophic mass-death event, so close to the end of their epic migration.

The area may then have experienced a second, equally powerful deluge, which would account for the jumbled-up carcasses and bones. Dr Bamforth has looked at modern animal behaviour for insight into this possible prehistoric tragedy: "There are many, many examples of wildebeest doing the same kind of thing in Africa. When the herds are moving across rivers in flood, if there are crocodiles there or anything to panic them, suddenly everything goes awry — and many individuals end up dying."

> A mass death event, while disastrous for one herd, can provide a valuable food source for other species.

THE EPIC MIGRATION

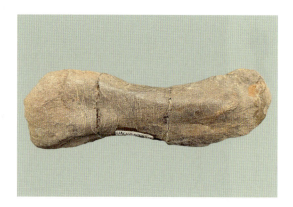

▲ **Bitten bones**
This Pachyrhinosaurus bone, part of the collection at the Phillip J. Currie Museum, shows bite marks over much of its surface.

SCAVENGERS' TREAT

The loss of so many animals was obviously a huge calamity for the local Pachyrhinosaurus population. However, a mass death event like this would have provided an easy, valuable food source for other animal species. As palaeontologist Jack Milligan notes; "It's a dinner bell for tyrannosaurs and other animals that could take advantage of all this available meat."

The evidence from Pipestone Creek backs this up. Bite marks have been found on some Pachyrhinosaurus bones and there are teeth embedded in others, suggesting that theropods had been scavenging the remains. And those animals that were buried rather than eaten made their own contribution to the food chain — as their carcasses decomposed, the nutrients within them were released back into the soil. There is a circularity in nature, which events like this bear out.

NESTING GROUNDS

So were the Pachyrhinosaurus herds completely wiped out in the Pipestone Creek catastrophe? Perhaps not. In the Kleskun Hills, a little over 40 km (25 miles) northeast of the Pipestone Creek bonebed, three fascinating fossil sites have been identified. The bones unearthed here are much smaller than any others discovered in the region. This leads scientists to suppose that these are the tiny bones of newly hatched dinosaurs, or perhaps even of embryos.

▶ **Kleskun Hills**
This formation in northern Alberta has been found to contain a variety of fossil remains of dinosaurs, early fish, mammals, and reptiles.

◀ **Next generation**
This scene from *Walking With Dinosaurs* shows how surviving Pachyrhinosaurus might have laid clutches of eggs and covered them with vegetation to help keep them warm.

These sites, the first of their kind found in this formation, could be nesting grounds, where dinosaur eggs were laid and hatched. The hatchlings here have been identified as belonging to both hadrosaurs and ceratopsians. So does this leave us with hope that at least some young dinosaurs in the area escaped the catastrophic flood and lived to fight another day? Well, there are other finds at this site that put paid to the idea that this story might have had a Disney-esque happy-ever-after twist. Some adults may indeed have found a suitable nesting site with ample supplies of food and laid their eggs ... but the fact that the bones of such young dinosaurs were discovered means, of course, that those youngsters didn't survive long enough to grow to maturity. Also found at the site were a number of teeth from troodontids – small, intelligent theropod predators. Perhaps, like many modern reptiles and amphibians, the dinosaurs laid large enough clutches of eggs to ensure that at least some of them were not predated, hatched successfully and made it to adulthood – but this is impossible for scientists to know.

These fascinating creatures, Pachyrhinosaurus and Edmontosaurus, were amongst the last dinosaurs to exist on Earth. Highly successful and well-adapted to their environment, a single flood – no matter how catastrophic – would not have wiped the species out. They carried on living alongside tyrannosaurs, ankylosaurs, and ceratopsians including Triceratops – right up until shortly (in the dinosaur timescale, at least) before the end of the Cretaceous, when that asteroid barrelled into our planet and changed the course of all life upon it.

THE EPIC MIGRATION

Mother and baby
In this scene from *Walking With Dinosaurs*, Albie the baby Pachyrhinosaurus is comforted by his mother after a too-close encounter with a predatory pterosaur.

THE EPIC MIGRATION

CHAPTER SIX
THE LAST DINOSAURS

> T.rex was an animal that, in every sense, could be called a natural born killer.

Tyrannosaurus rex is definitely not the world's cutest dinosaur (according to polls, Scutellosaurus is in the running for that accolade) or the one people would choose as a pet (Stegosaurus, since you ask). The most beautiful? Gigantoraptor is a front-runner for that crown. But while many people won't have heard of those three dinosaurs, let alone agree on their ranking, the one that *everyone* knows is T.rex, as it is universally known. Despite being a ruthless, baby-killing predator, it is the undisputed OG, a hero of popular culture, the most fearsome and famous dinosaur of all time.

At around 4 m (13 ft) tall and 12.5 m (41 ft) long (almost half of which was taken up by the tail), the sheer size of T.rex would have terrorized almost every other creature living alongside it. And that's before you add in all its other attributes. The sharpest eyesight (even in the dark); a powerful sense of smell; huge jaws large enough to swallow a baby Triceratops in one bite; razor-sharp teeth. This was an animal that was, in every sense, a natural born killer. After being hidden in the dust for millions of years, the first discovery of T.rex, almost 150 years ago, opened a window into the world of these extraordinary predators – and we are still exploring that world today.

▼ **Late Cretaceous North America**
Around 66 million years ago, the Western Interior Seaway was slowly shrinking. T.rex dominated a small part of what would become North America.

PIONEERS OF PALAEONTOLOGY

Arriving relatively late onto the dinosaur scene, the earliest T.rex first appeared on the planet less than 70 million years ago. Its fame might suggest that it reigned over the entire globe, but in fact its kingdom was confined to a relatively small part of what would become North America. Back then, the landmass looked markedly different, split in two by a vast inland sea known as the Western Interior Seaway. This body of water was 3,000 km (1,864 miles) long and almost 1,000 km (621 miles) wide, and covered much of what is now the American Midwest. Bordering the western edge of this relatively shallow sea was a huge landmass

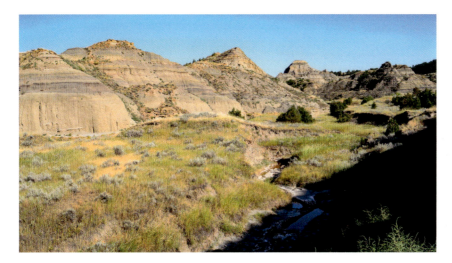

◀ **Hell Creek Formation**
This area's deep layers of sandstone, siltstone, and mudstone were formed during the Late Cretaceous.

called Laramidia — and it is here that T.rex made itself at home in an area we now know as the Hell Creek Formation.

Today, this distinctive formation of rocky layers spreads across North and South Dakota to the east and into Wyoming and the badlands of Montana to the west; it was in the western reaches of Hell Creek that the first skeleton of this legendary dinosaur emerged from the dust.

The road to this discovery began in the middle of the 19th century; the American Civil War had just ended and the settlers' drive to head west was in full flow. Newly built railroads cut across previously unreachable land, with settlements popping up in wild and remote areas across the western plains. Driven by access to government funds, several scientific expeditions set out to survey and map these new, unexplored areas of America. This glut of information helped not only to establish the first-ever National Park at Yellowstone, Wyoming, in 1872, but also added enormously to scientists' understanding of the geology of North America.

One of the biggest of these discoveries was evidence of the ancient presence of the Western Interior Seaway. This sea ebbed and flowed over millions of years and when levels fell, it exposed a strip of land that joined the landmasses to the west and east, temporarily allowing animal species on either side to mix. Then, when the water level rose, flora and fauna were separated again for millions of years. Finding this seaway provided valuable clues to a new breed of fossil-hunters, pointing them towards striking palaeontological gold.

DIG DEEPER

Lewis and Clark
The bonanza of fossil finds in the American West was made possible in part by the work of Meriwether Lewis (left) and William Clark (right). In 1804, they led an expedition to find a route west from the Missouri River to the Pacific Ocean. The pair made notes of the flora, fauna, and natural features they encountered en route.

THE LAST DINOSAURS

T.REX

T.rex was one of the most powerful predators ever to stalk the Earth. Though by no means fast, forward-facing eyes and a large brain allowed it to execute an ambush perfectly. T.rex was adapted to tackle even heavily armoured prey — its immensely strong teeth and jaws could bite through almost anything, making it a deadly foe to virtually any animal unlucky enough to encounter it.

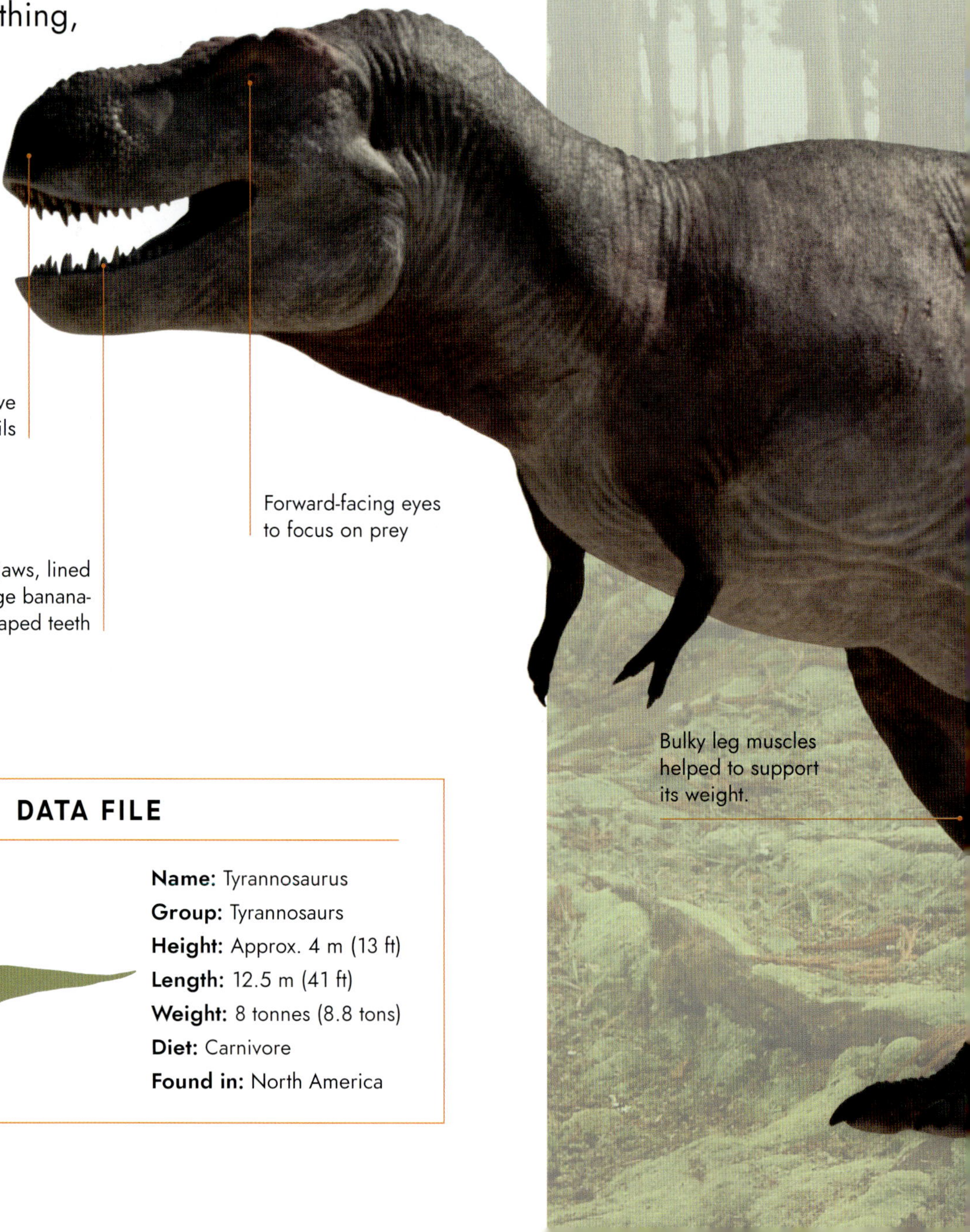

Ultra-sensitive nostrils

Powerful jaws, lined with huge banana-shaped teeth

Forward-facing eyes to focus on prey

Bulky leg muscles helped to support its weight.

DATA FILE

SCALE

Name: Tyrannosaurus
Group: Tyrannosaurs
Height: Approx. 4 m (13 ft)
Length: 12.5 m (41 ft)
Weight: 8 tonnes (8.8 tons)
Diet: Carnivore
Found in: North America

TRIASSIC	JURASSIC	CRETACEOUS
252 MYA	201 MYA	145 MYA

T.REX TIMELINE: 68 – 66 MYA

Long, muscular tail to counterbalance the heavy head

ARMS AND THE T.REX

T.rex's tiny, muscly arms have long puzzled scientists. One theory, that they helped the huge dinosaur get up if it fell over, is alas unsupported by physics. Other proposals are that the arms were used as weapons, or for grooming or nesting. Yet another theory suggests that their small size ensured counterbalance between the heavy head and tail. It is also a possibility that the arms had no use whatsoever and would have eventually disappeared, if T.rex had been allowed more time to evolve.

Two sharp, curved claws at the end of each arm

Exceptionally short arms compared to other tyrannosaurs

Three-toed feet up to 1m (39 in) long

THE FIRST DISCOVERY

The discovery of the first T.rex was not exactly a "Eureka!" moment — it was much messier than that. But before we come to that historic moment, we first have to understand the "dinomania" that was gripping the United States in the latter half of the 19th century. This golden age of palaeontology had already delivered several complete dinosaur skeletons, including the duck-billed *Hadrosaurus foulkii*. When this specimen went on display at the Academy of Natural Sciences of Philadelphia, it was the first time a mounted dinosaur had ever been exhibited in public. The response was off the scale, with huge numbers of visitors flocking to the museum. The exhibit transformed the popular perception of dinosaurs from creatures of myth to living, breathing animals that existed in nature.

▼ **Hadrosaurus skeleton**
This restoration of a Hadrosaurus skeleton discovered by American palaeontologist Joseph Leidy was first exhibited in 1868.

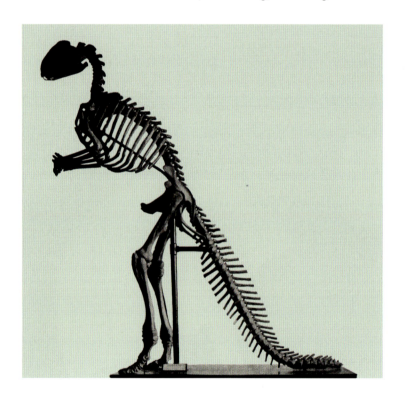

Fossil-hunters vied to become the person who would provide the next great discovery to thrill the expectant public. But in the rush for bones, many a specimen came out of the ground with little or no further investigation. If a fossil was not of immediate, obvious interest, it could find itself in the back of a cupboard for years. We now know some of those cupboards contained the bones and teeth of a T.rex, but at the time they were found, nobody suspected that there might be an extraordinary new animal waiting to be identified among this jumble of bones. That all changed at the turn of the 20th century, when a palaeontologist by the name of Barnum Brown rolled up his sleeves and set to work.

Responding to the public's appetite for dinosaur discoveries, Barnum Brown, then working for the American Museum of Natural History, led an expedition to the Hell Creek Foundation. It was 1902 when Brown and his crew of just three men began working at three separate sites across this isolated, inhospitable corner of Montana. Conditions were tough and during the dig, Brown developed severe gout. It gave him so much pain that he could barely ride his horse and he needed help to get into bed each night. But with the dream of a world-changing fossil in his sights, it would have taken much more than gout to make him give up.

By July 1902, the team had already unearthed a Triceratops skull in good condition. However, without its horns, this was not the career-changing showstopper the team was striving for. They pushed on through the gruelling summer heat, hoping that the magical combination of luck and perseverance would deliver that elusive golden find. And so that brings us to a day in August, a hill the team called Sheba Mountain, and a pile of explosives laid and ready to blow apart the rocks. The timer was set, the area cleared, and the team waited for the thunderous roar of rocks being blasted. When the dust finally settled in Quarry Number 1, Brown's men were confronted with the bones of a monster, making them the first humans to lay eyes on this creature.

Touched by sunlight for the first time in 66 million years, the world's most infamous dinosaur was beginning its journey into public consciousness. Barnum Brown wrote of that first discovery in his notebook: "Quarry Number 1 contains the femur, pubes, humerus, three vertebrae and two undetermined bones of a large carnivorous dinosaur … I have never seen anything like it from the Cretaceous."

However, removing the bones from the rock would prove anything but easy. As Brown wrote to his colleague Henry Osborn: "The bones are separated by two or three feet of soft sand usually, and each bone is surrounded by the hardest blue sandstone I ever tried to work … There is no question but what this is the find of the season so far for scientific importance."

Brown returned to the quarry and, as was common practice then, used dynamite to blast away the hard rock sitting on top of the skeleton. He could only hope that the fragile, fossilized bones would not be damaged in the process.

This hard toil all proved worth it and Brown's permanent place in history was secured, as the discoverer of the first documented remains of T.rex. Although Brown, nicknamed "Mr Bones", knew his findings were big, he could not have imagined on that day that this would turn out to be the dinosaur discovery of the century. He had well and truly unearthed the beast.

The T.rex that Brown and his team uncovered at that site amounted to just 10 per cent of a complete skeleton. It was transported to the American Museum of Natural History,

▼ **Prolific hunter**
Before his T.rex discovery, Barnum Brown had already made significant finds. This photo is of one his digs in a dry lake in Wyoming.

THE LAST DINOSAURS

DIG DEEPER

Dino dandy
Even when engaged in the dirty work of unearthing fossils, Barnum Brown was a recognisable personality, sometimes appearing on site in a full-length fur coat. Finding T.rex made him a major celebrity, with fans flocking to his lectures.

▶ **Name that dinosaur**
Henry Fairfield Osborn (centre) named several other dinosaurs besides T.rex, including Oviraptor, Velociraptor, and Struthiomimus.

where it was put on show until 1941. When the USA entered World War II, the specimen was thought to be unsafe in New York. It was sold to the Carnegie Museum in Pittsburgh, where it remains to this day.

After his big find, Brown continued to search for dinosaurs. In 1904 he married schoolteacher Marion Raymond, and just a year later the couple headed to Hell Creek, where Brown discovered another two T.rex specimens. Right up until the 1950s, Brown's discoveries remained the only T.rex remains to be found. Two world wars and a deep economic depression largely prevented any major digs and expeditions.

Brown, however, continued well into his eighties to search for specimens in the field. Several of his expeditions were funded by the Sinclair Oil Company; the US firm's interest in fossil-hunters came from a prevalent idea that oil deposits were formed from the remains of long-dead dinosaurs. Sinclair Oil even adopted a long-necked sauropod for its famous DINO logo — at first thought to be a Brontosaurus, but later acknowledged by the company as an Apatosaurus.

It wasn't Brown who gave his dinosaur discovery its name but Henry Osborn, president of the American Museum of Natural History and a leader of the now-discredited eugenics movement. He borrowed from Greek for the generic name: *tyrannos* means tyrant and *sauros* means lizard. For the species name he added the Latin word *rex*, which means king. The whole name translates as "tyrant lizard king" — a fitting title for such a formidable beast. Interestingly, a variety of other animals have since been given the taxonomic moniker "T.rex" to reflect their comparatively huge size, including an African mole rat (*Tachyoryctes rex*), a New Zealand leaf beetle (*Tyrannomolpus rex*), and a North American land snail (*Tropidoptera rex*).

CULTURAL PHENOMENON
So just how did T.rex become so incredibly famous? When it was discovered, T.rex was the largest predatory dinosaur anyone had ever found, and this created a palpable sense of excitement among fossil-hunters. As more examples were uncovered and the animal's height, length, and the scale of its enormous skull

and jaws became apparent, the fascination around it began to spread beyond the world of palaeontology.

With only partial skeletons to go on, palaeontologists and the public alike were desperate to visualize what dinosaurs like T.rex might have looked like when they were alive. Dinosaurs became a favourite subject for palaeo-artists such as Charles R. Knight. A painter and sculptor hailed as "one of the great popularizers of the prehistoric past", Knight was legally blind as a result of both the astigmatism he inherited and an eye injury sustained as a child. However, thanks to specially designed glasses, Knight was able to pursue his career in art — often painting with his face just centimetres from the canvas.

Knight was a frequent visitor to the American Museum of Natural History and there he met Osborn, the museum's head. Osborn wanted to display the dinosaur skeletons alongside portrayals of them living in their prehistoric habitats. So the two formed a team with Dr William Diller Matthew; Osborn and Matthew mounted the skeletons and Knight painted them as they might have looked when alive. This idea quickly caught on and soon became the gold-standard way of bringing the age of dinosaurs to life. Other museums decided they wanted a piece of the action and in 1926, Chicago's Field Museum of Natural History commissioned Knight to paint a series of 28 dinosaur murals. For this, Knight produced one of his finest and most famous works: a mural of T.rex confronting Triceratops. This work would help elevate both T.rex and Triceratops to an iconic status in the minds of the public.

At the same time as the trend took hold for displaying skeletons and dino-art together, another cultural phenomenon was gathering pace that would help cement T.rex in the hearts and minds of the public. The movies were coming to town. T.rex first hit the

▼ **Dinosaurs in action**
Charles Knight brought dinosaurs to life by placing them within their own world, as in this painting of T.rex approaching Triceratops.

THE LAST DINOSAURS

▶ **Slumber Mountain**
A poster for *The Ghost of Slumber Mountain* depicts a scene in which T.rex fights Triceratops before attacking the hero, played by Herbert M. Dawley.

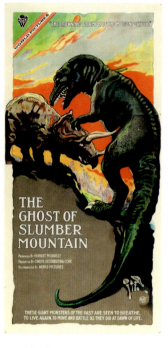

▼ **The Lost World**
The T.rex on this movie poster has powerful arms, quite unlike the puny forelimbs of the real beast!

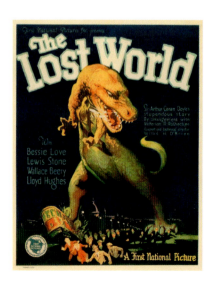

silver screen in the 1918 silent movie, *The Ghost of Slumber Mountain*. The film was the brainchild of special-effects pioneer Willis "Obie" O'Brien, who wrote and directed it, as well as starring along with the producer, Herbert M. Dawley, and models of T.rex and Triceratops. Barnum Brown was a technical advisor on the film and O'Brien based his models on the artworks of Charles R. Knight. This was the first movie in which human actors and stop-motion animations of animals appeared together on screen and it proved a box-office success, grossing over $100,000. This might not seem much, but with a return of more than 30 times its budget of $3,000, it is a slam-dunk success when measured against today's big-budget blockbusters.

The film's success propelled O'Brien to greater stop-motion triumphs. In 1925 he created the animations on another silent movie, *The Lost World*, based loosely on Sir Arthur Conan Doyle's 1912 novel of the same name. In the film, a rescue mission is set up by the daughter of an explorer who has been lost on an expedition to a mysterious plateau in South America. When the rescuers arrive, they find the place overrun with prehistoric creatures and encounter the true stars of the film: Triceratops and Allosaurus, the lion of the Jurassic, which existed long before T.rex. A long-necked sauropod, Brontosaurus, also makes an appearance, as does T.rex itself in murderous mode — brutally killing another ceratopsian and the flying reptile Pteranodon. The rescuers eventually manage to bring the Brontosaurus back to civilization with them — a plot twist that will be familiar to moviegoers today.

The Lost World opened to rave reviews in 1925 and a century later, O'Brien's special effects are still critically acclaimed — although the acting less so. The movie scores an enviable 100% on Rotten Tomatoes; Don Druker of the *Chicago Reader* sums it up as combining "incredible special effects (the monsters) and unbearable melodrama (the actors)". As the movie world advanced technically, introducing sound from 1927, O'Brien's ambitions grew, too. 1933 saw the release of the classic monster movie *King Kong*. Not only did it have one of the first feature-length musical scores written for a "talkie", but the film's climactic scene has also become one of the most memorable in movie history — King Kong astride the top of the Empire State Building, clutching Ann (played by Fay Wray) and swatting away biplanes. According to film historian Ray Morton, this scene would never have reached cinemas at all if it hadn't been for T.rex.

Morton claims that the film was so over budget the studio wanted to stop production. So the director, Merian C. Cooper, invited the studio heads to a screening of the fight scene between T.rex and the gorilla. They were so wowed by what they saw that they agreed to allow Cooper to finish filming. This was a wise decision as, although the budget was sky-high for the time at almost $675,000, *King Kong* took $5.3 million at the box office — around $125 million in today's money.

> "These giant monsters of the past are seen to breathe, to live again, to move and battle as they did at dawn of life!"

More recently, *Jurassic Park* has become a famous and successful franchise. A series of blockbuster movies, originally created by author and screenwriter Michael Crichton, the films play fast and loose with scientific facts, featuring huge Velociraptors which in reality would have been the size of turkeys and which, like T.rex, wouldn't even have existed in the Jurassic Period, both being creatures of the Cretaceous. But perhaps this is unnecessarily picky — the movie franchise is a fun, rollercoaster ride that continues to feed our appetite for dinosaurs and, in particular, the classic anti-hero T.rex.

◀ ***King Kong***
Although the dinosaur in *King Kong* was, according to the director, based on Allosaurus, publicists knew that calling it T.rex would go down much better at the box office.

As well as T.rex at the movies, there have been innumerable television series as well as T.rex-inspired kids' clothing, toys, and even edible versions, including ice lollies and chicken nuggets. This dinosaur's wide cultural reach stretches from a chart-topping 70's glam-rock band of the same name to the beloved children's TV character, Barney. The tyrant lizard king is firmly embedded in every level of our culture.

ULTIMATE PREDATOR

Perhaps T.rex captured the public imagination so comprehensively because it seemed to be the quintessential dinosaur — the fiercest, most powerful carnivore ever to walk the Earth. In addition to its intimidating dimensions, T.rex was impressively powerful, sporting a thick, barrel-shaped torso and thick, muscle-packed legs.

A HUMID SWAMP

T.rex and Triceratops shared the habitat of what we now call the Hell Creek Formation in northern USA. The warm sea that ran through the two landmasses that would become North America helped to make this area hot and swampy, populated by coniferous trees and flowering plants. The ground was covered by cycads, ferns, horsetails, and mosses.

ZALAMBDALESTES
This shrew-like animal lived in the forest undergrowth. Recent fossil discoveries suggest it was what is known as a transitional form of mammal, with key physiological differences to modern mammals.

HELL CREEK ANIMALS

As well as a wide range of dinosaurs, small mammals could also be found in abundance hiding in undergrowth on the forest floor, keeping clear of predators. The rivers teemed with fish, and pterosaurs, crocodiles, turtles, and lizards also formed part of this incredibly rich biosphere.

THEN AND NOW

Today, the wetlands of southern USA are a similar environment to Cretaceous Hell Creek. However, average oxygen levels today are around 21 per cent, compared to 35 per cent back then; so although the climate and vegetation might suit the dinosaurs, they would be so unaccustomed to such "thin" air that they would struggle to breathe.

Like T.rex's Hell Creek, the Loxahatchee river-swamp in Florida, USA, is warm and wet all year round and supports a large diversity of plant and animal life.

Hell Creek today is much drier, with vast, dusty prairies and rocky cliffs. Summers are warm and winters are cold, with temperatures frequently falling below freezing.

THE LAST DINOSAURS

T.rex's feet had a soft, cushioned pad on the underside, which would have helped the dinosaur approach prey relatively quietly — less stomp, more stealth. Like most predatory dinosaurs, it had three main toes, with a fourth toe starting further up the foot. The foot, typically for a theropod, looks similar to those of many modern birds — the closest in size and shape to a living bird is probably that of an emu.

A strong, muscled tail made up almost half of T.rex's length and this was probably used as a counterweight for balance when the creature was moving relatively quickly: the tail would have been pulled in the direction of the foot that was moving forward, so if the T.rex moved its right foot forward, the tail would have swished to the right.

▶ **Walk like an emu**
With three forward-facing toes and padded soles, an emu's foot looks remarkably like that of T.rex.

T.rex had the eyes of a hunter — at the front of the head and facing forwards, giving it binocular, stereoscopic vision. This means that each eye independently collected data, which the brain then interpreted in order to accurately perceive depth and the relative distances between objects. This in turn enabled the animal to judge the exact location of prey and move towards it with accuracy for a successful ambush. The plant-eating dinosaurs on which T.rex preyed tended to have eyes on the sides of their heads, giving them a greater range of vision to watch out for predators, but lacking the precision needed by hunters. The distinctive thick crests above T.rex's eyes could have been for display, to further intimidate its prey.

PIECING IT ALL TOGETHER

We now know a lot about the various parts of T.rex and how they were connected, but in the early days, it was a different story. When the first T.rex skeleton was being assembled for display, Henry Osborn and his team must have deliberated long and hard about how the creature moved — and no doubt involved the artist Charles Knight in their discussions. Their answer, whilst impressive, was not accurate. Towering over the public, that first T.rex was posed to stand up straight like a giant kangaroo, balancing on its tail.

This incorrect pose was recreated when T.rex was reassembled in the Carnegie Museum in the 1940s. It took two decades for scientists to finally work out that, in engineering terms, such an upright stance couldn't work. Instead, the tail and head were like the opposite ends of a see-saw, balancing on huge legs that acted like a fulcrum. With the body pretty much horizontal, the dinosaur's height would have been around 4.5 m (15 ft), while its length was about 12 m (39 ft). But of course, by the time scientists worked this out and museums set about re-posing their T.rex skeletons, the vision of an upright T.rex had already taken firm hold in the minds of generations of dinosaur enthusiasts.

The public stubbornly held on to the tall, towering version of T.rex that they had seen in countless movies, books, comics, and merchandise. Even as late as 2006, a Cornell University palaeontologist asked hundreds of students to draw a picture of what they thought T.rex looked like. He found that 72 per cent of college-age students drew an upright T.rex.

STAN'S STORY

In the 1950s, when prosperity returned after wars and recessions, the hiatus in important T.rex discoveries ended as dinosaur-hunters finally had the time and funds to take up the search again. However, T.rex finds have still proved elusive. Only about 30 relatively complete skeletons have been found to date — and far fewer documented fossilized footprints. Of those skeletons, fewer than 10 were more than half-complete. In 1987, a 70 per cent complete skeleton was uncovered and named Stan after its discoverer, amateur palaeontologist Stan Sacrison. Like most T.rex finds, it was unearthed in

> T.rex's front-facing eyes enabled it to judge the exact location of prey and move towards it with precision.

▼ **Stand up, T.rex**
The upright pose of the Carnegie T.rex suggested an awkward, lumbering animal dragging its tail behind it.

THE LAST DINOSAURS

▼ **Tyrannosaur track**
This footprint is a "negative" — a cast that was made when sediment filled the depression left by a tyrannosaur's foot.

▶ **Stan for sale**
Stan's skull went on display at Christie's auction house, New York, in September 2020. The skeleton sold for nearly four times the expected price.

the Hell Creek formation, near the town of Buffalo, South Dakota. Sacrison was searching for the fossilized remains of plants when he came across a T.rex pelvis. After he reported his find to the Black Hills Institute of Geological Research, it took a further five years for them to complete the excavation.

As well as the large number of Stan's bones that were found, what made this specimen so special was the skull. In excellent condition and the most complete T.rex skull ever discovered, it has provided scientists with a huge amount of information to support their research, including working out the bite force of this apex predator.

A T.rex skull is an extraordinary sight at 1.47 m (4.5 ft) long and 81 cm (31 in) wide. To expert eyes, the skull offers a tantalizing glimpse into the life story of its owner. For instance, Stan's skull had huge, tooth-shaped puncture wounds on the back, which suggested to researchers that the animal had been attacked and bitten by another T.rex.

The neck bones bear witness to another major injury, with more bite marks at the base of the skull and a couple of fused vertebrae, which indicate the neck could have been broken. Following this injury, Stan may have suffered constant pain and trouble moving its upper spine. But this skull tells us

CHAPTER SIX

something more — that this injury was not the cause of Stan's death. How can we know that? Because there are small areas of bone growth around the site of the injury, indicating that Stan survived at least long enough for new bone to form, healing the damage. There are other holes, too, around Stan's jaws that also show signs of having healed. It looks as though Stan led quite an eventful life, even by Late Cretaceous standards.

With T.rex firmly established as the world's favourite dinosaur, it's no surprise that its skeletons are among the most sought-after by buyers and collectors. In October 2020, Stan was put up for auction by the Black Hills Institute and sold to a mystery buyer for $31.8 million. This made it the most expensive fossil ever sold at the time, holding the record until July 2024, when a Stegosaurus sold for a staggering $44.6 million.

▼ **Running replica**
Visitors to the Manchester Museum, UK, can view an impressive replica of Stan, posed as if running full pelt.

Casts were made of Stan's bones — including the skull — and there are now more than 60 replicas around the world. However, if you want to see the original Stan, you will have to go to Abu Dhabi. The Department of Culture and Tourism was recently revealed as the acquirer of Stan and the T.rex is due to go on display at a newly constructed natural history museum.

UNRAVELLING MYSTERIES
As an apex predator, T.rex could potentially kill pretty much any other creature in its domain. But how exactly did it manage to move its huge bulk to catch prey in the first place? When it moved, T.rex didn't just have its two huge legs to take into account, there was also that massive tail. Vertebrae ran from the base of T.rex's skull to the tip of the tail and, just like human vertebrae, they were held together and kept stable by ligaments made of fibrous connective tissue. Such a huge tail had to have a significant effect on the animal's locomotion. In 2021, a team from the Netherlands looked in detail at this; to aid their research, they created a virtual model of a tail, which was treated as though it was a large rod suspended by springs. With every step T.rex took, the tail would "bounce" up and down, meaning that it would also have had a natural frequency at which it resonated. The Dutch team reckoned that T.rex would have walked more efficiently by timing its footsteps with the rhythm of the tail. They built

THE LAST DINOSAURS

▶ **Tail reconstruction**
By scanning a T.rex's tail bones, scientists worked out how the muscles were attached and how the tail might have moved.

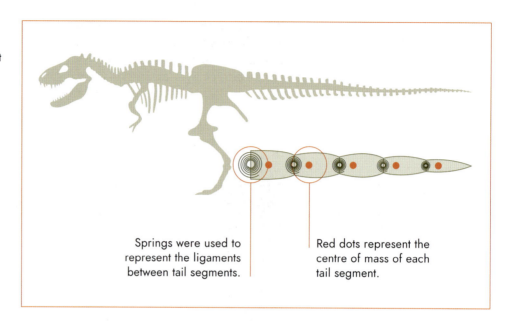

Springs were used to represent the ligaments between tail segments.

Red dots represent the centre of mass of each tail segment.

computer models to reconstruct the dinosaur's gait, compared it to other models, and calculated that the normal walking speed of a T.rex was likely to be 1.28 metres per second, which is just under 4.8 kph (3 mph). That is certainly not fast — a human could comfortably walk alongside a T.rex. So to catch prey, was this predator able to break into a run? Well, whilst it would have been capable of moving much faster than this preferred speed, its massive weight of up to 8 tonnes (8.8 tons) meant that it couldn't run flat out for fear of its legs breaking under the added strain; its top speed was likely around 24–32 kph (15–20 mph). In the film *Jurassic Park*, there is a scene in which a T.rex chasing a jeep is clearly going much faster than that. Apparently, when the jeep shots were combined with the visual effects of the T.rex, the result looked completely unrealistic. To run that quickly, the animal's legs had to spin so fast that, according to one animator, it looked "like Road Runner when he's going off a cliff". So they slowed T.rex to about 26 kph (16 mph), but made the chase look faster than that by adjusting the speed of the scenery they shot to go behind the action. The magic of the movies!

If T.rex wasn't sprinting after prey, it likely relied on another tactic — the element of surprise. It is thought that T.rex was an ambush hunter. Padded feet acted as shock-absorbers, keeping the approach of the stealthy predator quiet — or, at least, as quiet as possible for a creature weighing several tonnes. Once its huge head was up close, the jaws would open wide enough to engulf a small dinosaur and then snap together with brutal force, delivering a fatal, bone-crunching bite.

A variety of researchers have attempted, at different times, to estimate the strength of the T.rex bite, using everything from fossils to hydraulics to aid their calculations. Recently, when one team of scientists decided to study living animals for clues, they looked to T.rex's closest modern relatives; birds and crocodiles.

◀ **Fruitless chase**
In this scene from *Walking With Dinosaurs,* T.rex is not nimble enough to chase down a young Triceratops.

BITE POWER

Dr Greg Erickson, Professor of Anatomy and Vertebrate Palaeontology at Florida State University, has studied the saltwater crocodile, which has the strongest recorded bite force of any living animal, at 260 kg/cm^2 (3,703 psi). Erickson's work involved lassoing a 5-m (16-ft) croc, then persuading it to clamp its jaws down on a bite meter — a hands-on form of research that is definitely not for the risk-averse. Using their understanding of the musculature of crocodiles, Erickson's team created a 3D model of a T.rex to work out just how strong its bite could have been. They were able to calculate a bite force of over 562 kg/cm^2 (8,000 psi), more than double that of any crocodile today. For comparison, an average adult human can only bite at 2.5 per cent of that force — a mere 14 g/cm^2 (198 psi).

T.rex's bite force was more than double that of any living species of crocodile.

THE LAST DINOSAURS

Graveyard of tyrants
T-rex's old Montana hunting ground is now prairie and rocks. Under the stones lies all that remains of these once all-powerful predators.

THE LAST DINOSAURS

▲ **Testing the bite**
An American alligator clamps down on a bite force meter held by Dr Greg Erickson. During an 11-year study, his team tested crocodilians of all 23 living species.

▼ **Serrated edge**
Two teeth from the T.rex Sue (shown next to a fossilized leaf) display the serrations that enabled the dinosaur to rip through its prey's flesh.

Unlike most carnivores, T.rex's 60 teeth were not thin and blade-like, but loosely banana-shaped and serrated, like steak knives. Their shape meant they were perfectly built to withstand force; Erickson's team found that the tips of the teeth could exert a pressure of an astonishing 30,302 kg/cm² (431,000 psi). This incredible power enabled T.rex to bite through even the thickest bones to get to the nutritious marrow inside.

LIFESTYLE CLUES

Dinosaur behaviour is a difficult area to research; as palaeontologists are fond of saying, "Behaviour doesn't fossilize". But scientists will go to almost any lengths to scour the landscape for what evidence there is — whether it is abseiling down vertical cliffs, hiking through bear country, or shaking scorpions out of their walking boots. They are prepared to swelter in the scorching Sahara Desert for weeks on end, or camp in freezing temperatures on misty mountain peaks. One form of evidence can tell you something very specific about a dinosaur's behaviour, and it comes in many shapes and forms. George Frandsen has made his name and reputation as the "King of Coprolite" — a world expert in preserved dinosaur faeces. The tantalizing thing about fossilized poo is that it contains the remains of that dinosaur's last meal on Earth, and this can give an intimate glimpse of dinosaur behaviour. A coprolite is a time capsule that contains important clues about that animal's world, its immediate environment and ecosystem.

It takes a certain sensibility to devote your life to collecting fossilized excrement, and the urge came over George Frandsen when he was 18 years old. He had been interested in dinosaurs since childhood — and when he visited a fossil and rock shop in Utah and encountered his first coprolite, he was instantly hooked. Over the years, Frandsen has built his collection of coprolites with impressive dedication. Some he discovered for himself, others he purchased. By 2015, he was the proud owner of almost 1,300 coprolites, which made him a Guinness World Record holder. Frandsen's coprolite collection has continued to grow and he now has around 10,000 pieces of prehistoric poo, cementing his collection as the largest in the world.

But George Frandsen not only has the largest collection, he also claims to own the biggest single coprolite ever found. Frandsen nicknamed this prized poo Barnum, a nod to the identity of its probable originator — a T.rex from the Hell Creek formation. How do we know this giant poo was made by the king of dinosaurs? Eric Lund of the North Carolina Museum of Natural Sciences has examined this coprolite, and concluded that, while most coprolites can't be attributed to any specific species, bone fragments within this fossilized dung reveal it was the waste product of a meat-eater. Then there is the matter of size. The specimen measures 15.7 cm (6 in) in diameter, which means it must have come from a creature with a very large cloaca — the multipurpose hole in its rear end through which T.rex would have urinated, defecated, and, if female, had sex and laid eggs. Lund concluded, "The only large-bodied carnivore that could have possibly dropped this [dung] would be a T.rex."

Other T.rex faeces have been found to contain bones that are small and smooth, which suggests that the prey were juveniles — the bones of babies. To a fully grown T.rex, a baby Triceratops would have been bite-sized and

◀ **Coprolite king**
George Frandsen poses outside the "Poozeum" — his purpose-built cathedral of coprolite, the only museum of its kind in the world.

THE LAST DINOSAURS 213

▶ **Giant coprolite**
Palaeontologist Eric Lund and fossil restorer Aubrey Knowles examine a giant coprolite, which is likely to have come from T.rex.

could easily have been devoured whole. In 2024, Frandsen realized his ambition to create "a dedicated space where coprolites could be prominently showcased and their scientific significance thoroughly explored". So he resigned from his corporate job, upped sticks, and headed to Arizona to open the doors of his Poozeum. The museum's strapline says it all: "No.1 for fossilized No. 2"...

SMALL BEGINNINGS

It might be hard to imagine a T.rex as one of a nest of tiny, vulnerable hatchlings, blinking as they stare up, wide-eyed, at a prehistoric sky. But that is exactly how the king of the Cretaceous would have begun life. After being tightly curled up in an egg about 43 cm (17 in) long, a newly hatched T.rex was probably around 61 cm (2 ft) long and weighed in at a measly 4.5 kg (10 lb) — the approximate weight of a month-old human baby.

Compare the size of an adult T.rex to even the most statuesque human: the tallest man ever recorded was 2.72 m (8.9 ft) tall, whereas the dinosaur routinely grew to 12 m (40 ft) or more in length. So we can see just how much growing a T.rex had to do in its early years, compared to humans, to reach its adult size.

▼ **Nesting site**
In the BBC's *Dinosaurs: The Final Day with David Attenborough* T.rex is shown with a ring of eggs. One egg is broken, which might have occurred whilst T.rex was covering the eggs with earth to keep them warm.

Like many animals, newborn dinosaurs were more capable of surviving alone than human babies. Dr Erickson has concluded that juvenile T.rex had comparitively long legs and the ability to run fast — a useful strategy when you're a young, relatively defenceless animal. Nonetheless, Dr Erickson estimates that only around 40 per cent of hatchlings would have made it to their first birthday.

214   CHAPTER SIX

A number of scientists have investigated the route T.rex might have taken from defenceless youngster to apex predator. Professor Peter Makovicky and his team, of the department of Earth and Environmental Sciences at the University of Minnesota, have investigated whether T.rex grew steadily across its lifetime or in growth spurts. To do this, they took a core sample from the femur of a T.rex skeleton named Sue and examined its growth rings — these occur in bones in much the same way as they do in trees.

▼ **How Sue grew**
Sue's growth spurt ended when it reached adulthood, at about 19 years. It lived to 28 or so, which is the estimated average lifespan of T.rex.

Using a diamond-tipped coring drill, they cut out a tiny cylinder from Sue's leg, then put the cross-section under a microscope. They examined the rings, also known as cortical growth marks, which showed where new bone had grown every year. Where the rings were further apart, this indicated that Sue had grown faster during that time; where they were closer together, it meant Sue had grown more slowly. The team then compared Sue's results with those of other two-legged, carnivorous dinosaurs. What they found was unequivocal — whereas the other tyrannosaurids' growth was steady, once T.rex hit adolescence, it underwent an absolutely massive growth spurt! The team reckoned that, in its teen years, T.rex must have gained up to 3 kg (6.5 lb) every single day: that's over 1,060 kg (2,340 lb) a year. This growth spurt tailed off when it reached adulthood. Tom Cullen, a lead author on the paper that the team published about their work, has said: "The amount of calories T. rex would have needed during its growth spurt would have been ridiculous!"

This huge growth rate set T.rex apart from other tyrannosaurs such as Albertosaurus and Gorgosaurus. And although it would have taken a lot of energy to do that much hunting and eating, getting much bigger very fast provided an advantage over the competition. The more it grew, the easier it was to hunt other animals — and young T.rex's size would also have provided it with increasing protection from attacks by other predators.

When Stan and Sue were discovered, the tools for investigating fossilized remains were not as advanced as they are now. These days, one of the best non-invasive ways of studying skulls is by CT scanning. The technique involves taking multiple X-rays and combining the data to

> It is estimated that fewer than half of all T.rex hatchlings would have survived beyond their first year.

THE LAST DINOSAURS

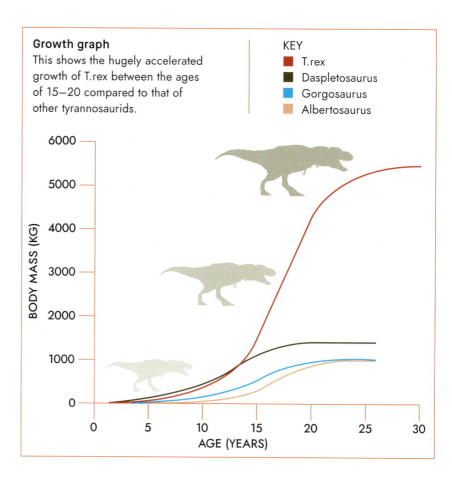

Growth graph
This shows the hugely accelerated growth of T.rex between the ages of 15–20 compared to that of other tyrannosaurids.

KEY
- T.rex
- Daspletosaurus
- Gorgosaurus
- Albertosaurus

DIG DEEPER

Two Sues

Sue, one of the largest, most complete T.rex skeletons ever found, was named after explorer and palaeontologist Sue Hendrickson, who discovered the fossil in 1990. Despite the name, scientists have not been able to ascertain the sex of T.rex Sue.

create a 3D image. (For more on palaeontolgists using CT technology, see page 173). Originally developed for medical use, it's not uncommon now to find scanners in universities and institutions, as they are a fantastic way to map the inside of a fossilized skull. Scanners used to investigate fossils use much higher levels of radiation than you'd ever want to experience as a living person — this is so that the X-rays can penetrate rock, which is much denser than the human body.

A CT-generated 3D image of the skull can now also be coupled with another very useful addition to the palaeontologist's toolkit — the 3D printer. Together, they can create an accurate physical representation of, for instance, the inside of a braincase, the bone that surrounded and protected the dinosaur's brain. This advance has allowed scientists to "hold" the brain of T.rex in their hands and has revealed some fascinating clues and possible insights into the predator's prodigious hunting skills.

In the early 20th century, a T.rex skull in Wyoming was unearthed with the braincase intact. Now part of a collection at the American Museum of Natural History, the skull was CT scanned by Professor Larry Witmer of Ohio University, who has been researching and working on skulls since 1983. The scan revealed the detailed shape of the inside of the braincase — following the contours of the brain itself. This showed that at the front of the brain, the olfactory bulbs — the parts that process information about scents picked up by the nose — were very large compared to those of other dinosaurs. So T.rex probably had one of the most sensitive noses of any dinosaur, able to pick up scents as diluted as a few parts per million. And it wasn't just the killer's sense of smell that was supercharged. In the middle part of the brain lies the area that controls vision, receiving signals from the eyes, and these were the size of an orange — the largest of any land animal. The closest living relatives of T.rex, birds and turtles, can see ultraviolet light, so it's likely that T.rex could too — perceiving electromagnetic radiation outside what we humans consider to be the visible spectrum. Predators able to do that are likely to be better at spotting prey, even under the camouflage of a dense forest.

▲ **Skull scan**
This CT scan, made in 1998, shows a top and side view of Sue's skull. The area occupied by the olfactory bulb can clearly be seen.

MEET TRICERATOPS
It's perhaps unfair to spend so much time looking at T.rex without considering the other, almost as famous, dinosaur with whom it shared habitats like Hell Creek. Certainly T.rex would have been intimately acquainted with, and reliant upon, this creature — particularly the juveniles. T.rex, with its voracious appetite, is probably responsible for the fact we have uncovered so few skeletons of this dinosaur's young. An adult T.rex would need to consume the weight equivalent of a baby dinosaur a day — and a young Triceratops would have fit the bill very nicely.

Triceratops was a ceratopsian; a member of a group of herbivore with large, bony frills around their head and hard beaks they used to pluck and shred the trunks and leaves of cycads and palms. Triceratops thrived alongside T.rex in the Late Cretaceous. We have relatively good knowledge about this dinosaur because skeletons of the animal at every stage of life, from hatchling to fully grown adults, have been unearthed.

> An adult T.rex would have needed to consume the weight equivalent of a baby Triceratops every day.

THE LAST DINOSAURS

Adult Triceratops would have made a formidable opponent for T.rex. Fully grown, it stood an impressive 8.5 m (28 ft) long and 3.5 m (11.5 ft) tall. It sported three large horns with the largest horn, above the eyes, around 1.5 m (5 ft) long. The neck frill acted as a shield and was held up by large muscles, which gave the animal a very thick neck. Fossilized portions of the frills have been found to have pits and grooves on the surface, suggesting the frill was peppered with channels for blood vessels, which would have covered the surface.

In *Walking With Dinosaurs*, Eric Lund mentions one hypothesis, that the frill may have had a function beyond being a shield. The thoery is that by flushing blood into the frill, Triceratops could change its colour pattern, warning off would-be attackers. For instance, if the blood vessels were in a circular pattern, it may have looked as though a huge pair of intimidating eyes was staring down the attacker. To increase the impact, Triceratops would probably have lowered its head; as well as showing off the entire frill, this would also mean that the horns were pointing straight at the would-be attacker. Then, if the enemy didn't back down, Triceratops would charge, inflicting considerable damage with those long horns.

▼ **Heavy herbivore**
With intimidating horns and a vivid warning pattern on its frill, Triceratops would have been a challenging prospect for most predators.

218   CHAPTER SIX

◀ **Huge head**
This specimen at the CosmoCaixa Museum of Science, Barcelona, shows the scale of Triceratops compared to the human visitors.

THE ASTEROID STRIKE

T.rex and Triceratops were two of the very last dinosaurs to exist on Earth (if you don't count modern birds). There's good evidence that they were still alive 66 million years ago when dinosaurs, along with three-quarters of all plant and animal species on the planet, died out. How can we be so sure of this date? Well, because of the way in which the reign of the dinosaurs was brought to an end – starting with a sudden, catastrophic event that left astonishing evidence behind that exists to this day. An asteroid about the same size as Mount Everest, at around 11.2 km (7 miles) wide, hurtled from space into Earth's atmosphere and struck the surface with shattering force.

On the day that asteroid struck, life would no doubt have been continuing as usual in places like the Hell Creek Formation. T.rex might have been hunting, trying to kill a young Triceratops; fish such as sturgeons would have been swimming and spawning in the rivers. All living things were oblivious to the imminent catastrophe. But in one area of North Dakota, palaeontologists might have uncovered evidence that could help to piece together the story of that fateful day and what happened to the dinosaurs there. Since 2012, Robert DePalma and a team of palaeontologists have been studying a Hell Creek site, which he has named Tanis.

> The end of the reign of the dinosaurs began with a sudden, catastrophic event that left astonishing evidence behind.

THE LAST DINOSAURS

TRICERATOPS

Triceratops was formidably built, with a skull that was one of the largest of any land animal. The skull was adorned with three imposing horns and an impressive neck frill that served as a shield. The horns may have been used to fight off predators like T.rex, or to impress other Triceratops. Despite its intimidating appearance, this slow-moving herbivore spent much of its day shearing off and chewing tough plants that other dinosaurs couldn't eat.

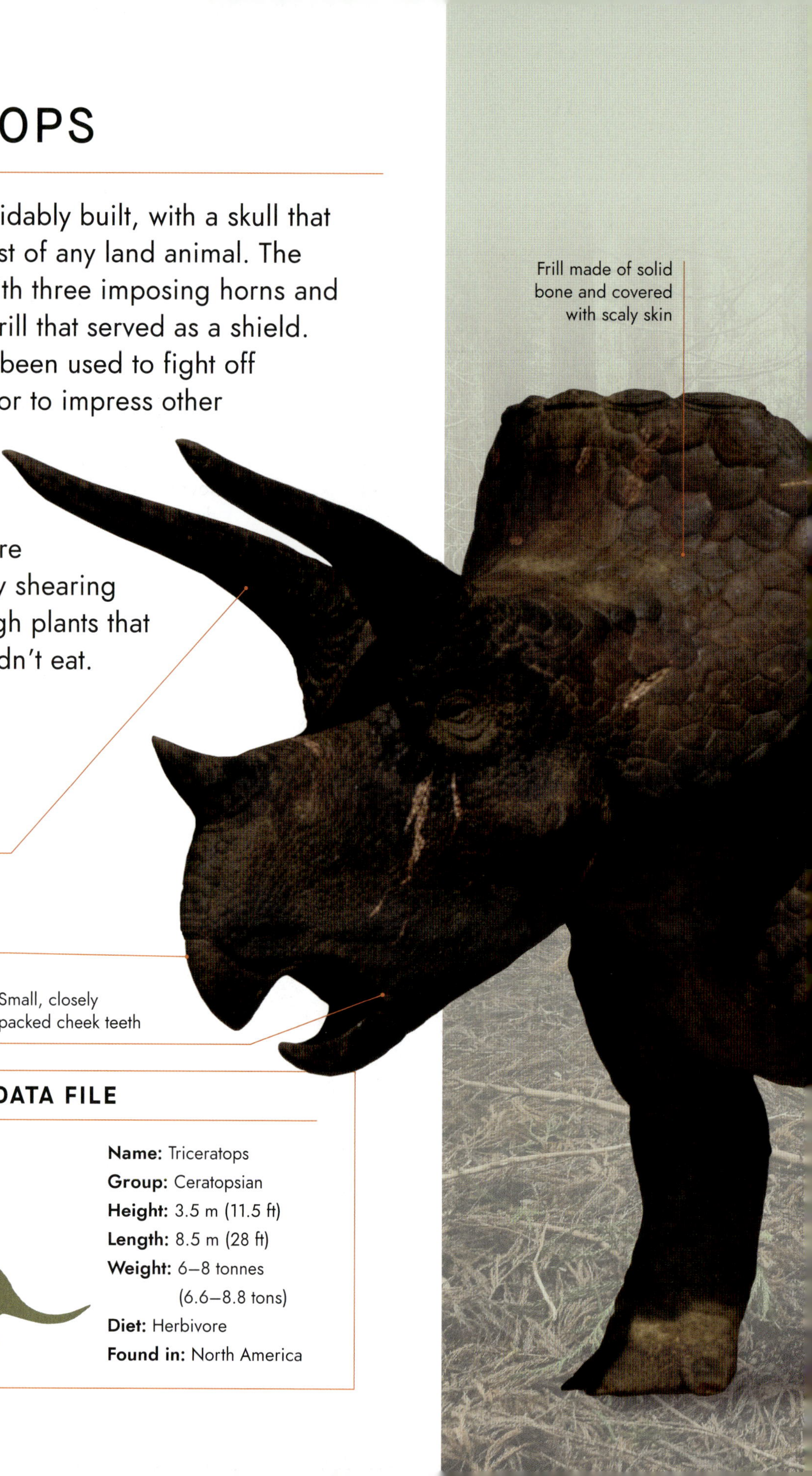

Frill made of solid bone and covered with scaly skin

Brow horns curved forwards and downwards and could reach lengths of 1.4 m (4 ft).

Parrot-like beak

Small, closely packed cheek teeth

DATA FILE

SCALE

Name: Triceratops
Group: Ceratopsian
Height: 3.5 m (11.5 ft)
Length: 8.5 m (28 ft)
Weight: 6–8 tonnes (6.6–8.8 tons)
Diet: Herbivore
Found in: North America

TRIASSIC	JURASSIC	CRETACEOUS
252 MYA	201 MYA	145 MYA

TRICERATOPS TIMELINE: 68–66 MYA

Large, saucer-sized scales

Bulky limb muscles helped to support body weight.

CHANGING WITH AGE

As young Triceratops grew to adulthood, the horns changed shape, the frill smoothed, and the nose horn fused to the skull. The changes were so marked that, at first, scientists thought fossils of younger and older Triceratops were from two different species.

Small horns curved upwards and backwards.

JUVENILE TRICERATOPS

DIG DEEPER

Naming Tanis
Robert DePalma, leader of the Tanis dig, named his site after a town in Ancient Egypt where important archaeological clues have been found. He hopes that the evidence found in his own Tanis will prove just as significant.

Much of DePalma's work is still to be published and he has kept the precise location of Tanis a closely guarded secret as the team thinks it could be a mass graveyard of creatures killed in the asteroid strike. A place where the remains of a long-lost world are frozen in time, allowing us a glimpse into what might have happened there on that day.

The asteroid, travelling at more than 72,000 kph (45,000 mph), pierced Earth's atmosphere, leaving a fiery trail as it crashed into the sea off Mexico. The asteroid has been named Chicxulub, after the modern town nearest to the centre of the impact. A 2020 study calculated that the asteroid came in from the northeast and hit the seabed at an angle of between 45 and 60 degrees. The depth of the water in that location at the time ranged from 100 m (328 ft) at the crater's western edge to more than 1,200 m (4,000 ft) at the north-eastern edge.

Striking relatively shallow water is thought to have contributed to the violence of the explosion, estimated to be bigger than a billion atomic bombs. At impact, the asteroid vaporized and more than 3 trillion tonnes (3.3 trillion tons) of superheated rock were thrown into the air. The impact would have caused a colossal earthquake, followed by a string of tsunamis. The blast would have generated winds of 1,000 kph (621 mph) near its centre. Any living thing within 1,400 km (900 miles) of the impact would have been destroyed almost instantly.

▶ **Strike location**
Theories linking an asteroid strike to the demise of the dinosaurs had been around since the 1970s. In 1990, researchers identified a crater off the Yucatán Peninsula as the impact site.

Hell Creek is around 3,200 km (2,000 miles) from the impact site. Here, the team has uncovered something that dinosaur-hunters are always incredibly keen to find – evidence of the impact itself. A thin layer of what looks like orange silt runs through part of the site. To palaeontologists, this fine band in the rock is extremely valuable, because it helps them to date the site they are working on. Chemical testing has shown that the layer found at Hell Creek is enriched with iridium, an element that is rare in Earth's crust but common in asteroids. It means that this layer is composed of dust and debris related to an asteroid impact – and further testing has has connected it specifically to the Chicxulub impact.

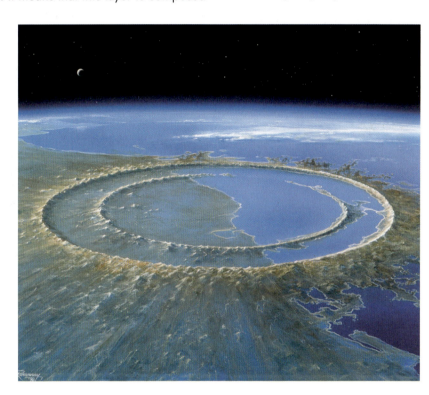

▼ **Chicxulub crater**
This illustration shows the crater's rings, which were caused by the devastating asteroid hit. These are not visible to the naked eye today, but can be seen on gravity maps.

This layer is known as the K-Pg (Cretaceous-Paleogene) boundary and has been found at many different locations across the globe. It marks the separation of two distinct eras – anything found below the dividing line is from the age of the dinosaurs, while the remains discovered above the line show no trace of dinosaurs and belong to the age of mammals. Finding evidence of the K-Pg boundary at Tanis tells the team that everything they find here will have been very close to the end of the age of the dinosaurs. And they have discovered more evidence that brings that date even closer to the day the asteroid hit...

TELL-TALE EVIDENCE
The team found carcasses of fish with ejecta spherules in their gills. Ejecta spherules are tiny balls that were once molten rock. After a large asteroid impact on earth, a mix of vaporized and molten rock is propelled into space. There it cools, solidifying into tiny, glass droplets (spherules) up to 5 mm (0.2 in) in diameter. Some spherules carry on deeper into space, but most fall back down to Earth, pulled by gravity. Then, over millions of years, pressure and chemical reactions in the ground turn most of them to clay.

THE LAST DINOSAURS

▶ **Border line**
The K-Pg boundary that relates to the asteroid impact — the lighter line in this image — can be found across the world, wherever rock formations of the right age are preserved.

Finding spherules in the gills of a fish suggests that the fish sucked them in while the spherules were still falling; so these creatures could have died around the time of an asteroid impact. It would require tests to determine precisely which asteroid strike had been responsible for these spherules, but the team found they had degraded to such an extent that they couldn't be tested. Fortunately, the team unearthed more spherules which had been encased in amber, perfectly preserving them as if in a time capsule. Chemical analysis linked these spherules with the Chicxulub asteroid impact.

> The team found that spherules of ancient molten rock in the gills of fossilized fish could be linked with the Chicxulub asteroid impact.

This was a hugely important finding for DePalma and his team. As he has claimed: "This date is key for the entire site, because once you have that link and you know which impact affected Tanis, then you essentially know that every object in that site — all the mammals and the plants and everything buried in those sediments — are linked to the last day of the Cretaceous."

If this dig site was linked to the final day of the dinosaurs, it would mean that the remains found here — of T.rex,

Triceratops, small mammals, the footprints of other dinosaurs, the leg of what looks to be a small bipedal herbivorous running dinosaur, possibly Thescelosaurus — could reveal what happened to them all. DePalma has unearthed a 1-m- (3.3-ft-) deep layer of sediment that shows evidence of an event involving a lot of water, which appears to have very quickly buried the animals — in much the same way as the lava from the eruption of Mount Vesuvius instantly buried the inhabitants of Pompeii and preserved them perfectly.

THE FINAL DAY
Based on these finds and the latest evidence from other scientists, this is how events on that tumultuous day might have unfolded at Tanis. Moments after the asteroid strike, as the devastation spreads out across the North American landmass, dinosaurs and other animals are obliterated by the blast, incinerated in a firestorm unlike anything seen since. Soon, it begins to rain fiery ejecta spherules. Their heat transfers to the air and temperatures rise with every passing second. As billions of tonnes of superheated spherules fall, the atmosphere becomes even hotter, igniting dead leaves and sparking wildfires.

While the blast from the impact doesn't reach Hell Creek, seismic shock waves travelling through the ground do. These waves are more powerful than any earthquake ever recorded, and shake the whole region. Some of the meandering rivers around Tanis may have responded with violent surge waves up to 10 m (33 ft) high.

◀ **Asteroid aftermath**
In this scene from the BBC's *Dinosaurs: The Final Day with David Attenborough*, a huge surge wave, triggered by the asteroid impact, is about to engulf a Hell Creek riverbank and its dinosaur inhabitants.

THE LAST DINOSAURS

Firm friends
This scene from *Walking With Dinosaurs* features Clover the young Triceratops finding protection — and a playmate — with a herd of passing Edmontosaurus.

THE LAST DINOSAURS

For many of the animals here, their stories might have ended by being caught in a swirling deluge of water that threw animals, plants, and mud together and dropped them into a silty grave site. Earthquakes. Fires. Floods. Devastation. The world here is changed forever.

> For many animals in Tanis, their stories may have ended with a sudden deluge of water and a silty grave.

Whilst painting such a vivid picture of what might have happened to the creatures at Tanis when the asteroid struck, it still begs the question – what happened to the rest of the world?

The impact would have triggered earthquakes and other catastrophic events all over the planet. And as the spherules continued to fall far and wide, more wildfires would have sprung up, possibly engulfing as much as 70 per cent of the world's forests. As that momentous day drew to a close, many of the world's dinosaurs would already have been dead.

Research suggests that the angle at which the asteroid hit, and the sulphur-rich rocks at the impact site, amplified the devastation. Billions of tonnes of sulphur were ejected into the atmosphere, blocking out sunlight and potentially reacting with moisture in the atmosphere, generating acid rain. Without light and water, most plants would have died, meaning no food source for herbivores.

As time passed, any dinosaurs not killed by the impact and its aftermath would be dying of hunger on land. In the oceans, it was the same story. Nearly all of the world's plankton disappeared, leading to the starvation of most marine creatures. It's thought that following the asteroid event, the global temperature dropped by at least 25°C (45°F). The planet was in semi-darkness for around a decade as dust and soot slowly fell to Earth.

A NEW AGE

The fossil record tells us that this huge change in climate was the main factor in the disappearance of three-quarters of all species, including the dinosaurs. But then came something wonderful – a new beginning. Once the dust had cleared from the atmosphere, light and warmth from the Sun could again reach the soil – enabling plant life to grow back. Ferns led the way, their spores having lain dormant, deep underground, during the darkest times. Gradually, the world began to turn green again.

▼ **Survivor plants**
Nutrient-storing rhizomes enabled ferns to wait it out underground, then bounce back when conditions improved.

Some animals survived. Not the large ones — they needed too much food to be able to stay alive in such lean times. But smaller mammals that could shelter in burrows and survive on seeds and insects made it through.

Did the impact kill all the dinosaurs? Well, birds evolved from the smallest, predatory, feathered dinosaurs and they are definitely still with us. So to be completely accurate, we should say that the asteroid rendered all the non-avian dinosaurs extinct.

However, the story of the dinosaurs is ultimately one of success, not failure. These were some of nature's most extraordinarily well-adapted creatures and after all, they dominated the planet for more than 150 million years. It's unlikely that we'll see creatures as spectacular as T.rex and Triceratops living here again, but by combining the clues they have left and the technology at our disposal today, we are at least able to recreate their lives and watch them walk the Earth again.

▲ **Rise of the mammals**
With no dinosaurs to either prey on them or compete for plants to eat, larger mammals such as Moeritherium were able to evolve after the extinction.

◀ **Clawed wings**
The hoatzin is the only living member of an ancient avian line. Its chicks have claws on their wings that resemble those of the prehistoric feathered dinosaur Archaeopteryx.

THE LAST DINOSAURS

CHAPTER SEVEN
MAKING WALKING WITH DINOSAURS

The image on the previous pages is a shot from an episode of the TV series *Walking With Dinosaurs*. In this scene Rose, the lilac lady at the back on the right, is defending her dinner (along with her boyfriend) against her arch-nemesis, the large matriarch and leader of Rose's pack. These three dinosaurs are Albertosaurus, an early and much less famous relative of … yep, you guessed it, T.rex.

What I hope you see when you look at this image, or watch the series, is a moment of incredible dinosaur drama, a young female Albertosaurus desperate to survive in a tough world. I hope you feel engrossed in the action, forget this is a story that happened millions of years ago, and fall in love with our dinosaur heroine! But I have to be totally honest with you, as the showrunner on *Walking With Dinosaurs*, what I see when I look at this is something totally different.

This is what I see:
- Three years of work
- 200 calls to palaeontologists in the field
- A team of over 40 directors, producers, and researchers
- At least 27 different discussions about dinosaur eye colour
- Thousands of hours of VFX design, by hundreds of artists
- And one very cold beach in Scotland

Let me explain…

▶ **Beach background**
The crew filming on a chilly Skye beach — the shots would become the background of the Albertosaurus scene on the previous pages.

CHAPTER SEVEN

◀ **Team work**
The film crew and our crack palaeontologists taking a break at the "Albie" dig site, doing our best impressions of a Pachyrhinosaurus…

HOW *WALKING WITH DINOSAURS* BEGAN

The story of how this series came about began back in 2021. However, the roots of the show stretch back much further in time than that; more than 25 years, in fact, when the original and totally fantastic series, *Walking With Dinosaurs,* was first aired in 1999. That series was what we all had in our minds when the development team at BBC Studios Science Unit was tasked with a top-secret mission — bringing the series back to the screen. How on earth were we going to reimagine one of the most visually stunning and successful series the BBC had ever made? Operating under the codename "Project Atlas" (I kid you not, it really was that hush-hush!), we knew we had our work cut out.

When the original episodes of *Walking With Dinosaurs* aired, no one had seen VFX (visual effects) like it, and more than 15 million people – almost a quarter of the UK's population – tuned in to watch the prehistoric predators stomp across the screen. But more than two decades later, high-end VFX is something we're all very used to, and so we knew that this alone wouldn't be enough to make people tune in and engage with the stories. Besides, the first series had been so innovative, we wanted to honour that legacy and do something fresh and new, too.

▲ **Then and now**
On the left is Utahraptor in the original series. Not only has VFX evolved but the science has, too. In our series, the leader of the Utahraptor pack (right) is fully feathered and brightly coloured.

So we began to explore what it would be like to film real dinosaur digs and base our VFX on the scientific evidence coming out of the ground. It was this germ of an idea that allowed us to start developing something totally original: telling the most amazing dinosaur stories, but allowing the audience to literally see for themselves scientists uncovering the specific evidence on which the dramatic narratives would be based.

▶ **Up close and personal**
Palaeontologist Eric Lund examining the excavated jaw bone of our little Triceratops, Clover, in Montana.

◀ **Digging the desert**
Dr Nizar Ibrahim and his team carefully unearth the remains of Sobek the Spinosaurus.

Nearly every dinosaur show I had ever seen showed generic dinosaurs fighting each other or stomping around (or chasing jeeps). But with the evidence from the dig sites and the ability to create all of our "natural history" moments in VFX, we realized we could tell the story in each of the six episodes not of a whole species, but of one single animal, such as Rose, our Albertosaurus, and make her into the living, breathing hero of her own personal story. Here was a chance to show these animals like never before: their real lives, their "loves", their losses, their ultimate battle for survival. We felt like we might just have a winning formula, and suddenly my trepidation turned to excitement! But that feeling wasn't to last long, because now we had to find our stars...

HUNTING FOR DINOSAURS
So how did we find the dinosaur dig sites that ended up being featured in the series? Every year, hundreds of fossilized dinosaurs are discovered, so finding just six individuals to focus on should be easy, right? Wrong. We soon realized that our dinosaur digs needed to have certain features if we were going to make each episode special. Firstly, we needed a dig that had already started. The palaeontologists had to have already unearthed some of the dinosaur, so we knew the species (the experts can't say for sure until they have examined the bones) but we also wanted to be at the heart of the

> Here was a chance to show dinosaurs like never before: their real lives, "loves", losses, and battles for survival.

MAKING *WALKING WITH DINOSAURS*

action, filming as the fossils were literally coming out of the ground. So that meant we also needed bones still in the ground – tricky because all palaeontologists want to do, understandably, is get their finds out safely and back to the lab as quickly as possible.

And we also didn't want just any dinosaurs, we wanted individuals with incredible stories to tell, which meant there had to be exciting scientific discoveries happening around their remains. Everyone has a favourite dinosaur, don't they? The long necked one, the spiky one, the bitey one … we wanted a dinosaur for everyone, so we knew we also had to get a good spread of species across the series. We quickly learnt this was a super tall order. Did you know that a T.rex found on private land can sell for up to $30 million? Who would want a film crew messing with a potential prize

▶ **Precious cargo**
The team of palaeontologists in Portugal transporting the fossilized leg bone of Lusotitan – the largest dinosaur ever found in Europe.

find like that? And did you know that armoured dinosaurs like Stegosaurus are so rare that they make up only a tiny fraction of all dinosaur fossils found? Nope, neither did I!

And finally, we wanted to convey a real sense of the global nature of this incredible palaeontological fieldwork, so we searched every continent, every time zone, and every type of environment to find the most exciting dig sites. Which is why, after our hundredth call to yet another expert, we were

◀ **Horse support**
No wheeled vehicles were allowed near the Triceratops dig we filmed; the team relied on local cowboys to help them heave out big fossils.

▼ **Hiking to the site**
In Alberta the film crew, laden down with heavy equipment, hike to Rose the Albertosaurus' dig site.

starting to feel that we may be on an impossible mission. But incredibly, by the time we had spoken to over 200 palaeontologists, we finally had our cast, including Rose the young Albertosaurus, who was discovered in (who would have guessed it?) Alberta, Canada. But Rose was not the first dinosaur we filmed…

FILMING THE DIGS

It's November 2022, and I've run outside the house, on my phone. I can't afford distractions and I'm struggling to hear the person on the end of the line. One of our directors, Stephen Cooter, is calling from the middle of the Sahara. He's just come down from a dig site at the top of what the crew called "Mount Doom". The name was earned due to the fact that to get to the summit, they had to drive for several hours

MAKING *WALKING WITH DINOSAURS* 237

▶ **Rocky climb**
The production team scrabbles across the rock face on their way up "Mount Doom" in Morocco.

across the desert, then hike for several more, while lugging about 180 kg (396 lb) of kit — all in relentless, burning heat.

But it was worth it. All of our dig-site experts were sure that there were more bones in the ground, but we knew there was no guarantee the team would find anything within the short windows of time we had to film. We were taking a big risk, but on the crackling phone line, Stephen tells me that they had just captured the first bone of the series being dug up, by Nizar Ibrahim. It's a metatarsal (a foot bone to you and me) of Spinosaurus, the largest predator to ever walk the earth (yep — T.rex isn't the top dog it would have you believe.) On the lonely summit of Mount Doom, we had the privilege of filming the unearthing of the only specimen of Spinosaurus on the planet today, and all in one of the most starkly beautiful places on Earth.

> We were privileged to film the unearthing of the only Spinosaurus specimen on Earth today.

We were off and running.

What we quickly learned, despite this first Spinosaurus shoot being in November, is that tricky weather conditions in remote places mean that a lot of digs have to take place during the summer months. So throughout 2023, our team steamed ahead with a punishing filming schedule, capturing the next five digs: a Lusotitan in Portugal — Lusotitan is the largest dinosaur ever found in Europe; in Montana, a very rare fossil of a young Triceratops; in Utah, an armoured Gastonia (the spikiest dinosaur to have ever existed) and his gang; in Canada, a baby horned Pachyrhinosaurus amongst his herd of thousands; and of course in Alberta, Rose — our teenage Albertosaurus, relative of T.rex. We had our six heroes.

I was lucky enough to be able to go on two of the six dig-site shoots, and I fully geeked out as I watched palaeontologists make their incredible discoveries. That year, the Portuguese experts pulled a single thigh bone

▼ **Stars of the show**
Clockwise from top left: Clover the Triceratops; George the Gastonia; Rose the Albertosaurus; Sobek the Spinosaurus; Old Grande the Lusotitan; Albie the baby Pachyrhinosaurus.

MAKING *WALKING WITH DINOSAURS*

▶ **Displaying the finds**
Arranging an Albertoasurus jaw, ready to point out, on camera, evidence of injuries that may be from "facebiting".

out of the ground that was bigger than me; in the US, part of a raptor as big as a grizzly bear was discovered next to our Gastonia gang; and at Rose's dig site, our team captured the experts discovering a baby Albertosaurus fossil — an incredibly rare find. They also filmed evidence of "facebiting". This suggested that, much like lions in a pride will squabble over a kill, Albertosaurus may have done the same thing, snapping at each other as they jostled for feeding rights. It was this evidence that partly inspired the storyline we developed for Rose. The image at the beginning of this chapter shows Rose defending her dinner. But after this quick standoff, the larger matriarch decides the meal is hers and attacks young Rose.

> During filming, a single thigh bone was pulled out of the ground that was bigger than me!

But whilst in every sense, the scientists were breaking new ground, our team faced some serious challenges. At one site, there was an amazing dinosaur trackway (fossilized row of footprints) but inconveniently, to say the least, it was halfway down the side of a sheer cliff. So in order to get footage of the plucky palaeontologist who went to inspect and measure the tracks, the crew had to get abseiling, too, and film him while hanging on ropes more than 100 m (328 ft) off the ground. At another site, the only way to get to some bones in a valley was by crossing rapids on a river. Not to be deterred, we came up with a practical, if none-too-high-tech solution, attaching a kids' inflatable dinghy to cords and pulling ourselves across, hanging onto the camera and sound kit for dear life as we went.

◀ **Getting the shot**
Cameraman Ben Sherlock gets ready to gear up and abseil down a cliff face to film a dinosaur trackway in the rock.

And at another dig site, I had an interestingly close encounter with a bear whilst going for a "comfort break" behind a bush. The animals you're not planning to film always turn up when you don't want them to! But creating the animals we did want to capture turned out to be one of the biggest challenges of this series…

DESIGNING THE DINOSAURS
One of the biggest differences between this series and the original *Walking With Dinosaurs* is the focus on individual hero characters. This meant that not only did the

◀ **Tough terrain**
In Canada, we hiked for hours, took boats, and even waded across rivers — all while keeping a lookout for the bears that made regular appearances.

MAKING *WALKING WITH DINOSAURS*

▼ **Pick a colour**
After consulting scientists, assistant producer Jay Balamurugan created colourway options for our VFX models.

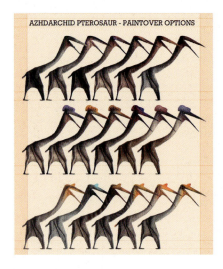

▼ **Building the environment**
This early model of Triceratops was tested moving on different terrains including sand (left) and rocks and leaves (right).

VFX creatures have to look amazing and be individually recognizable, but they also had to be able to evoke genuine emotion in viewers as they watched the dinosaurs' life stories unfold. It was also, of course, essential to be absolutely true to the science. So how do you set about creating a giant killer lizard that could also move you to empathetic tears?

Well, we started with the people who know these animals better than anyone else: the experts. Our incredible team spent countless hours speaking not only to palaeontologists but palaeobotanists, locomotion experts, modern zoologists, and animal behaviourists. You name the experts, we talked to them. We wanted to know everything about the very latest science. What colour would they have been? How would they move their arms? What would their toenails look like? These are easy questions when you're recreating living creatures, but when you're examining bare bones millions of years old, it's anything but simple.

The results of all this research went into what came to be known as the "Dino Bibles": documents, sometimes hundreds of pages long, that detailed every possible bit of information on our dinosaur stars. In the course of amassing this information, a lot of "known facts" were debunked: as you now know from reading this book, T.rex was useless at running; it's likely that no dinosaur actually roared; and the "giant" killer Velociraptor was actually smaller than a turkey. Once every single piece of information had been checked and double-checked, we finally handed over our Dino

▲ **Family portrait**
This scene, in which the Spinosaurus dad settles down to sleep with his baby, reflects the incredible attention to detail in every shot.

Bibles to the VFX artists, who painstakingly transformed all this information into our cast of "living, breathing" prehistoric animals.

Once we had built our stars and their supporting cast, we started work on making them move and the process began all over again. How did they walk? How would their tail move? What would it look like when they blinked? We went through rounds and rounds of VFX refinement, editorial discussion, and expert approval and then ... we started all over again. But this time it was all about behaviour.

Our brief was to create narratives rooted in the evidence from the digs, true to the science, and full of the drama that we knew these animals would have experienced in their lives. But as we've noted in a previous chapter, behaviour rarely fossilizes — so, working with palaeontologists and modern zoologists, we often turned to modern animals, looking to the descendants of dinosaurs to understand how our stars may have navigated their prehistoric world. We left no dinosaur rock unturned, and the scale of our research endeavour really hit home when one of our series experts told us that the data we had pulled together may be one the largest and most cutting-edge collections of information on these species in existence today.

After three years of incredibly painstaking work creating our dinosaurs, the result was something that we hope everyone who watches it will love and get involved with. We show dinosaurs in a whole new light — the giant sauropod (left) dancing to impress his lady, a single father (previous page) willing to sacrifice his life for his young, and of course our Albertosaurus Rose cuddling — yes, cuddling — her boyfriend under the night sky. But whilst our dinosaurs were VFX, the world in which we placed them was all too real — and that's where that cold beach in Scotland I mentioned at the beginning came in.

RECREATING ANCIENT WORLDS

From the very beginning of this project, we knew we wanted viewers to be so fully immersed that they would feel as if they were watching a natural history series that had been filmed today, and not animals that lived tens and hundreds of millions of years ago. To create that level of realism and beauty, we strongly felt this could only be achieved by filming the backgrounds for our dinosaurs in epic real-world locations, rather than creating computer-generated backdrops. This seemed like a great idea — until we realized that finding locations that could scientifically pass for Cretaceous Earth was going to land us in a whole world of pain. Apparently my face was a picture when I was told for the first time that grass hadn't evolved back then. You try finding a place on the planet today without grass — we might as well have decided to film on the Moon!

▲ **Sunset scene**
A VFX shot from the Lusotitan episode. The "backplate" for the shot was filmed in Gran Canaria.

But the team members were just as tenacious in finding locations as they were in getting our dinosaur stars exactly right. After scouring the planet, tearing our hair out, and saying some things about grass I won't repeat, we found our dinosaur worlds. So which exotic places did we film, I hear you ask? Which glamorous, far-flung corners of the globe did we trek to? Drum roll please: Scotland, Spain, and ... Slough.

In all seriousness, we found some incredible locations, including more distant spots like the stunning mountains of Canada, the tropical islands of the Azores, and the sweeping red rocks of Utah. But to our amazement, some of the best locations really did turn out to be on our doorstep. And whilst we may have laughed about Slough, we were in good company; the movie *Deadpool & Wolverine* was filming in the same forest whilst we were shooting. And that cold beach in Scotland? Well, it transported us back 71 million years in time and became the setting for of the most dramatic sequences in the Albertosaurus episode.

Once we'd found our dinosaurs' homelands, there came the challenge of shooting them. I've been lucky enough to film animals all over the globe; elephants in Kenya, lions in Zambia, orangutans in Borneo — but filming animals that aren't actually there and are often the size of buses? Well, that's interesting. Without real animals in shot we had to shoot what we call backplates over and over again. These were the shots to which we would later add our dinosaurs. It was essential to ensure the framing was right so that our behemoths, when added later, would actually fit in the shot. Cue producers running around with high-tech broom handles taped together with cardboard cutouts of dinosaur heads stuck on the ends — this was our size-reference shot. This meant that the director could see roughly how the dinosaur would eventually look when placed in the shot. Was the camera up high enough? Could we see the dinosaur's feet as well as the head? Would it make for a beautiful composition? These are just some of the questions our size reference shot helped us answer.

▼ **Making waves**
Assistant Producer Sam Wigfield swims a life-size Spinosaurus head through the water to create real ripples in the water.

We had to get shadows into the visuals — enter the team plodding about the place carrying huge screens to block out the light and cast a shadow across the floor. We sometimes created them in VFX but if we could add a sense of shadows in the real world, this just helped add an extra layer of authenticity to the footage. This shot is called a shadow pass.

We were doing a lot of computer-generated movement in the dinosaurs' environments, such as water splashes and sand compressing under the feet of our creatures, but we also wanted some real-world movement from plants, to make it feel even more like these huge creatures were interacting with their environment. So, in came the team pretending to be dinosaurs, crashing through bushes and hiding behind logs to move trees with wires. This type of filming is called a practical pass.

◀ **Invisibility cloak**
One of our VFX supervisors wearing a blue suit. Acting as a stand-in dinosaur, he moved through the ferns — making them shake as if a baby Triceratops was running through them!

And then we needed the shot clean. This meant filming a totally empty shot of the

MAKING *WALKING WITH DINOSAURS*

landscape. No shadows, no moving plants, no producers rushing around pretending to be dinosaurs. There were nearly 1,200 VFX shots in the series, and creating all those different versions meant we had to film each one at least four times. Once each version was filmed, they would all be brought together by the VFX team into one single image. Then the dinosaurs were added, creating a shot with swaying plants, moving shadows, and perfect framing, which we hoped would look absolutely stunning — and, more importantly, be totally believable.

The team never faltered in getting stuck in to do whatever the shot required — whether it was pouring themselves into a wetsuit to swim with a giant Spinosaurus head through the water, stomping around in the pouring rain being "the foot" of a T.rex, or donning a highly flattering all-in-one blue spandex body suit, which meant the crew member could stand in shot to shake a plant or kick up dirt, and be easily painted out

▼ **Setting the scene**
Sketches like the one below, called storyboards, were created as a narrative guide for the production team to use whilst filming each shot on location.

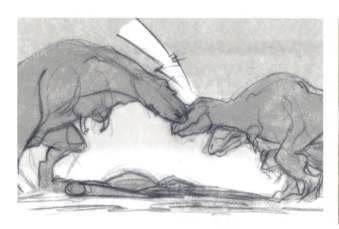

▶ **Taking shape**
VFX "greyscale" dinosaurs were then placed in shot (above right) before being replaced with coloured, textured versions of the characters (right).

246   CHAPTER SEVEN

later. I wasn't exempt from mucking-in duty either, scampering around in bushes, face hidden and holding a cardboard cut-out of our baby Triceratops. Finally, the filming was over. With all that footage in the can you'd be forgiven for thinking we were on the home stretch, but you'd be wrong. Now the work really began…

CREATING SHOTS AND EDITING

It was time for the team to hit the edit. Cutting the dig site scenes required endless scientific dedication from the team as well as incredible creativity, but editing the dinosaur VFX into the programme was a whole different ballgame. We had to take our real-world backplates and add in our dinosaur stars to bring their world to life. But this wasn't merely a copy and paste job; every single shot had to be created from scratch, evolving from a storyboard drawing of the scene to a moving grey blob of a dinosaur; and finally to a textured, coloured dinosaur imbued with layer upon layer of painstakingly created detail, which we checked — and checked — and checked again.

▲ **Piercing gaze**
This close-up of the matriarch from the Albertosaurus episode shows the level of detail achieved by the team.

Every single shot was created initially by our VFX team, cut, discussed, recut, tweaked, discussed, recut, and then on to the next round. Watching every single shot at every single stage, I don't know how many thousands of images we all looked at, but by the end we all knew every frame of each episode inside out.

As we finalized the images, our attention then turned to sound. We worked with talented sound engineers and our dinosaur experts to create a realism and depth to the dinosaur sounds that we could never have imagined when we started out on this journey. We took inspiration from the natural world, mixing sounds from living descendants of dinosaurs, such as geese and crocodiles, with engineered sounds to create the exact noises the experts believe these animals may have made. The result was not only something that was as scientifically accurate as we could have made it, but an extraordinarily impactful and atmospheric audio-scape.

The production team worked tirelessly to make this landmark series; be it ploughing through reams and reams of scientific papers, hiking in remote locations, or sitting in the dark for hours on end squinting at a huge screen, scrutinizing every centimetre of it for the wrong speck of dust or the right glint in a dinosaur's eye. Making this series was exciting, tough, exhausting, euphoric, and ultimately an absolute privilege. Looking back, even standing on that cold Scottish beach filming "invisible" dinosaurs fighting seems 100 per cent worth it now.

MAKING *WALKING WITH DINOSAURS*

GLOSSARY

ACID RAIN
Rain that contains large amounts of pollutants, such as sulphur dioxide. Acid rain harms plants by destroying nutrients in the soil.

APEX PREDATOR
A predatory animal at the top of a food chain. Apex predators kill other animals for food, but have no natural predators of their own.

ARTICULATED
Describes fossilized bones that are found in the same position as they would have been in life.

BADLANDS
Dry, plantless areas where erosion over long periods of time has created distinctive, often dramatic rock formations.

BINOCULAR VISION
In binocular vision, information from both eyes is combined by the brain to form a single image. Animals with binocular vision have excellent depth perception.

BONEBED
A layer of rock containing large numbers of fossilized bones.

CAUDAL VERTEBRA
A vertebra from an animal's tail.

CERATOPSIANS
A group of herbivorous dinosaurs mostly from the Cretaceous Period. They had parrot-like beaks and bony frills at the back of their skulls. Many also had horns.

CLADE
A group of organisms sharing a common ancestor, including the ancestor itself.

COPROLITE
A piece of fossilized faeces. It is considered a "trace fossil" because it is not part of an animal's body.

COVERT FEATHERS
Small, fluffy feathers that cover a bird's (or dinosaur's) larger flight feathers. They act as insulation and help with streamlining.

CYCADS
Primitive plants with thick, woody trunks topped by a crown of evergreen leaves. They were abundant in prehistoric times and still exist today.

DENTAL BATTERIES
Rows of teeth stacked up in columns within the jaw. Every time a tooth wears down and is shed, the next tooth in the column moves up to take its place.

DROMAEOSAURS
A group of agile, swift-running predatory dinosaurs from the Cretaceous period. They probably had feathers, and may share an ancestor with birds.

ECOSYSTEM
A group of animals, plants, and other organisms that live and interact with each other and with the particular geographical area in which they exist.

ECOTONE
A zone where two different ecosystems overlap. An ecotone includes flora and fauna from both adjacent ecosystems as well as that unique to itself.

EXTINCTION EVENT
The dying out of many species at or around the same time.

FENESTRAE
Natural openings in an animal's skull that help to reduce its weight. The openings for eyes and nostrils are not classed as fenestrae.

FERMENTATION
A process by which herbivores get the maximum nutrition from their food. Bacteria in the gut turn the cellulose in plant matter into valuable nutrients.

GENUS
Part of a broader family of dinosaurs that includes closely related species.

GIZZARD
A muscular organ in the digestive tract where food is ground up. Modern animals with gizzards include crocodiles, earthworms, birds, and some fish.

HADROSAURS
A group of herbivorous bipedal dinosaurs that lived in the Cretaceous Period. Their broad, flat, toothless beaks have earned hadrosaurs the nickname "duck-billed dinosaurs".

HOLOTYPE
The single specimen of an animal or plant that is used as the standard for a new species, and on which the species' name is based.

KERATIN
A fibrous protein that forms animal hair, feathers, nails, horns, hooves, beaks, and tortoise shells. Keratin also forms the outermost layer of skin, the epidermis.

K-PG BOUNDARY
A thin band of iridium-rich rock laid down between the end of the Cretaceous Period and the beginning of the Paleogene. It marks the mass extinction event that wiped out the dinosaurs.

NATURAL SELECTION
The process by which a species adapts to its environment. Individuals with traits more suited to the environment thrive and reproduce more successfully, thereby passing on their genes.

NEANDERTHALS
A short, stocky species of humans that died out about 40,000 years ago. Neanderthals lived in Europe and southwest Asia, and coexisted with modern humans (Homo sapiens) for some time.

NEURAL ARCH
The back part of a vertebra, from which the neural spine projects. It is sometimes referred to as the vertebral arch.

NEURAL SPINE
A bony projection that extends upwards from each vertebra.

OSTEODERMS
Pieces of bone that grow in an animal's skin and serve as protective armour. Crocodiles have osteoderms, as do many lizards.

OSTEOPHAGIA
The chewing of bones. Animals that are otherwise herbivorous may practise osteophagia if their diet is lacking in essential minerals.

PANGAEA
A supercontinent that formed about 300 million years ago. Tectonic plate movement caused Pangaea to eventually break apart, forming the continents we know today.

PLATE TECTONICS
The process by which activity under the Earth's surface causes parts of its crust to slowly move.

PRIMARY AND SECONDARY FEATHERS
The long, stiff feathers on a wing that enable a bird to fly. The primary feathers are closest to the wing tip and the secondaries are closer to the animal's body.

PROSAUROPODS
A group of large, long-necked, bipedal dinosaurs that lived in the Triassic and early Jurassic Periods. They are the probable ancestors of sauropods like Lusotitan.

PTEROSAURS
Flying reptiles closely related to dinosaurs. They were the first animals other than insects to fly by flapping their wings. Pterosaur wings were formed by a membrane extending from their elongated fourth finger to their legs.

ROSTRAL
In biology, "rostral" means situated towards the front of the animal.

STEREOSCOPIC
Relating to the way space is perceived in a three-dimensional way by combining two images of the same object viewed from slightly different angles.

STRATA
Layers of rock or soil. The singular form is "stratum".

TAXONOMIC
Relating to a system of naming and classifying animals and plants.

TEMPERATE
Having a climate where there are no extremes of temperature.

TROODONTIDS
Small, slender, predatory dinosaurs from the Cretaceous. Troodontids had large braincases in relation to their body size.

VESTIBULAR APPARATUS
The part of the inner ear involved in an animal's balance and sense of body position.

INDEX

A
Acrocanthosaurus 40
Aegpytosaurus 30
Africa 10, 18, 19, 35–36, 38, 53, 54, 65
Albertosaurus 11, 183, 216, 232, 244, 247
   anatomy of 138–139, 140–141
   behaviour of 143–144, 151–152, 179, 240
   fossils of 141–145, 150, 172, 240
   habitat of 136–137, 140, 148–149
   "Rose" 146–147, 150, 152–154, 232, 235, 237, 239, 240
Algeria 37, 38, 47
Allosaurus 22, 66, 76, 77, 81, 91, 94, 110, 165, 200, 201
Alvarez, Rogerio 85
Alxasaurus 11
amber 25, 224
American Museum of Natural History 67, 92, 141, 196, 198, 199, 217
ammonites 23
angiosperms 148
ankylosaurs 11, 15, 119, 122–123, 126, 187
antelopes 183
Apatosaurus 73, 92, 198
Archaeopteryx 229
Argentina 10, 16. *See also* Ischigualasto Formation (dig site)
Argentinosaurus 70
Asia 19
asteroid 11, 21, 187, 219, 222–229
   See also extinction events; Tanis (dig site)
Atlantic Ocean 10, 95
Australia 19, 65

B
Bahariya Oasis (dig site) 29, 30
Bahariyasaurus 30
Bamforth, Emily 169, 173–178, 184, 185
Barosaurus 67, 70
Baryonyx 40, 51, 58

beaks 14, 15, 93, 123, 162, 166, 176, 218, 220
Berlenga Horst 65, 74, 75
Bighorn Basin, the (dig site) 81
binocular vision 141, 182, 183, 204
birds 11, 14, 15, 33, 59, 77, 78, 80, 90, 107, 113, 116, 204, 209, 217, 229
   carrion crows 144
   emus 204
   frigatebirds 93, 94
   geese 247
   golden eagles 116
   hoatzin, the 229
   hummingbirds 58
bone bite marks 143, 186, 207, 240
bone density 57–58, 78, 150
bone growth rings 147, 150, 215
Bone Wars, the 71–73, 76–77
bonebeds
   Dalton Wells Quarry 127
   Dry Island 142, 144–147, 157
   Pipestone Creek 168, 169, 183, 184, 186, 172
bootlace worm 70
Boreonykus 165, 172
Brachiosaurus 10, 67, 93, 94
brain size, dinosaur 67, 100, 112–113, 132, 165, 173, 174, 194, 217
Brontosaurus 71, 198, 200
Brown, Barnum 141, 142, 144, 157, 196–198, 200
Brusatte, Steve 121
Buckland, William 45
buffalo 176
Burge, Donald 106

C
Camarasaurus 73, 79
Canada 136–137, 140–141, 156–157, 161, 166, 170–171, 180–181, 186, 237, 241. *See also* Horseshoe Canyon Formation (dig site); North America; Wapiti Formation (dig site)
Canestrari, Daniela 144

Carcharodontosaurus 30, 38
caribou 174, 176, 177
Carnegie, Andrew 82–83
Carnegie Museum of Natural History 82, 198, 205
Cedarosaurus 104
ceratopsians 15, 137, 150, 151, 160, 163, 165, 187, 200
Ceratosaurus 66, 95
China 41, 65, 117, 120–121
Citipes 151, 152
climate change 11, 13, 18–19, 228
coelacanth 38, 54
Coelophysis 10
Colbert, Ned 105
Como Bluff (dig site) 73, 81
Compsognathus 24
conifers 20, 108, 170, 202
Cooper, Merian C. 201
Cooter, Stephen 237, 238
Cope, Edward 71–73, 76–77
coprolite *see* fossilized poo
crabs 36
crests 15, 17, 138, 205
Cretaceous period 11, 16, 19, 51, 53, 72, 149, 197, 201, 244
   Early 99, 103, 108, 113, 118, 120, 122, 132, 148
   Mid 102, 104
   Late 28, 35, 36, 38, 47, 64, 140, 161, 164, 170, 177, 192, 193, 207, 218
   the end of the 11, 19, 187, 222–225, 228–229
Crichton, Michael 106, 201
crocodiles 33, 55, 56, 57, 58, 60, 80, 185, 202, 209, 212, 247
CT scanning 56, 173, 174, 216–217
Cullen, Tom 215
Currie, Philip J. 91–93, 142–144, 145, 169
cycads 20, 66, 74, 108, 202, 218

D
Dal Sasso, Cristiano 58
Daspletosaurus 216

250

Darwin, Charles 44, 48
Dawley, Herbert M. 200
Deinonychus 106
D'Emic, Michael 150
Demitrodon 77
DePalma, Robert 222–225
Diplodocus 15, 71, 73, 77, 78, 79, 81, 83
   "Dippy" 82, 84
Drescheratherium 66
dromaeosaurs 100, 101, 105, 106, 121, 165

E
Earth's creation, theories on 42–43, 44, 45
earthquakes 223, 228
Edaphosaurus 77
Edmontosaurus 11, 144, 151, 165, 178–179, 182–183, 187, 227
Egypt 29, 30, 31, 35, 54, 222
   See also Bahariya Oasis (dig site)
ejecta spherules 224, 225, 228
Elasmosaurus 11, 72
elephants 58, 64, 70, 90–91
Eodromaeus 16
Eoraptor 16, 17
Erickson, Greg 209, 212, 215
Europe 19, 40, 48, 65, 67, 83, 85, 94, 95
extinction events 10, 11, 21, 36, 110, 219, 222–229. See also Permian-Triassic extinction, the

F
Falcarius 104
feathers 11, 17, 116–117, 120–121
ferns 25, 66, 74, 108, 202, 228, 229
fish 33, 38, 54, 172, 186, 202, 222, 224, 228. See also coelacanth
floods 184–185, 225, 228
forest fires 108, 125, 133, 225, 228
fossil sales 198, 206, 207, 236
fossilization 21, 22–23, 24–25, 126, 150. See also amber; total preservation

fossilized eggs 25, 66, 186–187
fossilized footprints 23, 25, 49, 81, 88–90, 206, 240
fossilized leaves 25, 164
fossilized pollen 74, 132–133
fossilized poo 212–214
fossilized waves 184
moulds and casts 25, 120, 206
Frandsen, George 212–214
frills 15, 166, 174, 176, 218, 219, 220, 221
frogs 36, 66, 93, 140

G
Galapagos Islands 80
Garros, Christiana 150
Gaston, Robert 106, 122
Gastonia 15, 115, 118–119, 122–123, 126–129, 132–133, 240
   "George" 239
Geminiraptor 104
Gertie the Dinosaur 84
Ghost of Slumber Mountain, The 200
Gigantoraptor 192
Gigantspionosaurus 15
Ginkgo trees 66, 170
giraffes 67, 78, 80, 94
Grand County (dig sites) 98, 102, 106, 109, 111–115, 126, 127, 130–131
   "megablock" from 122–123
   uranium in 126–127
Gondwana 18, 36
Gorgosaurus 151, 152, 165, 216
Guanlong 10
gymnosperms 20

H
hadrosaurs 11, 137, 165, 178, 182, 187, 196
Hadrosaurus 196
hatchlings, dinosaur 58, 187, 214, 215
Harvard University 60, 61
Hell Creek Formation (dig site) 193, 196–198, 202–203, 206, 210–211, 213, 217

Hendrickson, Sue 216
Herrerasaurus 10, 16
hip shape, dinosaur 14
horns 15, 17, 166, 174, 176, 179, 197, 218, 219, 220, 221
Horseshoe Canyon Formation (dig site) 136, 141, 142, 145, 148–149, 161
horsetails 79, 170, 202
Hotton, Carol 132–133
Hylaeosaurus 48

I
Ibrahim, Nizar 49–61, 235, 238
ichthyosaurs 10, 11, 54
Ichthyovenator 51
Iguanodon 15, 48, 112, 113, 114
insects 11, 20, 108, 148, 229
Irritator 51
Ischigualasto Formation 16

J
"jacketing" bones 153–154
Jurassic period 10–11, 16, 18, 22, 42, 64–65, 74, 80, 81, 87, 94, 95, 110, 201
Jurassic Mile see Bighorn Basin, the (dig site)
Jurassic Park 105–107, 201, 208

K
Kem Kem, the (dig site) 35–40, 46–47, 49, 51, 53–55, 59
killer claws 99, 101, 106, 116
King Kong 201
Kirkland, Jim 106, 107, 110–117, 122, 127, 132
Kleskun Hills (dig site) 186
Knight, Charles R. 199, 200, 205
Knowles, Aubrey 214
Komodo dragons 151

L
Lakusta, Al 167–168
Laramidia 140, 161, 193
Laurasia 18
Leidy, Joseph 71

Lewis and Clark Expedition, the 193
Lhwyd, Edward 41
lions 128
Lively, Josh 127, 132
lizards 14, 66, 151, 172
Lost World, The 200
Lourinhã Foundation (dig site) 65, 66, 74–75, 87
Lü, Junchang 121
Lund, Eric 213, 214, 218, 234
Lusotitan 65–69, 74, 80, 85, 87, 88, 94, 95, 236, 240
    "Old Grande" 239

M

Madsen, Scott 113
Maganuco, Simone 51
Majungasaurus 150
Makovicky, Peter 215
Malafiaia, Elisabete 88, 95
mammals 66, 91, 172, 186, 202, 225, 229
    the age of 223
mammoths 73
marginocephalians 15
Markgraf, Richard 29, 30, 35
Martharaptor 104, 105
Marsh, Othniel 70–73, 76–77
Matthew, William 199
McIntosh, Annie 153
Megalosaurus 45, 48
Mesozoic Era 10–11, 16, 17, 18–19, 20, 44
Mexico 21, 222. *See also* North America; Tanis
mice 58
migrations 80, 151, 176–177, 184–185
Milligan, Jack 186
mineralization *see* fossilization
Miragaia 66
Moeritherium 229
monkey-puzzle trees 108, 170
Mongolia 121
Morocco 49, 50, 54, 238
    See also Kem Kem, the (dig site)
Mortimer, Beth 90–91
mosasaurs 10, 11, 58
Mosasaurus 11

mudstone 22, 184, 193
Myhrvold, Nathan 91–93

N

Nanuqsaurus 165
nasal bosses 160, 162, 176
Natural History Museums
    London 48, 82, 84
    Madrid 83
    Milan 49, 51
    Pittsburg 83
nesting grounds 186–187
Nissen-Meyer, Tarje 90–91
North America 10, 48, 65, 67, 71, 72, 94, 108, 110, 164, 170, 193, 196, 202. *See also* Canada; Mexico; USA
    geography of 19, 95, 102, 137, 140, 161, 192, 225
Nyasasaurus 14

O

O'Brien, Willis "Obie" 200, 201
onchopristis 38, 56
osteoderms 123, 173
osteophagia 80
ornithischians 14
ornithorpods 11, 15
Ortega, Francisco 88, 89
Osborn, Henry 197, 198, 199, 205
Oviraptor 198
Owen, Richard 48

P

pachycephalosaurs 15
Pachycephalosaurus 15
Pachyrhinosaurus 15, 137, 150, 160
    "Albie" 152, 188–189, 232, 239
    anatomy of 166, 176
    behaviour of 172–175, 176–177, 179, 183, 185–187
    fossils of 166–169, 172, 175, 177, 186, 187
    habitat of 161, 163–165, 170–171
Pangaea 10, 13, 18, 20
Palaeontological Museum of Europe (Munich) 29, 34
palaeontology tools 145, 184. *See also* CT scanning

Patagotitan 70
Peabody, George 73, 77
Permian-Triassic extinction, the 13
Phillips, John 44
Planicoxa 104
plateosaurus 10
plates 15, 123
plesiosaurs 10, 11, 58, 72
Plot, Robert 41
Poozeum 213–214
Portugal 65, 66, 85–90, 92, 236
    See also Berlenga Horst; Lourinhã Foundation (dig site)
Powell, John Wesley 76
Powers, Mark 143, 144–146
predator trap 114
Pteranodon 200
pterosaurs 11, 38, 49, 66, 189, 202
Puertasaurus 70

Q, R

quicksand 113, 114, 125
Red Deer River 141, 142, 145, 156–157
redwood trees 170
Rhamphorhyncus 66
Rocky Mountains 137, 140, 142, 164, 165, 170
Russell, Dale 35, 36, 37, 40

S

Sacrison, Stan 206
Sahara Desert 38, 212
St Mary River Formation (dig site) 161, 165
salamanders 140
salt tectonics 102–103, 126
sandstone 47, 53, 98, 111, 112, 113, 193, 197
    hoodoos 137
saurischians 14
sauropods 10, 15, 42, 64–70, 78–81, 90-94, 198, 244
Sauroposeidon 67
Scelidosaurus 10
Scott, Max 174, 176
Scutelloraurus 192
seals 58, 93
seismic vibrations 90–91

Sellers, Bill 81
sequoia trees 179
sharks 54
Sharpe, Henry 144–146
Sheeley, Harry 14
Siberian Traps, the 13
siltstone 193
Sinclair Oil Company 198
Sinosauropteryx 117
Smith, William 43–45
Smithsonian Institution 72, 76
snakes 66
South America 18, 19, 65, 70, 83
Spielberg, Steven 106, 107
spikes 15, 118, 119, 123, 129
spines 17, 30, 31, 32, 33, 34, 40, 52, 79, 123
Spinosaurus 245, 246
    anatomy of 32–33, 36, 54–61
    behaviour of 54–61
    fossils of 28, 30–37, 40, 48–54, 59, 238
    habitat of 38–39
    "Sobek" 235
stegosaurs 11, 15
Stegosaurus 14, 73, 77, 95, 192, 207, 236
Sternberg, Charles M. 166
Sternberg, George F. 166
Sternberg, George M. 166
Stikes, Matt 111
strata of rock 43–44
Stromer, Ernst 29, 30–31, 34–35, 36, 37, 40, 51, 54
Struthiomimus 198
Suchomimus 40, 51, 58

T
tail club 15, 123, 119
Tanis (dig site) 222–225, 228
Taquet, Phillipe 27
Tethys Ocean 18, 19
theropods 10, 11, 15, 16, 66, 90, 94, 104, 141, 150, 186
Therizinosaurs 104
Thescelosaurus 225
thyreophorans 10, 15
tortoises 80–81
Torvosaurus 66, 95, 110

total preservation 25
trackways *see* fossilized footprints
T.rex. 15, 90, 192, 218, 219, 220, 225, 229, 239, 246
    anatomy of 16, 32, 54, 78, 136, 140, 192, 194–195, 204–205, 207–212, 214–217
    behaviour of 214–217, 222, 242
    fossils of 141, 196–198, 205–206, 212–214, 215–217, 236
    habitat of 192–193, 202–203
    in popular culture 198–201
    "Stan" 206–207, 216
    "Sue" 212, 215, 216, 217
    "Tyra" 136
Triassic period 10, 13, 14, 16, 18, 20, 170
Triceratops 160, 192, 199, 200, 209, 214
    anatomy of 166, 173, 242, 218–219, 220–221
    "Clover" 227, 234, 239, 247
    fossils of 21, 77, 197
    habitat of 187, 202–203, 217–218, 219, 222, 225, 229
    in popular culture 199, 200
trilobites 25, 50
Troodontids 165, 187
turtles 10, 36, 140, 202, 217
tyrannosaurs 10, 136, 138, 142, 144, 147, 151, 152, 172, 187, 195, 215, 216
Tyrell, Joseph 141

U
United Kingdom 41, 42, 43, 45
US Geological Survey 73, 76, 77, 110
USA
    Arizona 20
    Colorado 73, 102, 107
    Montana 193, 196, 210–211, 234, 239. *See also* Hell Creek Formation (dig site)
    North Dakota 193, 222
    South Dakota 121, 193, 206
    Utah 103, 104, 107. *See also* Grand County (dig sites)
    Wyoming 73, 82, 179, 193, 197, 217. *See also* Bighorn Basin, the

(dig site); Como Bluff (dig site)
Ussher, James 43
Utahraptor 98, 105
    anatomy of 99–101, 106, 115–117, 121, 234
    behaviour of 114–116, 122
    fossils of 103, 106, 111–113, 122
    habitat of 102–104, 108–109, 110, 113–115, 118, 125, 128, 132, 133
    in popular culture 107

V, W
Velociraptor 14, 100, 104–106, 165, 198, 201, 242
volcanic eruptions 10, 13, 22, 120, 225
Walking With Dinosaurs (original series) 233, 234, 241
Walking With Dinosaurs (new series)
    film crew of 233, 237
    filming of 235–241, 245
    locations of 237, 239, 244
    sound effects of 247
    visual effects (VFX) of 117, 232, 234–235, 242–244, 245, 247
Wapiti Formation (dig site) 161, 164
    Nose Creek 177
    Pipestone Creek 167–171, 172, 174, 176–177, 183, 184, 186
Wapiti River 167, 169, 171
Western Interior Seaway 102, 136, 137, 140, 148, 149, 165, 170, 192, 193
wildebeest 179, 185
Witmer, Lawrence 173
whales 58, 64, 70, 78
Whipsnade Zoo 90

X, Y, Z
Yale Peabody Museum 73
Yurgovuchia 104
Zalambdalestes 202
zebras 179
Zhenyuanglong 121

ABOUT THE AUTHORS

ANDREW COHEN

Andrew Cohen is Head of the award-winning BBC Studios Science Unit and the co-executive producer of the BBC series *Walking With Dinosaurs*. The Science Unit has produced hit shows for broadcasters around the world including BBC, Netflix, Nat Geo, Discovery, Channel 4 and Channel 5. As Executive Producer, Andrew has been responsible for a range of premium documentaries, including *Einstein and the Bomb*, *Earth*, *Our Universe*, *The Anthrax Attacks* and *The Surgeon's Cut* (Netflix); *The Wonders* trilogy, *Universe,* and *8 Days: To the Moon and Back* (BBC). He has won numerous awards including Emmy, BAFTA, Grierson Awards, RTS, Broadcasting Press Guild, Peabody and BANFF. Andrew is author of nine best-selling science books.

HELEN THOMAS

Helen is Cornish. She is a multi-award-winning Senior Executive Producer and the co-executive producer of *Walking With Dinosaurs*. This is her third dinosaur documentary, after *Secrets of the Jurassic Dinosaurs* and the Broadcast and Rockie Award-winning *Dinosaurs: The Final Day with David Attenborough*. She has worked on science programmes for a range of global broadcasters and her BAFTA nominations include *Stargazing: Live* and *Extinction The Facts* with Sir David Attenborough. With experience in many genres of programme-making, Helen also made the Arthur Clarke Award-winning series *Astronauts: Do You Have What it Takes?* and the science/orchestral performance film *Holst: The Planets with Professor Brian Cox*. This is the first book she has co-authored.

KIRSTY WILSON

Kirsty is an award-winning showrunner and director with a strong background in natural history filmmaking. Before showrunning *Walking With Dinosaurs*, she made films for a range of international broadcasters and was lucky enough to travel the globe, filming in some of the most incredible places on Earth. From the Emmy Award-winning *First Life* with David Attenborough, to the Grierson-nominated *The Burrowers: Animals Underground* for the BBC, Kirsty enjoys pushing the boundaries of documentary filmmaking and bringing enthralling stories to the screen.

AUTHORS' ACKNOWLEDGEMENTS

When it comes to dinosaurs appearing on TV, *Walking With Dinosaurs* is a giant. A massive global hit when it first launched back in 1999 and still much-loved by dino fans around the world, the task of bringing it back to our screens was a monster-size challenge. The first tiny development steps began back in 2022, lead by Nicola Cook and Thomas Scott, it was their brilliant work (supported by so many others in the BBC Science Unit) that began the creative journey that would eventually lead to the new series.

To deliver a series of this scale and ambition would require worldclass production, storytelling, and visual effects and we have been extraordinarily lucky to work with so many talented people to bring the new series to life. We are hugely grateful for all the hard work, passion, and craft that so many people have brought to this project across almost three years of production. This is just a small chance for us to say a very big thank you.

Great ideas go nowhere without great production management and so we would particularly like to thank our two line producers, Max Brunold and Libby Hand, who have lead the production with such tenacity, skill, and good humour, throughout the many challenges we faced. And a very special thanks to Laura Davey, our endlessly supportive and wise Head of Production for everything you have brought to the management of such a massive project. We are also deeply indebted to Rob Harvey and the amazing team at Lola Post Production, who have partnered us all the way through this production. Their craft and vision have been instrumental in bringing these extraordinary creatures back to life in such astonishing detail.

We have also been incredibly lucky to have a world-class team of filmmakers working with us, with Stephen Cooter, Tom Hewitson, and Owen Gower producing and directing what are without doubt a stunning series of films. We are very lucky to work with such talented people. They were supported by a hugely talented production team who have grappled with so many different challenges that have been overcome in endlessly creative ways. So a very big thank you to Jay Balamurugan, Sam Wigfield, Mairead MacLean, Natalie Coles, Thomas Barnett-Welch, Pete Levy, Tom Heyden, Mark Atwill, Martin West, Russell Leven, Ged Murphy, Ben Lavington Martin and Gary McMath, Tom Kelpie, Saul Budd, Adam Douglas, Neil Harvey, Julius Brighton, Patrick Acum, Sharon Ricketts, Su Pennington, Krish Thind, Katherine Farrell, Sophie Guttner, Stuart Krelle, Andrew Downey, Ami Jah, Selena Harvey, Marie O'Donnell, Emma Chapman, Gail Padron, Jessica Springthorpe, Andrew Boateng, Molly Yeo, Nyima Jarra, Marie O' Donnell, Vicky Edgar, Robyn Gollifer, Johndy Surio III, Lydia Bird, and the many, many other people who have supported this production. A big thank you also to the team at Envy Post Production, composer Ty Unwin and our commissioners at the BBC, Jack Bootle and Tom Coveney. An extra thank you to Jay, Sam, Tom, and Andrew for all the time and support they have given to us in the production of this book.

Recreating worlds and creatures that have been lost for a hundred million years or more has required the guidance of so many palaeontologists and experts. We are enormously grateful for the time and effort that so many people have put into guiding us though our depictions of prehistoric life. We would particularly like to thank Nizar Ibrahim, Jim Kirkland and Josh Lively, Mark Powers, Eric Lund, Emily Bamforth and Francisco Ortega, Elisabete Malafaia and Pedro Mocho, Thomas Holtz, Scott Hartman, and Steve Brusatte.

Finally, a big thank you to the team at Dorling Kindersley. You have created the most beautiful and informative book in such a short space of time and it has been an utter pleasure to partner with you all on this project.

ACKNOWLEDGEMENTS

DK would like to thank the BBC Studios team for their help, especially Andrew Boateng, Jan Paterson, Krishandeep Thind, and Tom Welch; authors Andrew Cohen, Helen Thomas, and Kirsty Wilson for their absorbing, authoritative text; Rona Skene and Nigel Wright for putting the book together; Craig Jelley for proofreading; Hannah Dolan for indexing and text contributions; Helen Murray for text contributions; Julia March for editorial assistance and text contributions; Sophie Dryburgh for editorial assistance; Craig Oldham and Eliza Hart for design assistance; Jo Walton for picture research; and our consultant, Dr Dean Lomax, for expert advice.

DK would also like to thank the following for their kind permission to reproduce their images:

(Key: a-above; b-below/bottom; c-centre; f-far; l-left; r-right; t-top)

1-8 BBC Studios. 9 BBC Studios: (t). 10 123RF.com: Corey A Ford (cl). Dreamstime.com: Linda Bucklin (b). 11 123RF.com: Mark Turner (tr). Dorling Kindersley: James Kuether (cr, fcr). Dreamstime.com: Mr1805 (br). Science Photo Library: Friedrich Saurer (bl). 12 Dreamstime.com: Wael Hamdan (t). Science Photo Library: Pascal Goetgheluck (b). 13 Dreamstime.com: Sergei Lebedev (t). 14 123RF.com: Linda Bucklin (tr). Science Photo Library: Mark Garlick (cl). 15 123RF.com: Corey A Ford (cra). Dorling Kindersley: Jon Hughes (tr); Peter Minister (tl); James Kuether (cr). 16 Alamy Stock Photo: imageBROKER.com. 17 Dorling Kindersley: James Kuether. 19 NASA: Norman Kuring, NASAs Ocean Biology Processing Group (t). 20 Dreamstime.com: David Smith. 21 BBC Studios. 22-23 Dorling Kindersley: Dan Crisp. 23 Dorling Kindersley: Gary Ombler / Oxford Museum of Natural History (tr). 24 123RF.com: Camilo Maranchón garcía (tr). Dorling Kindersley: Colin Keates / Natural History Museum, London (tl, bl). Science Photo Library: Dirk Wiersma (br). 25 naturepl.com: Adrian Davies (tr). Science Photo Library: Philippe Psaila (br). 26-27 BBC Studios. 28 Alamy Stock Photo: Photo 12. 29 Alamy Stock Photo: Archive Farms Inc (b); colaimages (t). 30 Alamy Stock Photo: Signal Photos (bl). 31 Biodiversity Heritage Library. 32-33 BBC Studios. 33 Dreamstime.com: Liliana Marmelo (background). 35 Courtesy of the Royal Tyrrell Museum, Drumheller, AB. 36 Colorado Plateau Geosystems Inc. (t). Dorling Kindersley: Gary Ombler / Senckenberg Gesellschaft Fuer Naturforschung Museum (b). 37 Alamy Stock Photo: Abaca Press. 38 Dorling Kindersley: Colin Keates / Natural History Museum, London (l). 38-39 BBC Studios: (t). 39 Alamy Stock Photo: Sophie Godefroy (br). Getty Images / iStock: Andrew Peacock (bl). 40 Staatliche Naturwissenschaftliche Sammlungen Bayerns. 41 Alamy Stock Photo: The Natural History Museum. Wellcome Collection: (b). 42 Alamy Stock Photo: Chronicle (t). Real Jardín Botánico, Madrid: (b). 43 Library of Congress, Washington, D.C.: (tr). Trustees of the Natural History Museum, London: (b). 44 Courtesy of The Linda Hall Library of Science, Engineering & Technology: (b). Wellcome Collection: (t). 45 Dorling Kindersley: Harry Taylor / Natural History Museum, London. 46-47 Alamy Stock Photo: Rachel Carbonell. 48 Wellcome Collection. 49 Alamy Stock Photo: Paolo Reda - REDA &CO (b). BBC Studios: (t). 50 Alamy Stock Photo: imageBROKER.com. 51 Dr Nizar Ibrahim: Andreas Jacob (t). Dr Nizar Ibrahim: (b). 52 Alamy Stock Photo: imageBROKER.com GmbH & Co. KG (t); Xinhua (b). 54-55 BBC Studios. 56 Dr Nizar Ibrahim. 57 Dr Nizar Ibrahim: Jon Betz (b). 58-60 BBC Studios. 61 Mike Hettwer www.hettwer.com. 62-63 BBC Studios. 65 Colorado Plateau Geosystems Inc. 66 Jay Balamurugan. 68-69 BBC Studios. 69 Getty Images / iStock: Oksana_Schmidt (background). 70 Science Photo Library: James Kuether. 71 Library of Congress, Washington, D.C.. 72 Alamy Stock Photo: GL Archive (t). 73 Alamy Stock Photo: Randy Duchaine (t). Getty Images: Universal History Archive / Universal Images Group (b). 74 naturepl.com: Ernie Janes (fcl). Science Photo Library: Dee Breger (cl). 74-75 BBC Studios: (t). 75 Dreamstime.com: Dynamoland (bl); Jose Goulao (br). 76 Courtesy of the Yale Peabody Museum. 77 American Museum of Natural History. 78 Dorling Kindersley: Gary Ombler / Senckenberg Gesellschaft Fuer Naturforschung Museum. 79 Dorling Kindersley: Gary Ombler / Senckenberg Gesellschaft Fuer Naturforschung Museum (t). 80-81 BBC Studios: Ideacom International Inc.. 82 Science Photo Library: Mark P Witton. 83 Alamy Stock Photo: Album (b). Dappled History: Dappled History / Libray of Congress / LCCN2017648759 (t). 84 Alamy Stock Photo: Guy Bell (b); Pictorial Press Ltd (t). 85 BBC Studios. 86-87 Shutterstock.com: Foreign Life. 89 BBC Studios. 90 Dreamstime.com: Antonio Ribeiro. 91 BBC Studios: Ideacom International Inc.. 92 Nathan Myhrvold. 93 Alamy Stock Photo: imageBROKER.com. 94 naturepl.com: Tui De Roy. 95-97 BBC Studios. 98 Alamy Stock Photo: David R. Frazier Photolibrary, Inc.. 99-101 BBC Studios. 101 Dreamstime.com: Geoff Arrowsmith (background). 102 Dorling Kindersley: Colorado Plateau System. 103 Dreamstime.com: Ronald L (r). 104 BBC Studios. 105 Jay Balamurugan: (t). Shutterstock.com: Murray Close / THA (b). 106 Ardea: Francois Gohier (t). BBC Studios: (b). 107 Alamy Stock Photo: Kristina Blokhin. 108 Dreamstime.com: Antonio Gravante (l). 108-109 BBC Studios: (t). 109 Alamy Stock Photo: Stephen Saks Photography (bl). Getty Images / iStock: Anne Lindgren (br). 110 Science Photo Library: Millard H. Sharp. 111-113 James Kirkland, Utah Geological Survey. 114 Julius T. Csotonyi. 115 BBC Studios. 116 Dreamstime.com: Ondrej Prosicky. 117 BBC Studios: (t). 118-119 BBC Studios. 119 Dreamstime.com: Maxine Hovell (background). 120 Getty Images / iStock: Flory. 121 Steve Brusatte. 122 Science Photo Library: Millard H. Sharp. 123 Dorling Kindersley: Colin Keates / Natural History Museum, London (b). Dreamstime.com: Cynthia Mccrary (t). 124-125 Getty Images / iStock: Steve Ranger. 126 Alamy Stock Photo: Jon G. Fuller / VWPics (b). Utah State Historical Society: (t). 127 James Kirkland, Utah Geological Survey. 128-135 BBC Studios. 136 Dreamstime.com: Ryan Marcotte. 137 Getty Images / iStock: brytta (t); Tomas Nevesely (b). 138-139 BBC Studios. 139 Dreamstime.com: Aivoges (background). 140 Colorado Plateau Geosystems Inc: (t). naturepl.com: Graham Eaton (b). 141 Courtesy of the Thomas Fisher Rare Book Library, University of Toronto: Joseph Burr Tyrrell Papers (t). Courtesy of the Royal Tyrrell Museum, Drumheller, AB.: (b). 142 BBC Studios: (b). Shutterstock.com: hecke61 (t). 143 BBC Studios. 144 Courtesy of the Royal Tyrrell Museum, Drumheller, AB. 145 Alamy Stock Photo: ZUMA Press Inc (t). BBC Studios: (b). 146 BBC Studios. 148-149 BBC Studios: (t). 149 Dreamstime.com: Viktorus (br). Getty Images / iStock: Lemanieh (bl). 150 BBC Studios: (t). Image of PR 2278 © Field Museum of Natural History: (b). 151 Alamy Stock Photo: Horizon International Images. 152 BBC Studios: (b). Courtesy of the Royal Tyrrell Museum, Drumheller, AB.: (t). 154-155 Courtesy of the Royal Tyrrell Museum, Drumheller, AB. 156-157 Alamy Stock Photo: Design Pics Inc. 158-159 BBC Studios. 160 BBC Studios. 161 Colorado Plateau Geosystems Inc: (t). 162-163 BBC Studios. 163 Dreamstime.com: Geoff Arrowsmith (background). 164 Alamy Stock Photo: Kevin Schafer (tl). Dreamstime.com: Sara Winter (b). Science Photo Library: Dirk Wiersma (tr). 165 BBC Studios. 166 Alamy Stock Photo: The Natural History Museum. 167 Anthony R. Fiorillo, Ph.D.: (t). Getty Images: Field Museum Library (b). 168 Alamy Stock Photo: All Canada Photos (t). Courtesy of the Royal Tyrrell Museum, Drumheller, AB.: (b). 169 BBC Studios: (r). 170-171 BBC Studios: (t). 171 Emily Bamforth: (br). Getty Images / iStock: NickJKelly (bl). 172 BBC Studios. 173 Getty Images: Lawrence M. Witmer, PhD: (b). 174-178 BBC Studios. 179 Dreamstime.com: Isselee. 180-181 Getty Images / iStock: Zsuzsanna Jenei. 182 Dorling Kindersley: Gary Ombler / Oxford Museum of Natural History (l). 183 naturepl.com: Suzi Eszterhas. 184 BBC Studios: (t). Philip J. Currie Dinosaur Museum: (b). 185 Getty Images / iStock: aksphoto. 186 Philip J. Currie Dinosaur Museum: (t). Shutterstock.com: Justin Hetu (b). 187-191 BBC Studios. 192 Colorado Plateau Geosystems Inc. 193 Alamy Stock Photo: Everett Collection Historical (cr); Zachary Frank (t). 194-195 BBC Studios. 195 Dreamstime.com: Nfcv (background). 196 Alamy Stock Photo: The History Collection. 197 Getty Images: Bettmann. 198 American Museum of Natural History. 199 Getty Images: Ron Testa / Field Museum Library. 200 Alamy Stock Photo: Bill Waterson. 201 Getty Images: Silver Screen Collection. 202-203 BBC Studios: (t). 203 Alamy Stock Photo: Zachary Frank (br). Dreamstime.com: Wilsilver77 (bl). 204 Dreamstime.com: Ken Griffiths. 205 Carnegie Museum of Natural History. 206 Alamy Stock Photo: ZUMA Press Inc (b). Science Photo Library: Millard H. Sharp (t). 207 Alamy Stock Photo: Sabena Jane Blackbird. 208 Pasha van Bijlert. 209 BBC Studios. 210-211 Alamy Stock Photo: Danita Delimont. 212 Dr. Gregory Erickson: (t). Getty Images: Field Museum Library (b). 213 Alamy Stock Photo: Associated Press. 214 BBC Studios. 215 Getty Images: Mark Wilson / Newsmakers. 216 Getty Images: Field Museum Library (l). 217 Getty Images: Field Museum Library. 218 BBC Studios. 219 Alamy Stock Photo: frantic. 220-221 BBC Studios. 221 Dreamstime.com: Kostiantyn Verovkin (background). 222 BBC Studios: (t). 223 Science Photo Library: D. van Ravenswaay. 224 Alamy Stock Photo: Rosanne Tackaberry. 225-227 BBC Studios. 228 Dreamstime.com: Gijsvdabeele. 229 Alamy Stock Photo: mark Turner (t). Dreamstime.com: Dmitrii Kashporov (b). 230-247 BBC Studios

Cover images: BBC Studios